GREGORY OF TOURS

THE MEROVINGIANS

edited and translated by

ALEXANDER CALLANDER MURRAY

broadview press

Library and Archives Canada Cataloguing in Publication

Gregory, Saint, Bishop of Tours, 538-594.
   Gregory of Tours : the Merovingians / edited and translated by Alexander Callander Murray.

(Readings in medieval civilizations and cultures ; 10)
Includes bibliographical references and index.
ISBN 1-55111-523-9

  1. Merovingians—History—Sources. I. Murray, Alexander C., 1946-   II. Title. III. Series.

DC65.G74 2005   944'.013   C2005-905166-3

Broadview Press Ltd. is an independent, international publishing house, incorporated in 1985. Broadview believes in shared ownership, both with its employees and with the general public; since the year 2000 Broadview shares have traded publicly on the Toronto Venture Exchange under the symbol BDP.
We welcome comments and suggestions regarding any aspect of our publications—please feel free to contact us at the addresses below or at broadview@broadviewpress.com.

North America:

PO Box 1243, Peterborough,
Ontario, Canada K9J 7H5

PO Box 1015, 3576 California Road,
Orchard Park, NY, USA 14127

Tel: (705) 743-8990;
Fax: (705) 743-8353
E-mail: customerservice@
broadviewpress.com

UK, Ireland, and continental Europe:

NBN Plymbridge
Estover Road
Plymouth PL6 7PY UK

Tel: 44 (0) 1752 202301
Fax: 44 (0) 1752 202331
Fax Order Line: 44 (0) 1752 202333
Customer Service:
cservs@nbnplymbridge.com
Orders: orders@nbnplymbridge.com

Australia and New Zealand:

UNIREPS,
University of New South Wales
Sydney, NSW, 2052
Australia

Tel: 61 2 9664 0999
Fax: 61 2 9664 5420
E-mail: info.press@unsw.edu.au

www.broadviewpress.com

Broadview Press Ltd. gratefully acknowledges the financial support of the Government of Canada through the Book Publishing Development Program for our publishing activities.

Book design and composition by George Kirkpatrick

PRINTED IN CANADA

GREGORY OF TOURS

READINGS IN MEDIEVAL CIVILIZATIONS AND CULTURES: X
series editor: Paul Edward Dutton

CONTENTS

LIST OF ILLUSTRATIONS

LIST OF GENEALOGIES

LIST OF MAPS

ABBREVIATIONS

a.	*anno, annis*, in the year(s)
ca	*circa*, around (the year)
GC	Gregory of Tours, *Liber in Gloria Confessorum*. Trans. Raymond Van Dam, *Glory of the Confessor* (Liverpool, 1998)
s.a.	*sub anno*, under the year
MGH	Monumenta Germaniae Historica
VM	Gregory of Tours, *Libri IV de Virtutibus Sancti Martini*. Trans. Raymond Van Dam, in *Saints and their Miracles in Late Antique Gaul* (Princeton, 1993)

References to the *Histories*:

Roman numerals refer to the book numbers, Arabic to the chapter number; IX 2, for example, would be Book Nine, chapter 2.

PREFACE

Abridging the *Histories* of Gregory of Tours has a long, and some will think ignoble, history. Gregory gravely anticipated the development. In the last chapter of the *Histories*, having listed his various writings, he adjured his successors, under threat of having to keep company with the devil at the last judgment, to leave his work intact. As Gregory conceded the privilege of turning selections into verse, his concern may not have been so much abridgement as such as the potential for an epitome to consign the real thing to oblivion. The *Histories* never found its poet, but not too long after Gregory's death, his history was abbreviated. It was reduced to its first six books, and numerous chapters of an ecclesiastical character excised. The popularity of the epitome seems to have long eclipsed the original. Fredegar in his *Chronicle* around 660 and the Neustrian author of a *History of the Franks* (*Liber historiae Francorum*) around 727 used the six-book epitome, neither aware of the ten-book version that Gregory had feared might suffer diminution. Both authors in turn abbreviated the epitome further in the composition of their own distinctive versions. Fortunately the ten-book version survived, acquiring in the Carolingian period the title *History of the Franks*, the name by which it was known for most of the medieval and modern periods.

The present abridgement has its own history too, brief as it is. It is a considerably expanded version of selections that started life as a chapter in *From Roman to Merovingian Gaul: A Reader*, a collection of original sources that I translated and compiled for Broadview Press in 2000 in the series Readings in Medieval Civilizations and Cultures. The thanks I rendered there to Walter Goffart and Joan Murray bear repeating here. Special acknowledgment is due Paul Dutton, the series editor, and Broadview Press for not only suggesting this new translation but patiently awaiting the arrival of a manuscript that, like the Reader before it, outgrew the modest dimensions that were first intended.

One can readily detect in the early abridgements of the *Histories* a response to the historical interests of the generations after Gregory's death. The configuration of the present selections differs significantly from previous medieval or modern epitomes, but no great claim can be made for it responding to some distinctive interest of the present age. This is, after all, a time in which the integrity of Gregory's work has been asserted and the designation *Histories* restored as the title of Gregory's historical books. The selections, nevertheless, will I hope fill a need, which for want of better words may be called utilitarian and even, if the term does not offend, pedagogical. The thought occasionally surfaced while translating that perhaps the world might benefit from another translation of the whole *Histories*. And then again perhaps not. Succumbing to the temptation was resisted for a simple reason: it would have undermined the purpose of the present edition, designed to focus the reader's attention on a central aspect of the *Histories* often difficult to grasp amid its complicated, tangled, and fractured narrative of secular and spiritual history. A more serious temptation was the almost irresistible desire to constantly add just another episode that might tweak the narrative perspective a little more—a process that by degrees would have restored all the complexity of the grand edifice and all of the difficulty of interpreting it. Whether in the end the right balance has been struck is for readers to determine.

I have enjoyed making the selections and my hope is that others will enjoy reading them and find them a useful introduction to a broader study of Gregory's work. A more detailed discussion of their context will be found in the Introduction.

On that, *caveat lector*. Editors of selections should I think strive to provide guidance, not issue directives, even if, in the mode of Chilperic, they sometimes imagine those reluctant to believe are only being "taken gently by the hair." The present work is not a Reader in the conventional sense, yet I hope I have not transgressed that principle by too much. While my views have been expressed most resolutely, I believe, on matters that are fundamental at the present time to reading the *Histories*, I am more likely to be an observer than a participant in the debates on these questions. Though I have pressed for some points of view, I hope I have clearly signaled the scope of interpretations as I understand them. Involved readers, incorrigible suspicious creatures as they are likely to be, will no doubt beat their own paths through the thickets of Gregorian scholarship.

Alexander Callander Murray
Orton, Ontario

INTRODUCTION

Among the Latin historians of the early Middle Ages, Gregory of Tours occupies a unique place as the age's most prolific recorder of contemporary events. This unrivaled position has not always been the reason his *Histories* has been prized, and it has rarely contributed to his reputation as an historian, or even fitted the interests of his readership. Soon after his death in 594, for example, Gregory's work was abridged and circulated in a version that eliminated much of its contemporary narrative. Among moderns, Gregory's standing as an historian has tended to suffer in comparison with the Northumbrian monk Bede, whose idealized, harmonious account of the development of the Christian church among the English grows notably silent as it coincides with his own lifetime. Because Gregory has commonly been thought to have been writing a history of the Franks, his halting (but in fact relatively exacting) search for monuments of their early history has seemed to many disappointing when set next to the deep, expansive, fictional evocations of the distant Germanic past in the Gothic history of Jordanes and the Lombard history of Paul the Deacon. In recent times, students and general readers sampling Gregory's work have likely done so through his famous account of the career of Clovis, a subject about which Gregory was imperfectly informed but with which he is indelibly associated. By comparison, his dense, fascinating descriptions of contemporary affairs have been left by and large to the attention of a small number of specialists.

This book is hardly about setting the record straight on Gregory. Recent magisterial studies have done this, providing the *Histories* with what it has always been thought to lack—a coherent perspective and a plausible 'philosophy of history'. Gregory's history has also at last been divorced from that slightly specious genre, 'national history', which moderns have readily imposed on the historical writing of the period; the extended recollection of the past that Gregory failed to provide for the Franks can now be ascribed to the cultural realities of Gallic and Frankish history, not a deep aversion to a thriving barbarian tradition on the part of Gregory. Even the criticism mounted against the credibility of Gregory's Clovis-narrative, though sometimes exaggerated, has had the merit of suggesting that the lasting value of the *Histories* might also lie somewhere else.

The present selection and translation has a utilitarian purpose: to present in a readable and ready form the political narrative of the *Histories* with the hope that readers, once they have traversed the well-known country of Clovis and the early kings, might be encouraged to spend a while with events that Gregory knew best and for which he is usually the unique source.

Gregory of Tours

Georgius Florentius Gregorius, better known to posterity as Gregory, bishop of Tours, was born about 538 to a highly distinguished Gallo-Roman family in Clermont in the region of Auvergne. A mark of the family's importance is its service to the church, which was a major outlet for the vocation and ambitions of the Gallic aristocracy. In the course of the sixth century at least a half-dozen of Gregory's kinsmen or ancestors were bishops, holding at various times the sees of Langres, Lyons, Clermont, and Tours; of the previous eighteen-odd bishops of Tours before him, Gregory claimed that he was related to all but five (V 49).

At the time of Gregory's birth, Auvergne was subject to the Merovingian Theudebert I (a. 534–48), the king of what in Gregory's day was known as Austrasia, the eastern kingdom of the Franks, and a ruler who in Gregory's retrospective evaluation was described as "thoroughly distinguished for good qualities" (III 25). The founder of the Frankish Merovingian state, Clovis I (a. 481–511), had been in his grave for over a quarter of a century. In Italy, a great and destructive war between the Ostrogoths and the Roman Empire, now based in Constantinople, had just begun in 536 and would last the better part of two decades. About a year before Gregory's birth, Provence had been transferred from Ostrogothic to Frankish control, bringing the Franks Marseilles and access to the Mediterranean. Theudebert had begun the impressive, but fruitless, Frankish interventions into the Italian peninsula.

Gregory's younger years, following the death of his father in the mid-540s (his mother lived to at least 587), seem to have been spent largely among the clergy of Clermont and Lyons, at first in the episcopal household of his paternal uncle Gallus, bishop of Clermont (a. 525–51), and then in the household of his maternal great-uncle Nicetius, bishop of Lyons (a. 552–73). Gregory also visited his maternal kinsman Eufronius, bishop of Tours (a. 556–73), whom he eventually succeeded as bishop. Gregory was a deacon (likely of Clermont) in 563 and may have been ordained that year when he had reached the canonically acceptable age of twenty-five. In 573, on the death of Eufronius, he was appointed bishop of Tours by the Austrasian king Sigibert I, who ruled both Clermont and Tours, and ordained by Egidius, bishop of Rheims. Gregory was about thirty-five years old. Even before his episcopacy, Gregory was not likely a stranger to the Austrasian court. He also listed among his acquaintances the queen, nun, and later saint, Radegund, and the poet, writer, and panegyrist, and later bishop, Venantius Fortunatus.

When Gregory was ordained bishop, serious conflicts had already arisen among Chlothar I's sons, who now ruled the Frankish kingdom; during the course of his episcopate, Tours was subject at different times to each of the brothers Sigibert (a. 573–75), Chilperic (a. 576–84), and Guntram (a. 584–85), and finally Sigibert's son, Childebert II (a. 585–94). The wars and disputes among the kings constitute much of the subject of the *Histories*. By the time of Gregory's ordination, the Italian Ostrogothic kingdom was rapidly becoming a mere memory, eliminated by Emperor Justinian's general Narses in 552/54. Imperial forces had also intervened in Spain in 551 and occupied the south-east coast. The Avars had appeared in the Hungarian plain in the mid 560s, invading Gaul and defeating Sigibert, and precipitating the entry of the Lombards into the Italian peninsula in 568.

Gregory's bishopric coincided with the *civitas*, or city, of Tours. The *civitas* (in plural, *civitates*) was a territorial unit, composed of a walled urban area and a surrounding dependent region of smaller centers and rural settlements. Among the smaller centers were *castra*, translated in the present selections as 'fortresses', but often being in fact fortified towns of a good size. Another was the villa, which I have left untranslated; the term, which had fiscal significance, embraced several kinds of rural units that might be in the possession of one or multiple owners. On the ground the community focus of many villas may have looked like a village, but the term did not represent one mode of settlement, proprietorship, or production.

In both Roman and Merovingian Gaul, the *civitas* was the basic unit of administration; since the late Roman period, it had also corresponded to a bishopric. Under the Merovingian kings, Tours was one of about 120 bishoprics or *civitates* in Gaul, most, with only a few exceptions, deriving from their Roman counterparts (see Map 1). The Merovingian kings also appointed over each *civitas* a secular official, called a count (*comes*), responsible for royal administration. Relations between bishops and counts were not always harmonious. The count of Tours in the last years of Charibert († 567) was Leudast, who on the death of the king gave his loyalty to Chilperic. Leudast was briefly in office in 573, the same year Gregory became bishop, and came back again under Chilperic from about 577 to 579. He was followed by Eunomius from 579 to 584. Willachar was count in 584/85 during the brief period Guntram held the city. The count under Childebert II was likely Gregory's friend Galienus (V 48).

In the Roman period, *civitates* were grouped into provinces, the leading *civitas* being called *metropolis civitas*—*metropolis* was in origin a Greek word, meaning literally 'mother-city'. The Merovingian kings, in sharing out the *civitates* among themselves, abandoned the province as a secular administrative unit. The province, nevertheless, did survive in large measure into the Merovingian period as an ecclesiastical unit led by the bishop of its metropolis. Gregory was not only bishop of Tours but also metropolitan of the old province of *Lugdu-*

nensis tertia or, at least, that part of it under Frankish control (some western parts were held by the Bretons). His relations with the other bishops of the province were not always good, to judge by his dealings with Felix, bishop of Nantes (V 49, Appendix V 5).

Although the old Roman Gallic provincial structures no longer functioned in the secular administration, a higher unit of royal government did exist under the Merovingian kings. This unit was composed of grouped *civitates* (and their counts) placed under the command of dukes. About a dozen of these ducal circumscriptions existed in Gregory's day. The configuration and number of *civitates* commanded by a duke varied; some groupings appear more or less fixed, others, flexible. Tours and Poitiers together were assigned to the command of a series of dukes: Gundovald, from the late 560s to 573, under Sigibert; Dracolen, ca 576 to 578, and Berulf, from 578 to 584, under Chilperic; Gararic in 584/85, under Childebert, though Gararic failed to secure his appointment against the forces of Guntram; and Ennodius from 585–87, under Childebert. Agynus was probably duke in 588. Under Berulf, in 583 at least, Angers and Nantes were included in the command. Gararic's intended command may have included Limoges. Dukes were (just as the Latin term implies) the generals of Frankish armies. The extent to which the office existed apart from particular circumscriptions of *civitates* is unclear.

Gregory's role as bishop of Tours extended beyond the spiritual realms of pastoral care, and even the practical requirements of church administration. The role of bishops in the administrative, judicial, and fiscal apparatus of the Merovingian state is real, but it cannot be defined with complete satisfaction. It is nevertheless clear that bishops represented their citizens and dependents before kings and royal officials and that their tribunals exercised jurisdiction over clergy and dependents, served as courts of arbitration, and participated in mixed tribunals with lay officials. Gregory's role also exceeded the commonplace functions of many of his fellow bishops. He traveled widely on ecclesiastical business and was involved in direct service to at least the Austrasian crown. In Coblenz in 585, for example, Gregory acted in Childebert's presence as the king's spokesman before an envoy of King Guntram of Burgundy (VIII 13), and three years later he was sent as Childebert's envoy to the Burgundian court (IX 20).

Like many historians, Gregory has been accused of retailing rumor as history. Determining rumor in Gregory can be a hazardous undertaking. In any case, what Gregory's biography, position, and role in affairs suggest is that the *Histories* in its contemporary, Gallic mode is not the tale of an outsider told at a distance, but an inside story related by a participant in the great events of his day. Identifying Gregory's relation to those events is an enduring sport open to readers who commit some time to unraveling the contemporary narrative of the *Histories* and Gregory's other writings.

Gregory wrote a number of works during his episcopacy. He chose to list most of them in the concluding chapter of the *Histories* (X 31): "I have written ten books of *Histories*, seven of *Wonders*, and one on the *Life of the Fathers*. I have composed one book of *Commentaries on the Psalms*. I also wrote one book on the *Offices of the Church*." Gregory's hagiographic works (*Wonders* and *Life of the Fathers*) document the good news of God's continuing work in the world and complement the generally grim picture of a fallen humanity whose strivings dominate much of the *Histories*. Gregory omitted from his list some minor works of compilation and adaptation—a collection of the masses of Sidonius Apollinaris and versions of the tale of the seven sleepers of Ephesus and the miracles and passion of Saint Andrew. Gregory's fame rests on the work that he placed first in his list—the *Histories*, which has long been prized as one of the most important sources of the early Middle Ages.

Gregory died in 594, roughly at the time he completed his *Histories*, at the age of fifty-six.

Contemporary Historians

Gregory of Tours was not the only writer of history in the latter part of the sixth century. In Britain around mid-century, the homilist and moralist Gildas prefaced a denunciation of his fellow countrymen with a brief outline of British history down to his own day that is an important source for our understanding of post-Roman events and the settlement of the English (Anglo-Saxons). Constantinople in the latter half of the sixth century was rich in historiography. The historians there who invite comparison with Gregory are Jordanes, Procopius, and Evagrius Scholasticus. Around 552, Jordanes composed his history of the Goths, which culminates in the overthrow of the Ostrogothic kingdom in Italy, as well as his *Romana*, a résumé of Roman history. Shortly thereafter, Procopius composed a public series of histories in Greek recounting the great wars of the emperor Justinian, while venting his spleen on the emperor (among others) in a vicious portrait drawn up in secret; Procopius's public histories were continued by Agathias down to 558. At the end of the century, Evagrius Scholasticus, almost the direct contemporary of Gregory, wrote an ecclesiastical history, which includes secular events, for the period 431 to 594. In Spain, the bishop John of Biclar wrote a brief chronicle of his times in 590, continuing the famous Chronicle of Jerome and two of its continuations, that of Prosper of Aquitaine and the African bishop Victor of Tunnuna, whose work ended in 567. John's treatment of Spanish affairs presents a very different account of the celebrated revolt of Hermenigild against his father Leovigild. In Gaul, Gregory had one colleague in the historian's craft that we know about—Bishop Marius of Avenches. Like John of Biclar, Marius wrote a modest continuation of the

famous Jerome Chronicle, including two of its fifth-century continuations—
Prosper's Chronicle and the Gallic Chronicle of 451. Marius's chronicle covers
the years 451 to 581. His episcopacy from 574 to 594 almost exactly corresponds
to Gregory's own. Gregory and Marius drew on similar sources on occasion,
but these are unknown.

Scope and Subject Matter of the *Histories*

The *Histories* is a big, complicated book that is not easily mastered. Its size can
be roughly gauged by the standard MGH Latin edition, which, with apparatus,
covers 537 pages; the modern Penguin translation renders the equivalent in
540 pages. It begins with Creation and with the earliest biblical and secular
history in the fashion of the Jerome Chronicle and history of Orosius and
comes down to the year 591. The complexity of the work derives not just
from its size and scope but also from its presentation. Gregory weaves together
spiritual and secular subject matter of ecclesiastical and conventional history in
a fashion structured by apparently fractured, discrete narrative segments which,
while engaging in their particularities, are hard to assimilate into harmonized,
conventional modes of historical meaning. The fractured sense of the narrative
is also affected by Gregory's practice of proceeding chronologically not only
year by year (with the reign of Childebert II each year is clearly delimited)
but even over the course of a year. The latter tendency can be helpful for determining the order and interrelation of events, though it is not a mechanical,
foolproof indicator of their sequence. Gregory's artifice clearly trumped mere
chronological consistency, as on occasion did narrative requirements. Whether
complexity at times got the better of Gregory himself is a moot point, but it is
likely that as he completed his *Histories* in the year of his death, some tasks of
polishing, harmonizing, and integrating still remained uncompleted.

The work is composed of ten books. Book I covers 5,596 years, from Creation
to A.D. 397 and the death of Gregory's hero, Saint Martin, bishop and patron
saint of Tours. Readers should note that Martin, an early bishop of Tours,
continues as a vital force to affect the course of events in subsequent books,
even those of Gregory's own day. Biblical history was central to Gregory's understanding of the theological significance of human history. Nevertheless, the
Histories is largely a record of Gallic affairs, particularly during Gregory's mature
years as bishop of Tours. From Book II onwards, the focus of the *Histories* is
predominantly, though not exclusively, Gaul. Book II covers 114 years, from the
death of Martin to 511 and the death of Clovis; Books III and IV between them
cover 64 years, from 511 to 575, the second year of Gregory's episcopate. The
remaining six books, well over half the entire *Histories*, cover a mere 16 years,
from 575 to 591. The epicenter of the narrative appears to be Books VII and

VIII. Book VII deals with about half a year, as does most of Book VIII.

Evaluating this narrative requires some idea of the broader historiographical issues raised by the *Histories*.

Interpreting the *Histories*

Despite the importance of the *Histories*, the perspective of its author has not been well understood. Moderns have generally viewed Gregory as a naïve and superstitious compiler, heaping up a confused medley of ecclesiastical and national history. Gregory's merit was thought to have been his attempt to write a 'History of the Franks', a title often applied to his work though never used by Gregory himself; and the value of the work was largely seen as an accidental consequence of its author's naïveté, a quality that was thought to help guarantee the veracity of the apparently depraved picture of Merovingian society presented in its pages. Recent appraisals suggest a different interpretation of the historian and his work. Gregory is no longer seen as the author of a national history of the Franks; a work conceived along these lines, the *Liber historiae Francorum* or *History of the Franks*, had to wait until much later (ca 727). His intertwining ecclesiastical and secular themes are increasingly recognized as integrated parts of a moral or theological perspective. Gregory is a moralist, setting the vain strivings of a corrupt human nature against the continuing story of the marvels of the saints and the church of Christ, and consciously selecting his material and shaping it to present these themes. In short, the *Histories* should not be regarded merely as a giant compendium of particular incidents, quaint religiosity, and raw unmediated bad behavior, but as the purposive work of a real historian.

There is an unavoidable irony in this evaluation. The more securely Gregory takes his place among the fraternity of major historians and the more his selection and presentation of events seem contrived to persuade the reader of a particular view of the human condition, the less direct appears to be the *Histories'* representation of reality. This circumstance is no cause for despair. It does not negate the value of the *Histories* as a source for sixth-century life and politics; it is simply a condition of reading it. Historians, especially those regarded as the great expositors of an age (and Gregory is surely one of these), are generally grand moralists in one way or another; even minor expositors, past and present, tend to have the same penchant but on a lesser scale. The new perspective on Gregory means that, like the work of all historians, the *Histories* takes careful handling. Reading it should cause reflection on not just what historians were doing in the sixth century but also what they are still doing in the present one.

These Selections of the *Histories*

This translation is composed of selections from Books II to X, following the political narrative of the *Histories* from the year of Clovis's death to the end of the work. Such a treatment of Gregory's text is intended to facilitate reading the narrative history of the sixth century and interpreting Gregory as the principal portrayer of sixth-century Gallic political events. But utility and focus are achieved at a cost. The selections cannot maintain Gregory's conjunction of the saints and the reprobate and, by its nature, precludes a full understanding of the moral and theological perspective informing the *Histories*. Those who wish to bring this perspective fully to bear on their interpretation of the narrative must avail themselves of the *Histories* in its entirety, as well as Gregory's other works devoted to the saints and their miracles (see Bibliography).

Not all the historiographical issues of purpose and perspective can be equally evaluated from the selections. Among the questions they may clarify is how to understand the term 'episodic' as frequently applied to the discrete narrative elements of the *Histories*. In the context of the work as a whole, Gregory's moral and theological purposes were clearly served by fragmenting his narrative, juxtaposing the political and topical, the secular and spiritual. To help decide if there was confusion or a lack of direction in the treatment of events on Gregory's part, as is often supposed, readers may here follow a narrative whose elements I have arranged to be read consecutively.

Many scholars have thought that the events coinciding with Gregory's episcopate were recorded just as they happened or shortly thereafter and reflect a more or less immediate perspective of the compiler. According to this understanding of the composition of the *Histories*, one can read into Gregory's account of events his outlook at particular times and chart his changing attitude toward the main characters, detecting in the process a record of the immediate interest or even the shifting political loyalties of the historian. By this method some scholars claim to have detected a Gregory friendly to Chilperic, supporting the Nogent agreements, backing Egidius of Rheims, and abetting the Gundovald party, and even hopeful of the future prospects of a unified kingdom under Chlothar II.

Readers will want to make up their own minds about the likelihood of such mysteries. The excerpts presented here, which are the chief basis for these conclusions, hardly bear out the approach that leads to them. There is little reason to see Gregory's selection of material as ad hoc; on the contrary, the narrative of the years in which Gregory was bishop seems consistently shaped from a retrospective position, especially that of the great events of the years 585, 587, and 590. The structure of Gregory's political narrative as set within the larger framework of the *Histories* was episodic; the contents were not. The size, scope, and complexity of the *Histories* do not suggest it was written at one point and over a short period of time. But its compositional history is lost to us. The conviction of many scholars that individual books and chapters can be dated is misplaced, as is their attempt to interpret the *Histories* on the basis of the compositional sequence this method produces. And detecting in the *Histories* traces of a concealed political career that had become an embarrassment, even a danger, to Gregory by the late 580s is, in my view, fanciful. It is sufficient to recognize that the *Histories* as a whole reflect Gregory's perspective by about 590 and the years following.

This vantage point ca 590 had implications for how Gregory presented the major characters and how we understand his own attitude and the limitations on his freedom of expression. Chilperic († 584), a king whom Gregory memorably described as the "Nero and Herod of our time" (VI 46), was gone from the scene. Gregory was free to condemn him as he saw fit. Instances where Chilperic's actions elicit approbation, or at least fail to produce condemnation, are no argument for composition during the king's lifetime and his control of Tours (a. 576–84); Gregory's view of humankind was not one-dimensional. In the circumstances of writing contemporary history, reticences and silences may be important. These are most apparent with respect to the ruling house of Austrasia, and especially the imperfect portraits of Childebert and Brunhild whom Gregory must have known well. The praise for Brunhild seems sparing, criticism indirect, and one cannot help wondering whether a portrait less out of keeping with the hostile portrayal of the queen in later historiography (see Epilogue and Postscripts) might have been the result if Gregory had chosen to express himself freely. Gregory was a man with a view of the world, and while he had his preferences and loyalties, his view was not wholly confined within narrow political or ecclesiastical allegiances. That he thought he was on the side of God may seem obvious, but what that really means in his own understanding and in the broader context of the late sixth century is a conundrum that defies easy solution.

Although the following excerpts of political narrative are lengthy, readers should be aware that political and topical material has had to be left out for reasons of space. I have tried to include as much of the history of Gallic events as possible, occasionally resorting to summary. Gregory's account of events in Italy and the empire—sometimes lengthy and often inaccurate—has not fared nearly as well (the affairs of the empire, for example, have been completely excluded). Gregory's treatment of these events has interesting implications for understanding his historical perspective, but given the choice of including narrative dealing with Frankish Gaul or that of its neighbors, I have chosen to stick with

Gaul and aim for, if not quite manage, completeness. Readers should at least bear in mind that Gregory's political horizon was not as narrow as the excerpts presented here might suggest. I have included events in Spain, not because I think Gregory's account of them should be endorsed, but because Visigothic politics are important for understanding the diplomatic dimensions of Frankish history; alas, Spanish affairs are a notable instance where Gregory's material is sometimes poorly integrated. Given the criteria set out above of emphasizing the big political picture, readers may wonder at the inclusion in the narrative of some ostensibly topical events (more of these appear in the Appendix). These selections generally tell us about important aspects of Gallic society and are valuable for that reason, but they are rarely just topical in a strict sense. Their leading participants are apt to be important players in the elite of Gallic society, and the events, which are often subtly linked to the larger narrative, tend to reveal the character, as Gregory saw it, of important players in the political life of the kingdom, not to mention the relentless course of providence.

Structure of the *Histories*, Structure of the Selections

Gregory was a subject of the kings of the Austrasian Franks—Clermont, Gregory's home town, and Tours, the city of his episcopate, being two of the many cities these kings controlled south of the Loire. His political allegiance has an important bearing on a number of aspects of the *Histories*, including its organization. Gregory structured his books with reference to the reigns of the Austrasian kings. Book II ends with the death of Clovis, the founder of a unified Frankish kingdom in northern, central, and southern Gaul. Book III ends with the death of Theudebert I, the greatest of Clovis's successors and ruler of the north-eastern (or Austrasian) Franks; and Book IV ends with the death in 575 of Sigibert I, ruler of this north-eastern kingdom, called Austrasia by the time Gregory was writing. Thereafter, for Books V–X Gregory adopted a dating system tied to the regnal years of the Austrasian king Childebert II. (This structure does not preclude further thematic treatment of individual books.)

The division of the selections largely follows Gregory's structure. The selections are divided into three parts that follow the narrative of Gregory's history, essentially in the order he presents it, but with a slight modification of its divisions. In Gregory's scheme, the death of Chlothar I, which looms large in subsequent accounts of Merovingian history, falls in the middle of Book IV. Modern historiography, with a different set of conventions in mind than Gregory's, tends to see the death of Chlothar and the partition of the unified kingdom among his quarrelsome sons as a new, or at least distinct, stage in the history of the Frankish kingdom. I have followed this perspective in arranging the present set of excerpts.

Consequently, Part I (Chapter One) on the early Franks and Clovis corresponds to Book II. Part II (Chapters Two and Three) corresponds to Books III–IV but is divided in the following way: Chapter Two on the reigns of Clovis's successors down to the death of the last surviving son, Chlothar I, in 561 accords with Book III and one-half of Book IV; Chapter Three down to the death of Sigibert I in 575 completes Book IV. Part III (Chapters Four to Eight) embraces the reign of Childebert II, whom Gregory regarded as the rightful ruler of Tours, with the years arranged according to his regnal dates. Each of Chapters Four to Seven corresponds to a Book of the *Histories* and Chapter Eight covers the final two Books, IX and X.

Contemporary histories by their nature are open-ended. I have added a final chapter briefly bringing to a close the biographies of the principal figures of the *Histories* still living at the time of Gregory's death in 594.

Names, Places, and Spelling

Consistency and accuracy in spelling and place-names are victories rarely won in the translation of early medieval texts without injury to some well-founded convention.

The spelling of names was not fixed in the early Middle Ages and manuscripts, of varying dates, often show an array of possible forms. I have chosen, where possible, forms that are a reasonable reflection of contemporary practice but that are also likely to be found in modern treatments of Frankish history: thus Chlothar, not the later form Lothar or the manuscript Chlothacharius. Minor names (and Latin ones) are most likely to survive the translation process in a way closely approximating a manuscript form. The names of major figures have long achieved conventional spellings in the literature that seemed presumptuous to alter. It appeared best to leave the modern preferences for Clovis, Clothild, Guntram, and Brunhild alone despite their distant resemblance to Chlodovechus, Chrodechildis, Gunthchramnus, and Brunechildis respectively. Another convention I have followed is reserving Theuderic for Franks (and one Breton) and Theoderic for Goths, though they are the same name and both forms appear in Merovingian texts. In short, readers searching the literature need to beware: neither early medieval nor modern practice is consistent.

Place names are only a modest problem. I have generally used modern and medieval names for places, as these derive for the most part from Roman and Merovingian forms and have the merit of being found on modern maps. Where Merovingian and medieval practice differs, I have been guided by prejudice and convention. For instance I have preferred the ancient name for Convenae rather than its later medieval reincarnation as Saint-Bertrand-de-Comminges, yet I render the ancient city of the Arverni (*civitas Arvernorum*) with its medieval (and modern) name Clermont, while referring to the region as Auvergne and its people as Arvernians.

The Merovingians, the Frankish Kingdom, and the *Histories*

This book has been called *The Merovingians*, not because Gregory used this title or because his book was only about Frankish kings, but because the Merovingian kings of Gaul stand at the heart of his narrative of events, and the selections have been made to illustrate this feature of his history.

Merovingian is the name for the dynasty of Frankish kings that united the Franks and took control of most of Gaul in the late fifth and early sixth century and ruled until 751, when the dynasty was replaced by the Carolingians. In that year Pippin III, son of the mayor of the palace Charles (in Latin, Carolus) Martel, whose name came to define the new Carolingian dynasty, assumed the Frankish throne with the sanction of the papacy. The last Merovingian, Childeric III (*a.* 743–51), was placed in a monastery and tonsured. Long hair was a mark of Merovingian kingship according to foreign sources and Gregory, who famously dubbed the early kings *reges criniti*, 'long-haired kings' (II 9). French and Germans have each looked upon the Merovingian kingdom as the origins of their own history. In modern French historiography the Merovingians are known as 'la première race' of French kings; Clovis, despite the opaqueness of the modern form of his name, was the real first Louis. Gregory of Tours is the historian of the first part of Merovingian rule.

The earliest source to use the term Merovingian is not Gregory but Jonas of Bobbio, writing around 640. Another seventh-century Frankish source, Fredegar (ca 660), and the eighth-century *Liber historiae Francorum* (ca 727) derive the name from Merovech/Meroveus: Merovingian means 'the descendants of Merovech'. According to Gregory (II 10), Merovech lived in the mid-fifth century and was the father of Childeric and grandfather of Clovis I (*a.* 481–511). Although Gregory does not use the dynastic name in his works, he was clearly familiar with it because he traced the descent of the kings of his own day back to this Merovech. At least three kings' sons were given the name Merovech in the late sixth and early seventh centuries. Some scholars reject the dynasty's association with an historical Merovech, arguing instead that the Merovingians traced their descent from a mythical ancestor called Mero, but there is no evidence for this re-evaluation of Gregory's testimony.

The founder of the Merovingian kingdom in northern Gaul was Chlodovechus, called Clovis in modern historical works. Later forms of the name include Ludovicus, Ludwig, and Louis. In 481 Clovis, aged about 15, succeeded his father Childeric, a Frankish king associated with Roman military and episcopal authorities in northern Gaul; Childeric's tomb, furnished with rich grave goods, was discovered in 1653 in Tournai (in present-day Belgium). In a letter to Clovis, Remigius, bishop of Rheims, described the young king as succeeding to the administration of *Belgica secunda*, the name for the Roman province. According to Gregory, Clovis defeated Syagrius, who was based in Soissons and was the son of the late Aegidius, Roman master of the soldiers. Clovis also achieved military victories against the Alamanni and extended his control over Frankish groups in northern Gaul and the middle Rhine. In 500 he defeated the Burgundians under King Gundobad, who nevertheless held on to power. He achieved permanent control of territories south of the Loire in 507 when he defeated the Visigoths under Alaric II at the battle of Vouillé. This defeat led to the eventual collapse of the Visigothic kingdom of Toulouse in southern Gaul and, as a result, Spain became the heartland of the Visigothic kingdom. Clovis established Paris, a city located in a Latin-speaking region of his kingdom, as his capital. He was baptized a Catholic by Remigius, bishop of Rheims, an event that has imprinted itself on the historical imagination of western Europeans. Clovis was not the first of the new kings ruling former provinces of the Roman Empire to reject the form of Christianity known as Arianism in favor of Catholicism, but he was by far the most important. What was thought to be the 1500th anniversary of this event was celebrated in France in 1996.

The main interpretative problems of Clovis's reign usually concern an evaluation of the famous account of Clovis's career in the *Histories* written more than seventy years after the king's death. A small number of sources contemporary with the king's reign exist, but only Gregory supplies a comprehensive, if schematic, chronology of events. He also recounts incidents designed to highlight the king's character and provides incidental information lacking in the contemporary sources. Scholars have gradually progressed from an uncritical acceptance of Gregory as the main source for Clovis's reign to varying degrees of skepticism about the bishop's sources, his motives, and his historiographical method. As a result, the chronology of the king's career, the circumstances and timing of his baptism, and the character of his religious sensibilities have all been the subject of dispute. On the question of the date of the baptism, for example, scholars are divided between those placing it between 496 and 500 (following Gregory and a letter of Nicetius, bishop of Trier, ca 564) and those who connect it with Vouillé and date it as late as 508 (arguing from a letter of Theoderic the Ostrogoth to Clovis, ca 506). Even skeptics of Gregory's account retain some of its elements.

On Clovis's death, the kingdom was divided among four sons: Theuderic I (a. 511–33), Chlodomer (a. 511–24), Childebert I (a. 511–58), and Chlothar I (a. 511–61). Around 532, Theuderic I and Chlothar I conquered the Thuringian kingdom; in 534 the kingdom of Burgundy was conquered by Chlothar I, Childebert I, and Theudebert II (the son of Theuderic I); in 537 the Ostrogoths relinquished their control over Provence, making Frankish Gaul a Mediterranean kingdom. The Franks under Theuderic I's son Theudebert I (533–48), and his son Theudebald (548–55), became involved in Justinian's wars in Italy, though without achieving lasting results. The Frankish kingdom was reunited briefly in 558 by Clovis's sole surviving son Chlothar I. It was again divided on his death in 561 between his four sons: Charibert (a. 561–67), Guntram (a. 561–92), Sigibert I (a. 561–75), and Chilperic I (a. 561–84). In the divisions of both 511 and 561, the principal seats of the kings lay north of the Loire (see Map 2 and Genealogy 1).

The civil wars and political conflicts of Chilperic, Guntram, and Sigibert figure prominently, and sometimes in remarkable detail, in the *Histories,* especially after the death of Sigibert and the succession of his son Childebert II in 575 (Books V–X). A thorough recapitulation here of Gallic history in the two generations following the division of 561 would be unnecessarily contentious and require detailed argument. What can be offered—and intrepid readers might wish to decline it—are a few of the main junctures in the story to help navigate the complexity of Merovingian politics and the narrative's sometimes unstated implications, which were much more evident to contemporary readers. The list hardly resolves all the cruxes of Gregory's account.

1) **Death of Charibert in 567 (IV 26).** The inheritance of Charibert, whose kingdom was based on Paris, was divided among his surviving brothers and an agreement reached that none of them would enter Paris. Gregory alludes to the outcome in IV 45, V 48, and VI 27 but only gives particulars in VII 6. Disagreements about the division of the *civitates* involved continued for the next two decades. Tours was originally part of Charibert's kingdom.

2) **Assassination of Sigibert of Austrasia in 575 and succession of his son Childebert II (IV 51).** The assassination occurred in the midst of a civil war between Sigibert and his brother Chilperic. Childebert was five years old and placed in the guardianship of court officials. His governor (*nutricius*) Gogo was likely one among a number so-called who supervised his upbringing and controlled his person. Sigibert's widow, Brunhild, rejoining the Austrasian court after an indiscreet marriage with Chilperic's son Merovech, was not without influence.

3) **Treaty of Stone Bridge, or Pompierre, in 577 (V 17).** By this agreement Guntram of Burgundy, having lost all his sons, allied himself with the

Austrasians against Chilperic, making his nephew Childebert an heir to his kingdom.

4) **Treaty of Nogent in 581 (VI 1, 3).** By this agreement Austrasia now allied itself with Chilperic against Guntram, repudiating the Treaty of Stone Bridge. A new governor Wandelen took charge of Childebert, and a group hostile to Brunhild assumed the leading role in Austrasian affairs. A prominent member of the group was Egidius, bishop of Rheims. As Chilperic had recently lost his sons, he agreed to make Childebert an heir to his kingdom. At the same time, Guntram's general Mummolus went over to Austrasia.

5) **Mutiny of the army of Childebert during the war against Guntram in 583 (VI 31).** The mutineers directed their wrath against Egidius and the Austrasian dukes, revealing resistance to the policy pursued by the Austrasian court since Nogent. Improved relations between Burgundy and Austrasia seemed to result, as early in 584 Guntram restored to Childebert the part of Marseilles taken from Austrasia after the death of Sigibert in 575 (VI 33).

6) **Assassination of Chilperic late in 584 (VI 46).** Chilperic left an infant son, eventually called Chlothar (II), who along with his mother Fredegund now came under the protection of Guntram. Guntram also invoked his claim to all of Charibert's kingdom by virtue of the terms of the agreements reached following the latter's death in 567 (VII 6).

7) **Gundovald's rebellion, also late in 584 (VII 10).** The rebellion followed directly on Chilperic's assassination. In southern Gaul near Limoges, Gundovald, who had been waiting in the wings since 582, was raised to the kingship by Mummolus, Guntram's former general who had defected to Childebert three years earlier, and by officials of the deceased Chilperic. Gundovald claimed to be a son of Chlothar I—an assertion that is most likely true in a strict sense, though he was never acknowledged by his father. Gundovald also maintained (certainly truthfully) that he had come to Gaul from Constantinople at the invitation of the Austrasians. Guntram shared his knowledge of the conspiracy personally with Childebert and put the rebellion down within a few months early in 585.

8) **Better relations between the Burgundian and Austrasian courts in 585, following the suppression of the rebellion.** At this time Guntram restored Tours to Childebert. For the first time since 575, Gregory now directly served the Austrasian house of Childebert (VIII 13). Wandelen died, and

Brunhild asserted control over her son (VIII 22), who came of age in the same year. Guntram acted as guardian of his nephews, Chlothar and Childebert, though neither was in his control.

9) **Plot to usurp power in the Austrasian kingdom in 587.** The leaders were Duke Rauching as well as Ursio and Berthefled, two members of the party previously hostile to Brunhild (IX 9, 12). The plot was detected by Guntram and communicated to Childebert, who quickly had the rebellion crushed.

10) **Treaty of Andelot in November 587.** As the Austrasian rebellion was being suppressed, a formal agreement was concluded between Austrasia and Burgundy. Differences of opinion on a number of matters, however, continued to dog Austrasian/Burgundian relations.

11) **Austrasian interventions in Italy to assist the empire in 588 (IX 25).** Austrasian disinclination to serve imperial interests (see VI 42, a. 584) seems to have faded after Ingund, the daughter of Brunhild and sister of Childebert, fell into the hands of the Byzantines in Spain, along with her son, following the failure of the rebellion of her husband Hermenigild against his father Leovigild in 584 (VI 43).

12) **Condemnation of Egidius, bishop of Rheims, for treason in 590.** Egidius was now brought to account for his dealings with Chilperic at the time of the Nogent agreements (X 9).

The modern shift from viewing Gregory as a naïve compiler of the events of his time to an artful commentator on the moral failings of his contemporaries has complicated our interpretation of his masterful portraits of kings and other figures of his age that animate the summary of events outlined above, though even before this change in perspective, Chilperic and his queen Fredegund, whom Gregory portrays scathingly, had been the subject of revisionist interpretations claiming to detect extreme clerical bias in Gregory's portrait of the pair. But beyond issues of partiality and bias, which the outlook of the *Histories* inevitably raises, are other problems touching on larger questions about the nature of the Merovingian kingdom and society. Unfortunately—and, it should be added, unsurprisingly—the *Histories* does not address constitutional, ethnic, or social themes directly in a way satisfying to modern sensibilities. Modern scholars have as a consequence interpreted the meaning of Gregory's narrative on these questions in a variety of ways, influenced often by ideological or national perspectives.

For instance, modern scholarship is divided on the character of Merovingian kingship, some arguing for its connection to archaic, supposedly sacral Germanic roots, others for its fundamentally contemporary character. As far as the institutions of the kingdom are concerned, an ample, if sometimes intractable, body of legal material survives that supplements Gregory's narrative. Long-standing arguments about Roman versus Germanic continuity of Merovingian institutions continue, but it should be noted that our understanding of what constitutes Germanic and Roman features have changed radically in the last half-century. A division of a slightly different kind exists among those scholars who readily find Gaul operating amidst structures of state and post-Roman social organization and those who locate the essential features of the Merovingian kingdom in personal relationships and ritual practices. Complicating the terms of these debates are problems of regional and institutional diversity within the kingdom; Gregory's perspective does not fall equally on all of Gaul, and scholars have often been inclined to imagine that the Frankish north and east conformed to distinctive norms about which Gregory was allegedly uninterested or ignorant. Finally, despite its importance for our understanding of the Merovingian kingdom, the Frankish (not the Gallic) aristocracy remains an enigma, with scholars divided on its origins and antiquity, the ideological underpinnings of its authority, and its relationship to the Merovingian monarchy. An enigma at the center of Gallic politics invites extreme speculation as to the meaning of events, but the riddle is ours, not Gregory's. His outlook required no expatiation on many matters that were obvious to himself and his contemporaries.

NOTE ON THE DRAWINGS OF JEAN-PAUL LAURENS

Jean-Paul Laurens was a major nineteenth-century painter of historical subjects. He was born in 1838 near Toulouse and died in 1921 in Paris. His best-known paintings were done from the 1860s to shortly after the turn of the century, a period that coincided with the rise of modernism. Laurens, who was closely associated with the Salon—an institution that came to symbolize conservative, academic, official art—had as a consequence the unhappy but not uncommon experience of living long enough to see defining taste shift decisively toward a new aesthetic that implacably rejected the values inspiring most of his work. Despite the temporary and intemperate vicissitudes of fashion, Laurens remains an important artist whose drawings, paintings, and decorative works are again attracting the attention they deserve.

The twenty-one drawings included in the present selections were selected from forty-two originally done for deluxe editions of Augustin Thierry's *Récits des temps mérovingiens* (Paris: Hachette, 1882 and 1887), a once wildly popular re-telling of episodes of sixth-century history largely based on Gregory of Tours's *Histories* and the work of Venantius Fortunatus, Gregory's friend. (A couple of drawings representing incidents in Venantius's life have been included.) Laurens seems to have been aware also of contemporary academic controversies over the nature of Merovingian society.

Representing the 'look' of the Merovingian period, even assisted by all its written sources and a limited number of architectural and material remains, is still largely an act of imagination. Laurens's work is worth contemplating not only for its artistic merit but also for its usually restrained and sober, yet still dramatic, depiction of Merovingian history, with a surprising sense of the scene that often differs from that of Gregory. The inclusion of Laurens's Merovingian world in this translation is not intended to define the appearance of the period, but merely to serve as another reference point for readers who find themselves pondering the mysteries of how it really looked and what really happened.

For a contemporary representation of a king of the early Merovingian dynasty, readers should direct their attention to the cover, which depicts the signet ring of Clovis's father, Childeric. The ring, made of gold and bearing the king's name, was found among the grave furnishings of a tomb uncovered in Tournai in 1653. Unfortunately the contents of the grave were stolen in 1831, and most of the objects, including the ring, were either melted down or lost. The cover depicts a detail of a modern casting in the Ashmolean Museum, Oxford. The casting, made not of gold but base metal, was reconstructed from impressions of the ring taken before it disappeared in 1831. Representations of late Merovingian kings also survive in the worn images on their wax seals.

BIBLIOGRAPHY

Editions and Translations

Histories

The edition used for the present translation is *Historiarum libri X*, ed. Bruno Krusch and Wilhelm Levison, MGH SRM I/1, 2nd ed. (1937–51).

The *Histories* have been translated into several European languages. All English translations have been published under the title of *History of the Franks*. Two give the complete *Histories*: that of O.M. Dalton (2 vol., Oxford, 1927) and Lewis Thorpe (Penguin, 1974). Translations are never perfect. Dalton's two-volume edition provides in the first volume a general introduction which can be useful if used with discretion; it is out of date in its general perspective and sometimes in its substance. The second volume has the translation and a still valuable commentary. Dalton, who appreciated Gregory's unclassical style, decided to cast the translation in a slightly archaic English to suggest, one guesses, a medieval provenance. Thorpe attempts to capture in English the common view that Gregory's Latin is colloquial; the result is occasionally distorting but the translation is readable and serves most purposes reasonably well. An abridged edition of the *Histories,* comprising its secular and spiritual themes, was produced by Ernest Brehaut for the Columbia Records of Civilization Series (New York, 1916, and reprinted many times since); its treatment of both themes is necessarily incomplete. All these English editions mistakenly assume that Gregory's work was issued in two editions: an original six-book version (ending with the death of Chilperic) and a later, expanded, ten-book version. This mistake was corrected in 1699 and in the authoritative Latin editions. The title of Gregory's work is best rendered as *Histories* (without reference to the number of books it contains).

These English translations have been consulted for the present rendering on a variety of points, as has the German translation of Rudolf Buchner/Wilhelm Giesebrecht, *Zehn Bücher Geschichten*, ed. Rudolf Buchner, 2 vols. (Berlin, 1955–56).

Gregory's Other Works

Gregory's books on the workings of the saints and the lives of the fathers have been translated in their various subdivisions in the following: *Life of the Fathers*, trans. Edward James (Liverpool, 1985); *Glory of the Martyrs* (Liverpool, 1988) and *Glory of the Confessors* [GC] (Liverpool, 1998), both translated by Raymond

Van Dam; in his *Saints and their Miracles in Late Antique Gaul* (Princeton, 1993), Van Dam also provides *The Suffering and Miracles of the Martyr St. Julian* and *The Miracles of the Bishop St. Martin* [VM]. Gregory's work on the offices of the church survives under the title *On the Course of the Stars*; the introductory section on the seven wonders (*miracula*) of the world is translated by William C. McDermott in *Monks, Bishops and Pagans: Christian Culture in Gaul and Italy 500–700* (Philadelphia, 1949; rpt. 1975), which also provides a version of the *Seven Sleepers of Ephesus*, now attributed to Gregory though he does not claim it for himself.

Contemporary Historical Works

Michael Winterbottom translates the works of Gildas in *The Ruin of Britain and Other Documents* (London and Chichester, 1978), which is alas out of print. Jordanes, *The Gothic History*, is translated by Charles Christopher Mierow (Princeton, 1915 – and later reprints). All Procopius's works are translated by H.B. Dewing, 7 vol., Loeb Classical Library (London, 1914–40); the *Secret History* is also available in several different translations. Agathias's *Histories* are translated by Joseph D. Frendo (Berlin and New York, 1975). The *Ecclesiastical History* of Evagrius Scholasticus is translated by Michael Whitby (Liverpool, 2000). John of Biclar is included in *Conquerors and Chronicles of Early Medieval Spain*, translated by Kenneth Baxter Wolf (Liverpool, 1990). Marius of Avenches is in Murray, *Reader* (see below).

Other Sources

Alexander Callander Murray, *From Roman to Merovingian Gaul: A Reader* (Peterborough, 2000), supplies a range of late Roman and Frankish historical sources, including Marius of Avenches and a translation of Fedegar's *Chronicle*, which completes Gregory's story of Chlothar II, Fredegund, and Brunhild. Tales by Fredegar and the author of the *Liber historiae Francorum* expanding Gregory's narrative are also included. Fredegar's *Chronicle* (without the early tales) is also translated by J.M. Wallace-Hadrill (London, 1960), and the *Liber historiae Francorum* is translated in its entirety by Bernard S. Bachrach (Lawrence, Kansas, 1973). *Vitae* of Genovefa (Childeric's and Clovis's contemporary) and of Radegund are translated in Jo An McNamara, John E. Halborg, with E. Gordon Whatley, *Sainted Women of the Dark Ages* (Durham and London, 1992). For a selection and discussion of Fortunatus's poems, see *Venantius Fortunatus: Personal and Political Poems*, trans. Judith George (Liverpool, 1995), and Judith George, *Venantius Fortunatus: A Latin Poet in Merovingian Gaul* (Oxford, 1992).

Guide to Further Reading

The following suggestions, and the alphabetical list of further reading that follows them, are by no means exhaustive. They are not guides to sixth-century Merovingian history, archaeology, and hagiography in the broad sense, nor to the corpus of Gregory's work or even the *Histories* in their entirety; their relevance is to the subject matter of the selections of the present translation and the questions that might arise from reading them. References (with one exception) have also been limited to English-language works.

In the alphabetical list of authors, individual works are cited chronologically.

As of this writing, a working online bibliography on Gregory is being maintained by Allen E. Jones (http://spectrum.troy.edu/~ajones/gotbibl.html). It contains, among much else, references to foreign-language works.

On the Histories

There are now two fundamental works on the *Histories* as an historical work: Goffart (1988), which is the starting point for the present-day, intensive re-evaluation of Gregory; and Heinzelmann (2001), which detects a theological perspective in the structure of the *Histories* and constitutes a virtual handbook to reading them. Both authors agree on many, but by no means all, of the issues of setting the *Histories* in context.

Other perspectives: Breukelaar (1994), which sees Gregory's work as a series of 'short stories', piled up over time; de Nie (1987), which interprets Gregory's works in literary/psychological terms; and Wood (1993, 1994*b*) and Halsall (2002*b*), which suppose a graduated composition and shifting political perspective. Various views can also be sampled in Mitchell/Wood (2002).

On Gregory's (and the *Histories*') relation to contemporary saints' cults, see Brown (1977, 1981), Corbett (1981, 1983, 1985) and Van Dam (1993).

On Gregory's circle and Venantius Fortunatus, see Brennan (1985*d*), Godman (1987), and George (1989, 1992); on Felix of Nantes, MacDermott (1975).

An interesting literary reflection on the narrative approach of the period is Pizarro (1989).

For the transmission of the *Histories* in the Middle Ages, see Goffart (1987), Contreni (2002), and Reimitz (2003).

General History

James (1982, 1988), and Wood (1994*a*).

Franks, Kings, and Politics

Issues in conceptualizing the Franks and their early history are outlined by Murray (2002). The problem of Frankish settlement and archaeology is treated by James (1979), Halsall (1992), and now by Fehr (2002), who deals with the modern political and historiographical context; on the Alamanni, see Brather (2002). On issues of ethnicity in general, see Gillett (2002b, 2002c) and the essays by contributors to Gillett (2002a). For Gregory's view of the subject: Goffart (1982, 1985), and James (1998).

On Merovingian long hair, see Cameron (1965), James (1984) despite its title, Diesenberger (2003), and Dutton (2004). The concept of sacral kingship as applied to the Merovingians is critiqued by Murray (1998b). On Childeric's ring, see MacGregor (1999).

On queens and politics, see Nelson (1978) and Stafford (1983). On the representation of Radegund, see Brennan (1985c), Kitchen (1998), and Moreira (2000).

The questions revolving around Clovis can be accessed through McCormick (1989), Daly (1994), Spencer (1994), and Fanning (2002).

On Clovis's grandson Theudebert, see Collins (1983), and on local politics, Wood (1983).

The affair of the pretender Gundovald has received two dedicated studies in English: Goffart (1957), and Bachrach (1994).

Institutions and Society

There is no modern comprehensive treatment of Merovingian institutions (even in the narrow sense of administrative structures) in English or any other language. Various aspects of law and administration are dealt with in the following: Lewis (1976), James (1983), Murray (1983, 1986, 1988, 1994, 2001), Barnwell (1992, 1997), and Wood (1986, 1990).

On war and military organization, compare the approaches of Bachrach (1970, 1972a, 1972b, 1994, 1997, 2002) and Halsall (2003); see also James (1997) and Murray (1988, 2001). Attitudes toward war and heroic virtues are explored by Muhlberger (1998), Wynn (2001), and Goffart (2002a).

The Merovingian church, its episcopacy, and its relationship to institutions and the guidance of local communities has not yet found a fundamental, modern exposition. Aspects are treated in James (1983), Wallace-Hadrill (1983), Wood (1983a), Nelson (2002), Noble (2002), Rosenwein (2002), and Smith (2002).

On the cult of the saints, the defining work is Brown (1977, 1981). But on Brown, now see Howard-Johnston/Hayward (1999) and especially Hayward (1999).

On general archaeology, see James (1988) and Périn (2002).

On the *civitates*, see Loseby (1998*a*), Gauthier (2002), and Périn (2002). For Marseilles, see Loseby (1998*b*), and for the Touraine, Stancliffe (1979) and Wood (2001).

On kinship and family ties, from a variety of perspectives, see Wemple (1981), Murray (1983), Lynch (1986), and de Jong (1998).

On the Gallic aristocracy and senators, see Brennan (1985*b*).

A treasure of references, with a classification and commentary on most aspects of Gregory's world, is Weidemann (1982).

Further Reading

Auerbach, Erich 1953. "Sicharius and Chramnesindus." Chap. 4 of *Mimesis: The Representation of Reality in Western Literature*. Trans. William R. Trask. Princeton.

Auerbach, Erich 1965. *Literary Language and Its Public in Late Latin Antiquity and in the Middle Ages*. Trans. Ralph Manheim. New York.

Bachrach, Bernard S. 1970. "Procopius, Agathias and the Frankish Military." *Speculum* 45: 435–41. Reprinted in *Armies and Politics in the Early Medieval West*, Aldershot, 1993, no. VIII.

Bachrach, Bernard S. 1972*a*. *Merovingian Military Organization*. Minneapolis.

Bachrach, Bernard S. 1972*b*. "Procopius and the Chronology of Clovis' Reign." *Viator* 1: 21–31. Reprinted in *Armies and Politics in the Early Medieval West*, Aldershot, 1993, no. VII.

Bachrach, Bernard S. 1994. *The Anatomy of a Little War: A Diplomatic and Military History of the Gundovald Affair (568–586)*. Boulder.

Bachrach, Bernard S. 1997. "The Imperial Roots of Merovingian Military Organization." In *Military Aspects of Scandinavian Society in a European Perspective, AD 1–1300*, ed. Anne Nørgård Jørgensen and Birthe L. Clausen, pp. 25–31. Copenhagen.

Bachrach, Bernard S. 2002. "Gregory of Tours as a Military Historian." In Mitchell/ Wood (2002), pp. 351–63.

Barlow, Jonathan 1995. "Gregory of Tours and the Myth of the Trojan Origins of the Franks." *Frühmittelalterliche Studien* 29: 86–95.

Barlow, Jonathan 1996. "Kinship and Fourth-Century Franks." *Historia* 45: 223–39.

Barnwell, P.S. 1992. *Emperors, Prefects and Kings: The Roman West, 395–565*. Chapel Hill and London.

Barnwell, P.S. 1997. *Kings, Courtiers and Imperium: The Barbarian West, 565–725*. London.

Brather, Sebastian 2002. "Ethnic Identities as Constructions of Archaeology: The Case of the Alamanni." In Gillett (2002*a*), pp. 149–76.

Brennan, Brian 1985*a*. "*Episcopae*: Bishops' Wives Viewed in Sixth-Century Gaul." *Journal of Church History* 54: 311–23.

Brennan, Brian 1985*b*. "Senators and Social Mobility in Sixth-Century Gaul." *Journal of*

Medieval History 11: 145–61.

Brennan, Brian 1985c. "St Radegund and the Early Development of her Cult at Poitiers." *Journal of Religious History* 13: 340–54.

Brennan, Brian 1985d. "The Career of Venantius Fortunatus." *Traditio* 41: 49–78.

Brennan, Brian 1985e. "The Conversion of the Jews of Clermont in AD 576." *Journal of Theological Studies* 36: 321–37.

Brennan, Brian 1992. "The Image of the Merovingian Bishop in the Poetry of Venantius Fortunatus." *Journal of Medieval History* 18: 115–39.

Brennan, Brian 1997. "'Being Martin': Saint and Successor in Sixth-Century Tours." *Journal of Religious History* 21: 121–35.

Breukelaar, Adriaan 1994. *Historiography and Episcopal Authority in Sixth-Century Gaul: The Histories of Gregory of Tours Interpreted in their Historical Context.* Göttingen.

Brown, Peter 1977. "Relics and Social Status in the Age of Gregory of Tours." *The Stenton Lecture, 1976.* Reading. Reprinted in *Society and the Holy in Late Antiquity*, London, 1982, pp. 222–50.

Brown, Peter 1981. *The Cult of the Saints: Its Rise and Function in Latin Christianity.* Chicago.

Brown, Peter 2002. "Gregory of Tours: Introduction." In Mitchell/Wood (2002), pp. 1–28.

Cameron, Avril 1965. "How Did the Merovingian Kings Wear their Hair?" *Revue belge de philologie et d'histoire* 43: 1203–16.

Cameron, Avril 1968. "Agathias on the Early Merovingians." *Annali della Scuola Normale di Pisa*, ser. II, 37: 95–140.

Collins, Roger 1983. "Theodebert I 'Rex Magnus Francorum.'" In *Ideal and Reality in Frankish and Anglo-Saxon Society*, ed. Patrick Wormald with Donald Bullough and Roger Collins, pp. 7–34. Oxford.

Contreni, John J. 2002. "Reading Gregory of Tours in the Middle Ages." In Mitchell/Wood (2002), pp. 419–34.

Corbett, John H. 1981. "The Saint as Patron in the Work of Gregory of Tours." *Journal of Medieval History* 7: 1–13.

Corbett, John H. 1983. "*Praesentium signorum munera*: The Cult of the Saints in the World of Gregory of Tours." *Florilegium* 5: 44–61.

Corbett, John H. 1985. "Hagiography and the Experience of the Holy in the Work of Gregory of Tours." *Florilegium* 7: 40–54.

Croke, Brian 2003. "Latin Historiography and the Barbarian Kingdoms." In *Greek and Roman Historiography in Late Antiquity, Fourth to Sixth Centuries A.D.*, ed. G. Masasco, pp. 349–89. Oxford.

Daly, William M. 1994. "Clovis: How Barbaric, How Pagan?" *Speculum* 69: 619–64.

de Jong, M. 1998. "An Unresolved Riddle: Early Medieval Incest Legislation." In Wood (1998a), pp. 107–40.

de Nie, Giselle 1987. *Views from a Many-Windowed Tower: Studies of Imagination in the*

Works of Gregory of Tours. Amsterdam.

de Nie, Giselle 2003. *Word, Image and Experience: Dynamics of Miracle and Self-Perception in Sixth-Century Gaul.* Aldershot, Hampshire, and Burlington, VT. [Collected articles.]

Diesenberger, Maximilien 2003. "Hair, Sacrality and Symbolic Capital in the Frankish Kingdoms." In *The Construction of Communities in the Early Middle Ages: Texts, Resources and Artefacts,* ed. Richard Corradini, Max Diesenberger, and Helmut Reimitz, pp. 173–212. Leiden and Boston.

Dill, Samuel 1926. *Roman Society in Gaul in the Merovingian Age.* London.

Dutton, Paul 2004. *Charlemagne's Mustache and Other Cultural Clusters of A Dark Age.* New York.

Fanning, Steven 2002. "Clovis Augustus and Merovingian Imitatio Imperii." In Mitchell/Wood (2002), pp. 321–36.

Fehr, Hubert 2002. "*Volkstum* as Paradigm: Germanic People and Gallo-Romans in Early Medieval Archaeology since the 1930s." In Gillett (2002a), pp. 177–200.

Gauthier, Nancy 2002. "From the Ancient City to the Medieval Town: Continuity and Change in the Early Middle Ages." In Mitchell/Wood (2002), pp. 47–66.

Geary, Patrick 1988. *Before France and Germany: The Creation and Transformation of the Merovingian World.* Oxford.

George, Judith 1989. "Poet as Politician: Venantius Fortunatus' Panegyric to King Chilperic." *Journal of Medieval History* 15: 5–18.

George, Judith 1992. *Venantius Fortunatus: A Poet in Merovingian Gaul.* Oxford.

Gillett, Andrew, ed. 2002a. *On Barbarian Identity: Critical Approaches to Ethnicity in the Early Middle Ages.* Turnhout.

Gillett, Andrew 2002b. "Introduction: Ethnicity, History, and Methodology." In Gillett (2002a), 1–20.

Gillett, Andrew 2002c. "Was Ethnicity Politicized in the Earliest Medieval Kingdoms?" In Gillett (2002a), pp. 85–121.

Gilliard, Frank D. 1979. "The Senators of Sixth-Century Gaul." *Speculum* 54: 685–97.

Godman, Peter 1987. "Orpheus among the Barbarians." Chapter 1 of *Poets and Emperors: Frankish Politics and Carolingian Poetry.* Oxford.

Goffart, Walter 1957. "Byzantine Policy in the West under Tiberius II and Maurice." *Traditio* 13: 73–118.

Goffart, Walter 1982. "Foreigners in the *Histories* of Gregory of Tours." *Florilegium* 4: 80–99. Reprinted in Goffart (1989), pp. 275–91.

Goffart, Walter 1985. "The Conversions of Avitus of Clermont and Similar Passages in Gregory of Tours." In *"To See Ourselves as Others See Us": Christians, Jews, "Other" in Late Antiquity,* ed. J. Neusner and E.S. Frerichs, pp. 473–97. Chico, CA. Reprinted in Goffart (1989), pp. 293–317.

Goffart, Walter 1987. "From *Historiae* to *Historia Francorum* and Back Again: Aspects of the Textual History of Gregory of Tours." In *Religion, Culture, and Society in the Early Middle Ages. Studies in Honor of Richard E. Sullivan,* ed. T.F.X. Noble and J.J.

Contreni, pp. 55–76. Kalamazoo. Reprinted in Goffart (1989), pp. 255–74.

Goffart, Walter 1988. *The Narrators of Barbarian History (A.D. 550–800): Jordanes, Gregory of Tours, Bede, and Paul the Deacon*. Princeton.

Goffart, Walter 1989. *Rome's Fall and After*. London and Ronceverte.

Goffart, Walter 2002a. "Conspicuously Absent: Martial Heroism in the *Histories* of Gregory of Tours and its Likes." In Mitchell/Wood (2002), pp. 365–94.

Goffart, Walter 2002b. "Does the Distant Past Impinge on the Invasion Age Germans?" In Gillett (2002a), pp. 21–37.

Halsall, Guy 1992. "The Origins of the *Reihengräberzivilization*: Forty Years On." In *Fifth-Century Gaul: A Crisis of Identity?* ed. J.F. Drinkwater and Hugh Elton, pp. 196–207. Cambridge.

Halsall, Guy 1995. *Settlement and Social Organization: The Merovingian Region of Metz*. Cambridge.

Halsall, Guy 1998. "Social Identities and Social Relationships in Early Merovingian Gaul." In Wood (1998a), pp. 141–76.

Halsall, Guy 2001. "Childeric's Grave, Clovis' Succession, and the Origins of the Merovingian Kingdom." In *Society and Culture in Late Antique Gaul: Revisiting the Sources*, ed. R.W. Mathisen and D. Shanzer, pp. 116–33. Aldershot, Hampshire, and Burlington, VT.

Halsall, Guy, ed. 2002a. *Humour, History and Politics in Late Antiquity and the Early Middle Ages*. Cambridge.

Halsall, Guy 2002b. "Nero and Herod? The Death of Chilperic and Gregory's Writings of History." In Mitchell/Wood (2002), pp. 337–50.

Halsall, Guy 2003. *Warfare and Society in the Barbarian West, 450–900*. London and New York.

Hayward, Paul Antony 1999. "Demystifying the Role of Sanctity in Western Christendom." In *The Cult of Saints in Late Antiquity and the Middle Ages: Essays on the Contribution of Peter Brown*, ed. J. Howard-Johnson and P.A. Hayward, pp. 115–42. Oxford and New York.

Heinzelmann, Martin 1998. "Heresy in Books I and II of Gregory of Tours' *Historiae*." In Murray (1998), pp. 67–82.

Heinzelmann, Martin 2001. *Gregory of Tours: History and Society in the Sixth Century*. Trans. Christopher Carroll. Cambridge.

Hen, Yitzak 1993. "Clovis, Gregory of Tours, and Pro–Merovingian Propaganda." *Revue Belge de philologie et d'histoire* 71: 271–76.

Hen, Yitzak 1994. *Culture and Religion in Merovingian Gaul, AD 481–751*. Leiden.

Hen, Yitzak 1998. "The Uses of the Bible and the Perception of Kingship in Merovingian Gaul." *Early Medieval Europe* 7: 277–90.

Hen, Yitzak 2002. "Paganism and Superstitions in the Time of Gregory of Tours: Une question mal posée!" In Mitchell/Wood (2002), pp. 229–40.

Howard-Johnston, James, and Paul Anthony Hayward 1999. *The Cult of the Saints in Late*

Antiquity and the Middle Ages. Oxford.

Hummer, H.J. 1998. "Franks and Alamanni: A Discontinuous Ethnogenesis." In Wood (1998*a*), pp. 9–32.

James, Edward 1979. "Cemeteries and the Problem of Frankish Settlement in Gaul." In *Names, Words, and Graves: Early Medieval Settlement,* ed. Peter H. Sawyer. Leeds.

James, Edward 1982. *The Origins of France: From Clovis to the Capetians.* London.

James, Edward 1983. "'Beati Pacifici': Bishops and the Law in Sixth-Century Gaul." In *Disputes and Settlements: Law and Human Relations in the West,* ed. John Bossy, pp. 25–45. Cambridge.

James, Edward 1984. "Bede and the Tonsure Question." *Peritia* 3: 85–98.

James, Edward 1988. *The Franks.* Oxford.

James, Edward 1993. "A Sense of Wonder: Gregory of Tours, Medicine and Science." In *The Culture of Christendom: Essays in Medieval History in Memory of Denis L. T. Bethel,* ed. E.A. Meyer, pp. 45–60. London.

James, Edward 1997. "The Militarisation of Roman Society." In *Military Aspects of Scandinavian Society in a European Perspective, AD 1–1300,* ed. Anne Nørgård Jørgensen and Birthe L. Clausen, 19–24. Copenhagen.

James, Edward 1998. "Gregory of Tours and the Franks." In Murray (1998), pp. 51–66.

Kitchen, John 1998. *Saints' Lives and the Rhetoric of Gender: Male and Female in Merovingian Hagiography.* Oxford and New York.

Lewis, Archibald 1976. "The Dukes in the Regnum Francorum, A.D. 550–751." *Speculum* 51: 381–410.

Loseby, S.T. 1998*a.* "Gregory's Cities: Urban Functions in Sixth–Century Gaul." In Wood (1998*a*), pp. 239–84.

Loseby, S.T. 1998*b.* "Marseilles and the Pirenne Thesis, I: Gregory of Tours, the Merovingian Kings and 'un Grand Port'." In *The Sixth Century: Production, Distribution and Demand,* ed. R. Hodges and W. Bowden, pp. 203–29. Leiden, Boston, Cologne.

Lynch, J.H. 1986. *Godparents and Kinship in Early Medieval Europe.* Princeton.

MacGonagel, Sarah Hansell 1936. *The Poor in Gregory of Tours: A Study of the Attitude of Merovingian Society towards the Poor as Reflected in the Literature of the Time.* New York.

MacGregor, Arthur 1999. "The Afterlife of Childeric's Ring." In *Classicism to Neo-classicism: Essays Dedicated to Gertrud Seidmann,* ed. Martin Henig and Dimitris Plantzos. Oxford.

Mathisen, Ralph W. 1984. "The Family of Georgius Florentius Gregorius and the Bishops of Tours." *Medievalia et Humanistica* 12: 83–95.

McCormack, Michael 1989. "Clovis at Tours, Byzantine Public Ritual and the Origins of Medieval Ruler Symbolism." In *Das Reich und die Barbaren,* ed. E.K. Chrysos and A. Schwarcz, pp. 155–80. Vienna and Cologne.

McDermott, William C. 1975. "Felix of Nantes: A Merovingian Bishop." *Traditio* 31: 1–24.

Miller, David Harry 1987. "Sacral Kingship, Biblical Kingship, and the Elevation of Pepin the Short." In *Religion, Culture, and Society in the Early Midddle Ages: Studies in Honor of Richard E. Sullivan*, ed. T.F.X. Noble and John J. Contreni, pp. 131–54. Kalamazoo.

Mitchell, Kathleen 1987. "Saints and Public Christianity in the *Historiae* of Gregory of Tours." In *Religion, Culture, and Society in the Early Middle Ages: Studies in Honor of Richard E. Sullivan*, ed. T.F.X. Noble and J.J. Contreni, pp. 77–94. Kalamazoo.

Mitchell/Wood (2002) = Mitchell, Kathleen, and Ian Wood, ed. 2002. *The World of Gregory of Tours*. Leiden.

Moreira, Isabel 1993. "*Provisatrix optima*: St. Radegund of Poitiers' Relic Petitions to the East." *Journal of Medieval History* 19: 285–305.

Moreira, Isabel 2000. *Dreams, Visions, and Spiritual Authority in Merovingian Gaul*. Ithaca, NY.

Muhlberger, Steven 1998. "War, Warlords, and Christian Historians." In Murray (1998a), pp. 83–98.

Murray, Alexander Callander 1983. *Germanic Kinship Structure: Studies in Law and Society in Late Antiquity and the Early Middle Ages*. Toronto.

Murray, Alexander Callander 1986. "The Position of the *Grafio* in the Constitutional History of the Merovingian Gaul." *Speculum* 61/4: 787–805.

Murray, Alexander Callander 1988. "From Roman to Frankish Gaul: *Centenarii* and *Centenae* in the Administration of the Merovingian Kingdom." *Traditio* 44: 59–100.

Murray, Alexander Callander 1994. "Immunity, Nobility and the *Edict of Paris*." *Speculum* 69/1: 18–39.

Murray, Alexander Callander, ed. 1998a. *After Rome's Fall: Narrators and Sources of Early Medieval History*. Toronto.

Murray, Alexander Callander 1998b. "*Post vocantur Merohingii*: Fredegar, Merovech, and 'Sacral Kingship'." In Murray (1998a), pp. 121–52.

Murray, Alexander Callander 2001. "'Pax et Disciplina': Roman Public Law and the Merovingian State." In *Proceedings of the Tenth International Congress of Medieval Canon Law, Syracuse, New York, 13–18 August 1996*, ed. Kenneth Pennington, Stanley Chodorow, and Keith H. Kendall, pp. 269–85. Vatican City.

Murray, Alexander Callander 2002. "Reinhard Wenskus on 'Ethnogenesis,' Ethnicity, and the Origin of the Franks." In Gillett (2002a), pp. 39–68.

Nelson, Janet L. 1978. "Queens as Jezebels: Brunhild and Balthild in Merovingian History." In *Medieval Women*, ed. Derek Baker, pp. 31–77. Oxford. Reprinted in Nelson, *Politics and Ritual in Early Medieval Europe*, London, 1986, pp. 1–48.

Nelson, Janet L. 2002. "The Merovingian Church in Carolingian Retrospective." In Mitchell/Wood (2002), pp. 241–59.

Newbold, R.F. 1983. "Patterns of Communication and Movement in Ammianus and Gregory of Tours." In *History and Historians in Late Antiquity*, ed. B. Croke and A. Emmett, pp. 66–81. Sydney.

Noble, Thomas F.X. 2002. "Gregory of Tours and the Roman Church." In Mitchell/

Wood (2002), pp. 145–61.

Périn, Patrick 2002. "Settlements and Cemeteries in Merovingian Gaul." In Mitchell/Wood (2002), pp. 67–98.

Petersen, Joan M. 1983. "Dead or Alive? The Holy Man as Healer in East and West in the Late Sixth Century." *Journal of Medieval History* 9: 91–98.

Pizarro, Martinez 1989. *A Rhetoric of the Scene: Dramatic Narrative in the Early Middle Ages.* Toronto.

Pohl, Walter 2002. "Gregory of Tours and Contemporary Perceptions of Lombard Italy." In Mitchell/Wood (2002), pp. 131–43.

Reimitz, Helmut 2003. "Social Networks and Identities in Frankish Historiography: New Aspects of the Textual History of Gregory of Tours' *Historiae*." In *The Construction of Communities in the Early Middle Ages: Texts, Resources and Artefacts*, ed. Richard Corradini, Max Diesenberger, and Helmut Reimitz, pp. 229–68. Leiden and Boston.

Reynolds, Burnam W. 1985. "*Familia Sancti Martini: Domus ecclesiae* on Earth as It Is in Heaven." *Journal of Medieval History* 11: 137–43.

Reynolds, Burnam W. 1987. "The Mind of Baddo: Assassination in Merovingian Politics." *Journal of Medieval History* 13: 117–24.

Riché, Pierre 1976. *Education and Culture in the Barbarian West from the Sixth through Eighth Century.* Trans. John J. Contreni. Columbia, SC.

Roberts, J. T. 1980. "Gregory of Tours and the Monk of St. Gall: The Paratactic Style of Medieval Latin." *Latomus* 39: 173–90.

Roberts, Michael 2001. "Venantius Fortunatus' Elegy on the Death of Galswintha (*Carm.* 6.5)." In *Society and Culture in Late Antique Gaul: Revisiting the Sources*, ed. Ralph W. Mathisen and Danuta Shanzer, pp. 298–312. Aldershot, Hampshire, and Burlington, VT.

Rose, Emily M. 2002. "Gregory of Tours and the Conversion of the Jews of Clermont." In Mitchell/Wood (2002), pp. 307–20.

Rosenwein, Barbara H. 2002. "Inaccessible Cloisters: Gregory of Tours and Episcopal Exemption." In Mitchell/Wood (2002), pp. 181–97.

Samson, Ross 1987. "The Merovingian Nobleman's Home: Castle or Villa?" *Journal of Medieval History* 13: 287–315.

Shanzer, Danuta 1998. "Dating the Baptism of Clovis: The Bishop of Vienne vs the Bishop of Tours." *Early Medieval Europe* 7: 29–57.

Shanzer, Danuta 2002. "History, Romance, Love, and Sex in Gregory of Tours' *Decem Libri Historiarum*." In Mitchell/Wood (2002), pp. 395–418.

Smith, Julia M.H. 2002 "Women at the Tomb: Access to Relic Shrines in the Early Middle Ages." In Mitchell/Wood (2002), pp. 163–80.

Spencer, Mark 1994. "Dating the Baptism of Clovis, 1886–1983." *Early Medieval Europe* 3/2: 97–116.

Stafford, P.A. 1983. *Queens, Concubines and Dowagers: The King's Wife in the Early Middle*

Ages. London.

Stancliffe, C.E. 1979. "From Town to Country: The Christianization of the Touraine, 370–600." In *The Church in Town and Countryside*, ed. D. Baker, pp. 43–59. Oxford.

Uhalde, Kevin 2001. "The Quasi-Imperial Coinage and Fiscal Administration of Merovingian Provence." In *Society and Culture in Late Antique Gaul: Revisiting the Sources*, ed. Ralph W. Mathisen and Danuta Shanzer. Aldershot, Hampshire, and Burlington, VT.

Van Dam, Raymond 1985. *Leadership and Community in Late Antique Gaul*. Berkeley, Los Angeles, Oxford.

Van Dam, Raymond 1993. *Saints and their Miracles in Late Antique Gaul*. Princeton.

Wallace-Hadrill, J.M. 1962. *The Long-Haired Kings and Other Studies in Frankish History*. London.

Wallace-Hadrill, J.M. 1971. *Early Germanic Kingship in England and on the Continent*. Oxford.

Wallace-Hadrill, J.M. 1983. *The Frankish Church*. Oxford.

Weidemann, Margarete 1982. *Kulturgeschichte der Merowingerzeit nach den Werken Gregors von Tours*, 2 vols. Mainz.

Wemple, Suzanne 1981. *Women in Frankish Society: Marriage and the Cloister, 500 to 900*. Philadelphia.

Winstead, Karen 1990. "The Transformation of the Miracle Story in the *Libri Historiarum* of Gregory of Tours." *Medium Aevum* 59: 1–15.

Wood, Ian 1977. "Kings, Kingdoms and Consent." In *Early Medieval Kingship*, ed. P.H. Sawyer and I.N. Wood, pp. 6–29. Leeds.

Wood, Ian 1983a. "The Ecclesiastical Politics of Merovingian Clermont." In *Ideal and Reality in Frankish and Anglo-Saxon Society*, ed. Patrick Wormald with Donald Bullough and Roger Collins, pp. 34–57. Oxford.

Wood, Ian 1983b. *The Merovingian North Sea*. Alingsås.

Wood, Ian 1985. "Gregory of Tours and Clovis." *Revue belge de philologie et d'histoire* 63: 249–72. Reprinted in *Debating the Middle Ages: Issues and Readings*, ed. L.K. Little and B.H. Rosenwein, Oxford and Malden, 1998, pp. 73–91.

Wood, Ian 1986. "Disputes in Late Fifth- and Sixth-Century Gaul: Some Problems." In *The Settlement of Disputes in Early Medieval Europe*, ed. Wendy Davies and Paul Fouracre, pp. 7–22. Cambridge.

Wood, Ian 1988. "Clermont and Burgundy, 511–53." *Nottingham Medieval Studies* 32: 119–25.

Wood, Ian 1990. "Administration, Law and Culture in Merovingian Gaul." In *The Uses of Literacy in Early Medieval Europe*, ed. Rosamond McKitterick, pp. 63–81. Cambridge.

Wood, Ian 1993. "The Secret Histories of Gregory of Tours." *Revue belge de philologie et d'histoire* 71: 253–70.

Wood, Ian 1994a. *The Merovingian Kingdoms, 450–751*. London and New York.

Wood, Ian 1994b. *Gregory of Tours*. Headstart History Papers. Oxford.

Wood, Ian 1995. "Defining the Franks: Frankish Origins in Early Medieval Historiography." In *Concepts of National Identity in the Middle Ages*, ed. Simon Forde, Lesley Johnson and Alan V. Murray, pp. 47–58. Leeds.

Wood, Ian, ed. 1998a. *Franks and Alamanni in the Merovingian Period: An Ethnographic Perspective*. Woodbridge.

Wood, Ian 1998b. "Incest, Law and the Bible in Sixth–Century Gaul." *Early Medieval Europe* 7: 291–304.

Wood, Ian 2001. "Topographies of Holy Power in Sixth–Century Gaul." In *Topographies of Power in the Early Middle Ages*, ed. M. de Jong, F. Theuws and C. van Rhijn, pp. 137–54. Leiden.

Wood, Ian 2002. "The Individuality of Gregory of Tours." In Mitchell/Wood (2002), pp. 29–46.

Wood, Ian 2003. "Deconstructing the Merovingian Family." In *The Construction of Communities in the Early Middle Ages: Texts, Resources and Artefacts*, ed. Richard Corradini, Max Diesenberger, and Helmut Reimitz, pp. 149–172. Leiden and Boston.

Wynn, Phillip 2001. "Wars and Warriors in Gregory of Tours' *Histories* I–IV." *Francia* 28/1: 1–35.

I am determined to seek little glory from history, especially because we church-men are rash if we publish our own affairs, and self-important if we deal with the affairs of others; we record the past without advantage and the present from imperfect knowledge; we write what is untrue to our disgrace and what is true at our peril. History is the kind of subject in which you win scant credit for mentioning good men and incur serious disfavor for referring to infamous ones. Thus from the outset the quality and spirit of satire blends with the historian's style. Historical writing, then, is quite incompatible with our religious profession: it begins with ill-will, is carried out through toil, and ends in hatred.

Sidonius Apollinaris, bishop of Clermont, ca 477
Letters, IV 2, declining a suggestion to write history

A great many mortals prone to the vain pursuit of earthly glory have sought to achieve what they thought would be enduring remembrance for their own names by penning the lives of famous men.... But this enterprise of theirs had no bearing on the blessed and eternal life beyond. How does the glory of their writings do them any good, since it will perish with this world? And what does posterity gain by reading about Hector fighting or Socrates philosophizing? For is it not only foolishness to imitate them but lunacy not to bitterly oppose them? Those who value human life for its present activities only consign their hopes to tall tales and their souls to the tomb.

Sulpicius Severus, ca 480
Preface, *Life of Saint Martin*

In making moral judgments on the past, historians have far more powerful rhe-torical and stylistic weapons at their disposal than mere denunciation: sarcasm, irony, the juxtaposition of rhetoric and reality, the factual exposure of hypocrisy, self-interest, and greed, the uncommented recounting of courageous acts of re-bellion and defiance. All of this can be achieved without the direct application of the transient moral vocabulary of the society the historian is living in.

Richard J. Evans, 1997
In Defence of History

PART I

FROM MEROVECH TO CLOVIS

CHAPTER ONE
ORIGINS OF THE MEROVINGIAN KINGDOM
(BOOK II)

The way of providence is a little rude.

Ralph Waldo Emerson, *The Conduct of Life*

Before Clovis

Gregory first broached the subject of the Franks in Book II in the context of the history of fifth-century Gaul and his own inquiry into the earliest references to their kings—an inquiry doubtless undertaken with the origins of the current Merovingian dynasty in mind. The Franks first appear in Latin sources around the year 300 as a generic name for a variety of lower Rhineland peoples; at the time the name was well-known but still relatively recent. Whether the subsequent currency of the term was mainly due to Roman and provincial perspectives or the Rhineland peoples themselves is unclear. In any case, Gregory of Tours knew nothing of the earliest sources or his search would have been rewarded, for they furnish the names of early Frankish kings. Gregory's efforts, nevertheless, preserve for us two valuable selections from the otherwise lost histories of Sulpicius Alexander and Renatus Profuturus Frigeridus (not translated here). The first kings Gregory could identify were the mid fifth-century kings Chlodio, Merovech, and Childeric. Merovech gave his name to the Merovingians; he was the father of Childeric and the grandfather of Clovis.

Chlodio and Merovech (II 9–10)

In the following passage, reference to a left-bank 'Thuringia' is puzzling: it is often thought that Tongres and the Tungri are meant. Dispargum is usually identified as Duisburg. Richimer the Frank is not the great Roman patrician Ricimer (a. 457–72), who was of Suevic and Visigothic descent.

As regards the kings of the Franks, many are unaware who their first king was.

Gregory then gives substantial extracts from the lost works of Sulpicius Alexander and Renatus Profuturus Frigeridus and a small misquotation from the Histories of Orosius. *These narrate Gallic military and political events of the late fourth and early fifth centuries.*

…This is the information that the above mentioned historians have left us regarding the Franks, without naming their kings.

3

Now many say that the Franks left Pannonia and at first inhabited the banks of the river Rhine. From there they crossed the Rhine and traversed Thoringia; and then they set over themselves in the territories and cities (*pagi vel civitates*) [of Gaul] long-haired kings, from their first, and as I would say, more noble, family. This was shown to be true later by Clovis's victories, as I shall subsequently narrate.

We read in the consular annals that Theudomer, king of the Franks, the son of Richimer, and his mother Ascyla, were put to the sword.

It is said also that Chlodio, skilled in war and the most noble among his people, was king of the Franks at the time; he lived in the fortress of Dispargum, which is in the region of the Thoringi. In those parts, that is toward the south, the Romans were living up to the river Loire. Beyond the Loire the Goths ruled. The Burgundians, followers of Arian doctrine, lived across the Rhône, near the city of Lyons. Chlodio sent scouts to the city of Cambrai; when they had surveyed everything, he followed, crushed the Romans, and took the city. Staying there for a short time, he extended his control to the Somme. Some say that king Merovech, whose son was Childeric, was of his line.

The Franks of that time, however, paid service to pagan religion and were entirely without knowledge of God.

A long homily against paganism follows.

...The Franks of that time did not at first understand [their error], but later they understood as the history that follows will tell.

Avitus and Aegidius (II 11)

The eastern emperor Marcian, mentioned below, was only sole emperor of east and west briefly in 457; the western emperor Majorian (a. 457–61) may be meant.

When Avitus, a senator, and as is quite well-known, citizen of Clermont, managed to attain imperial rule [a. 455–56], he set about acting wantonly but was overthrown by the senators and ordained bishop of Placentia. When he learned that the senate, still incensed with him, was going to deprive him of his life, he made for the basilica of Saint Julian, the martyr of Clermont, bringing many gifts with him. But the course of his life reached its end while he was still on the road, and he died. He was taken to the town of Brioude and buried at the feet of the aforesaid martyr. Marcian succeeded him [as Roman emperor]. In the Gallic provinces, the Roman Aegidius was made master of the soldiers.

4

Childeric and Basina (II 12)

As for Childeric, since he was hopelessly undone by wantonness and reigned over the Franks, he began to violate their daughters. The Franks were incensed at this and drove him from power. When he learned that they also intended to kill him, he made for Thuringia, leaving behind a man dear to him who could mollify with smooth words those who were enraged with him. Childeric also gave the fellow a token that would indicate when he could return home—that is to say they divided between themselves a single gold coin, Childeric taking one half with him and his friend keeping the other.

"When I send this half to you," said the friend, "and the parts fit together to make a single gold piece, then you can confidently come home."

So Childeric went away to Thuringia and took refuge with King Bisinus and his wife Basina.

Then the Franks, now that they had thrown out Childeric, unanimously accepted as their king Aegidius, who, as we said above, had been sent by the empire as master of the soldiers. When he had ruled them for eight years, that faithful friend secretly placated the Franks and sent messengers to Childeric with half the gold coin he had retained. Childeric recognized the clear sign that the Franks wanted him and were even themselves asking for him and so he returned from Thuringia and was restored to his kingship.

During the reigns of Bisinus and Childeric, Basina, whom we mentioned above, left her husband and came to Childeric. He very carefully questioned her as to why she had come.

"I know your warlike qualities," she said, "and that you are quite restless, and so I have come to live with you. And you should know that were I to find out about someone more warlike than you across the seas I would have no qualms about seeking out his companionship."

He cheerfully married her. She conceived and gave birth to a son whom she called Clovis. He was a great man and an outstanding warrior.

Gregory recounts episcopal successions and the building of churches in Clermont, Tours, and Autun (II 13–17), before returning to Childeric.

Childeric, Aegidius, and Odoacer in the Annals of Angers (II 18, 19)

Because of its paratactic style (parataxis is the juxtaposition of elements without indicating their interconnection), the following passage regarding Childeric, Aegidius, and Odoacer is generally thought to be an excerpt from a now lost set of annals from Angers. Gregory apparently expunged a yearly dating scheme that clearly accompanied the original annals, which in the excerpt covered the period from 463 to around 470. It is difficult to say how long after the events the annals of Angers were compiled, but they were certainly not contemporary.

The succinctness of the annals makes them difficult to interpret, and the basic questions of who is doing what to whom and on whose behalf cannot be answered with absolute confidence. With the exception of the Goths, all the participants may have been ostensibly in Roman service; the annals may be recording a falling out among allies, occasioned in part by the succession of the emperor Severus (a. 461–65) and then the death of Aegidius.

The battle of Orleans, fought in 463, was a victory over the Goths of southern Gaul won by Aegidius, who had been appointed by either Avitus or Majorian. He was not accepted by the emperor Severus.

Childeric is described as in Roman service in the excerpt. Not all Franks were subject to Childeric.

Odoacer is generally believed to be the commander who deposed Romulus Augustulus in 476 and who ruled Italy from 476–93 as patrician and king, until his death at the hands of Theoderic the Great. The Saxons whom he commanded in the excerpt had occupied islands on the Loire as pirates. It is generally thought that in the excerpt Odoacer and the Saxons begin as Roman enemies and are brought into an alliance by the Franks only at the end; but it is more likely that they had agreements with Roman authorities prior to Aegidius's death.

The Britons were in Roman service under a certain Riothamus, who is attested in other sources.

Count Paul is clearly a Roman commander, but his death is problematical. Was he killed by the Saxons? The Latin can be construed to mean that Childeric's forces killed him.

The reference to the Alamanni has been considered a mistake for the Alani, or misdated. If there is an error here, it is not likely Gregory's.

Then Childeric fought at Orleans [a. 463].

Odoacer came with Saxons to Angers. This was a time when a great epidemic ravaged the population.

Aegidius died [a. 465], leaving a son called Syagrius. After his death Odoacer took hostages from Angers and other places.

The Britons were driven out of Bourges by the Goths, and many of them were killed at Bourg-de-Déols [ca 468].

Count Paul led Romans and Franks in a campaign against the Goths and carried off plunder.

Odoacer came to Angers. The next day King Childeric arrived and took the city after Count Paul had been killed. On that day the cathedral manse was burned in a violent fire [a. 469?].

After these events there was war between the Saxons and Romans. But the Saxons retreated leaving many of their men to the swords of the pursuing Romans. The Franks captured and ruined their islands, killing a large number of people. In the ninth month of this year, there was an earthquake.

Odoacer entered into a treaty with Childeric and they subdued the Alamanni who had invaded part of Italy.

Clovis, a. 481–511

The headings here are Gregory's.

Clovis Becomes King (II 27)

On Childeric's death [a. 481/82, at Tournai], his son Clovis reigned in his place.

In the fifth year of Clovis's reign [a. 486/87], Syagrius, king of the Romans and son of Aegidius, had his headquarters in the city of Soissons, which the late Aegidius had held. Clovis, along with his kinsman Ragnachar, who himself also held royal power, marched against Syagrius and challenged him to make ready a field of battle. Syagrius wasted no time, nor was he afraid to stand his ground. And so both sides joined battle, and Syagrius, when he saw his forces crushed, turned tail and slipped off at great speed to King Alaric [II, 484–507] at Toulouse. But Clovis sent Alaric an ultimatum to hand Syagrius over or to expect an attack for harboring him. Alaric was afraid to run afoul of the anger of the Franks for Syagrius's sake—it is the habit of the Goths to tremble with fear—and handed him over bound to the envoys. Clovis ordered his prisoner held in custody, but, when he had taken possession of Syagrius's kingdom, he had him put to the sword in secret.

In this period, many churches were plundered by the army of Clovis, because he was still enveloped in the errors of paganism. It happened that his forces took from a certain church a ewer of marvelous size and beauty, along with other items used in religious services. The bishop of that church sent messengers to the king, asking that, if his church could get back no other sacred vessel, might it at least obtain the ewer.

When the king heard this, he said to the messenger, "Follow us to Soissons, for there all the spoils are to be divided. When I get the vessel during the sharing of the spoils, I will grant what the bishop wants."

They came to Soissons, and when all the plunder was laid out in the open, the king said, "I ask you, most valiant fighting men, do not refuse to grant me that vessel"—he meant by this the above mentioned ewer—"over and above my share."

"All we see before us is yours, glorious king," said the more sensible ones when they heard the king's words. "Even we ourselves have been brought under your lordship. Go ahead and take what you desire, for no one can stand up to your power."

When they had spoken like this, one unthinking, envious, fool raised his ax and drove it into the ewer.

"You shall get nothing from here but what a regular division awards to you," he cried in a loud voice.

All were astounded at this act. The king covered his sense of outrage with a show of gentle forbearance. He took the ewer and restored it to the church messenger, keeping the wrong he felt buried in his breast.

A year passed. He commanded every unit to assemble with full equipment in order to exhibit on the March field the good condition of their arms. The king's intention was to inspect everyone, and he came to the man who had struck the ewer.

"No one carries weapons as poorly maintained as you," said the king. "Neither your spear, your sword, nor your ax are any good."

The king grabbed the man's ax and threw it to the ground. As the man started to lean over to pick it up, the king raised his own ax in both hands and planted it in the fellow's head.

"This is what you did to that ewer in Soissons," said the king.

With the fellow lying dead, the king dismissed the rest, having gained a considerable amount of fearful respect by his act.

Clovis waged many wars and won many victories. For instance, in the tenth year of his reign [a. 491], he made war on the Thuringians and subjected them to his rule.

Clovis Marries Chlothild (II 28)

Another king at the time was Gundioc, king of the Burgundians [a. 455–73/74?], from the lineage of that [Gothic] persecutor [of Christians] Athanaric [† 381]. He had four sons: Gundobad, Godigisel, Chilperic, and Godomar. Gundobad put his brother Chilperic to the sword, tied a stone around the neck of Chilperic's wife, and drowned her. He sentenced her two daughters to exile. The elder of the daughters was called Crona; she put on the habit of a religious. The name of the younger was Chlothild.

Clovis often used to send delegations into Burgundy where his envoys discovered the young Chlothild. They reported to King Clovis how they had observed that she was refined and intelligent and had learned that she was of royal descent. The king lost no time in sending an embassy to Gundobad, asking to marry her. Gundobad was afraid to refuse and handed her over to the envoys, who took the girl and quickly brought her before the king. He was quite delighted when he saw her and took her for his wife. He already had by a concubine a son by the name of Theuderic.

Baptism of their Firstborn Who Dies in his White Robes (II 29)

The king had by Queen Chlothild a firstborn son. The mother wanted the boy baptized and constantly gave instruction to her husband.

"The gods you worship are nothing," she would say. "They could help neither themselves nor others, since they were fashioned of wood, stone, or metal. As for the names that you have given them, these were the names of men, not gods. Saturn, for example, was a man who, so it is said, fled from his son to avoid being deprived of royal power. And Jove also, the filthiest practitioner of every indecency, defiler of men, mocker of kinswomen, was someone who couldn't even keep himself from sex with his own sister, as she herself said, 'both sister and wife of Jove' (Virgil, *Aeneid* I 46 f.). What were Mars and Mercury capable of? They were endowed with magical arts rather than in possession of power of the divine kind.

"Who should be worshipped is He who at a word created out of nothing heaven and earth, the sea and everything within it; who caused the sun to shine and adorned the heaven with stars; who filled the waters with reptiles, the earth with animals, the air with birds; He, at the nod of whose head the lands are adorned with fruits, the trees with apples, the vines with grapes; He, by whose hand the human race was created and by whose largesse every creature was made to render service and support to the human whom He created."

Although the queen would say this, the king's spirit was brought no nearer to believing.

"By the command of our gods," he would say, "all things are created and come forth. And as for your God, he plainly can do nothing, and what's more, he turns out not to be descended from the gods."

In the meantime, the faithful queen presented her son for baptism and had the church adorned with hangings and drapery, so that he who could not be prevailed upon by instruction might more readily be brought to believe by this mystery. The boy was baptized and called Ingomer, but he died, still wearing the white robes of his baptism.

The king as a result became bitter and was not slow to reproach the queen.

"If the boy had been dedicated in the name of my gods, he would surely have lived; after baptism in the name of your God, he was utterly incapable of living."

"To almighty God, creator of all things," replied the queen, "I give thanks. He has judged me not at all unworthy and has seen fit to admit to His kingdom a child born of my womb. My heart is untouched by grief at this event, because I know that those called from this world in their white baptismal robes will be cherished in the sight of God."

Afterwards she bore another son, who was baptized and whom she called Chlodomer.

When he too began to grow ill, the king would say, "There can only be the same outcome for him as for his brother—having been baptized in the name of this Christ of yours, he will die right away."

But the mother prayed, and by the will of God, the child recovered.

War against the Alamanni (II 30)

Now the queen never ceased instructing the king to recognize the true God, and to abandon his idols. But in no way could she bring him to believe, until at last, when waging war upon the Alamanni, he was forced by necessity to confess what of his free will he had denied. It happened that, when the two hosts joined battle, the slaughter was fierce and the army of Clovis was in danger of annihilation.

When he saw this, the king raised his eyes to heaven and, with a change of heart, began to weep.

"Jesus Christ," he said, "You who Chlothild proclaims are the Son of the living God, who are said to give aid to those in distress and to grant victory to those that put their hopes in You, I humbly implore Your glory for help. If You grant me victory over these enemies, and if I experience the power that people dedicated to Your name claim to have proven is Yours, then I shall believe in You and be baptized in Your name. For I have called upon my own gods, but as I am finding out, they have stopped helping me; so I don't think they have any power, if they don't come to help their servants. I now call upon You and wish to believe in you, provided I am rescued from my enemies."

As he said this, the Alamanni turned tail and started to run away. And when they saw that their king was killed, they yielded themselves to Clovis.

"We beg you," they cried, "stop the destruction of our people, now that we are yours."

The king put an end to the conflict, and having admonished the people and returned home in peace, he recounted to the queen how he had been found worthy of victory by calling on the name of Christ. This happened in the fifteenth year of his reign [a. 496].

The Baptism of Clovis (II 31)

At that point, the queen gave orders for the holy Remigius, bishop of the city of Rheims, to be summoned in secret and persuaded him to impart the word of salvation to the king. The king was brought to a private meeting and the bishop began to teach him to put his faith in the true God, maker of heaven and earth, and to abandon idols, which were of no use to either himself or others.

"Most holy father," said the king, "I myself have willingly listened to you; but there is still a problem. The people who follow me will not accept abandoning their gods; still, I will go and speak with them as you have taught me."

He met with his followers. Before he could speak, God's powers having preceded him, all the people shouted out together, "Dutiful king, we shall drive away our mortal gods, and we are ready to follow that immortal God preached by Remigius."

The news was brought to the bishop, who, filled with great joy, ordered the font to be prepared. The streets were canopied with colored hangings, the churches adorned with white drapery, the baptistery was set in order, the smell of incense spread, fragrant candles sparkled, and the whole baptismal church was filled with the divine fragrance. God granted such grace to those present there that they thought they had been transported amidst the fragrances of paradise.

To begin, the king asked to be baptized by the bishop. The new Constantine advanced to the font to wipe out the disease of the old leprosy, to wipe away in new waters the filthy stains borne from ancient times.

As the king entered the water, the saint of God eloquently addressed him with the words, "Gently bow your head, Sicamber; worship that which you have burned; burn that which you have worshipped."

Now Holy Remigius the bishop was extraordinarily learned and especially proficient in rhetoric; in addition, he was so outstanding in holiness that he was the equal of holy Silvester in performing miracles. There is now a book of his life that tells how he raised a man from the dead.

Then the king, acknowledging almighty God in the Trinity, was baptized in the name of the Father, the Son, and the holy Spirit, and anointed with holy chrism under the sign of the cross of Christ.

As for his army, more than three thousand men were baptized.

His sister Albofledis, who not long after passed on to the Lord, was also baptized. When the king was depressed over her death, holy Remigius sent him a letter of consolation, which began like this: "I am sorry, deeply sorry for the cause of your sadness, the death of your sister of good memory, Albofledis. But we can take comfort that, when a such a person departs from this world, she should be held in high regard rather than mourned."

Another sister of the king was also converted. Her name was Lantechildis, and though she had fallen into the heresy of the Arians, she acknowledged the Son and the Holy Spirit as equal to the Father and received the holy chrism.

War against Gundobad (II 32)

At this time the two brothers Gundobad and Godigisel were in possession of a kingdom in the area of the Rhône and Saône, including the province of Marseilles. Both they and their people were followers of the Arian sect.

Since the brothers were at odds with each other, Godigisel, who had heard of the victories of King Clovis, secretly sent envoys to him to say, "If you give me help to go after my brother, so I can either kill him in battle or drive him from the kingdom, I will pay you each year such tribute as you may wish to impose."

Clovis gladly took the offer and promised him aid whenever it was required. At the appointed time, he brought his army against Gundobad.

On hearing the news, Gundobad, unaware of his brother's treachery, sent him a message: "Come to my assistance, for the Franks have mustered against us and are approaching our territory to take it. Let us be of one mind against a people who are our enemies to avoid suffering separately what other peoples have gone through."

"I shall come with my army," said Godigisel, "and give you aid."

The three kings put their forces in the field at the same time—Clovis marching against Gundobad and Godigisel—and came to the fortress of Dijon with all the accoutrements of war. Battle was joined on the banks of the Ouche [a. 500]. Godigisel joined Clovis, and their united forces crushed the army of Gundobad. Observing his brother's treachery, which he had not suspected, Gundobad turned his back and, fleeing along the bank of the Rhône, entered the city of Avignon.

As for Godigisel, with victory achieved, he promised Clovis a part of his kingdom and went away in peace, entering Vienne in triumph, as if he were already master of the entire kingdom. Clovis reinforced his troops, and went in pursuit of Gundobad, intending to drag him from Avignon and kill him.

When Gundobad heard about this, he was terrified, fearing the sudden approach of death. He had in his company, however, Aridius, a man of illustrious rank, energetic and intelligent, whom he summoned to a meeting.

"I'm hemmed in on all sides and don't know what to do," said the king. "These barbarians have attacked me with the intention of killing me and bringing ruin to the whole country."

"You have to soothe the wildness of this man, if you're to avoid destruction," answered Aridius. "So, providing this plan meets your approval, I shall now pretend to desert you and go over to his side. Once I am in his confidence, I shall make sure that they bring ruin neither on you nor on this country. For your part, you must ensure that whatever demands he makes of you on my advice are carefully fulfilled, until such time as the Lord sees fit, in his goodness, to have your cause succeed."

"I shall do whatever you tell me," said the king.

After this discussion with the king, Aridius said farewell and, taking his leave, went off to King Clovis.

"See, most dutiful king," he said to Clovis, "I come into your power as a humble servant, abandoning that most wretched man Gundobad. If your goodness will see fit to receive me, you and your offspring will find in me an honest and faithful servant."

Clovis accepted him quite readily and kept him by his side. Aridius was a delightful story-teller, full of advice, fair in judgment, and faithful in his duties.

Then, while Clovis was investing the walls of the city with his army, Aridius said to him, "King, if your majesty would kindly listen to a few humble words of mine, I would like to furnish advice and, though you have little need of it, it is completely in your interest; it would also suit both you and the cities through which you decide to pass.

"Why," asked Aridius, "do you keep this army in the field, when your enemy is protected by stout fortifications? You lay the fields waste, consume the meadows, pull apart the vines, cut down the olive trees, and destroy all the products of this region; still, you can do nothing to hurt him. Instead, send emissaries to him and impose tribute that he will pay to you every year. In this way the country can be saved, and you will be lord over a tribute-payer forever. If he refuses that, then you may do what you want."

The king took the advice and gave orders for his army to return home. At that time he sent envoys to Gundobad, imposed tribute on him and ordered him to pay it every year. Gundobad paid it immediately and promised to pay it hereafter.

The Destruction of Godigisel (II 33)

After these events, Gundobad restored his forces. Then disdaining to pay the promised tribute to King Clovis, he brought an army against his brother Godigisel, shut him up in the city of Vienne and besieged the city.

When provisions began to run out among the lesser folk, Godigisel became afraid that the shortage might reach all the way to himself and so he ordered them driven from the city. When this was done, among those driven out was the artisan who looked after the aqueduct. Resentful at being driven out with the others, he went in a fury to Gundobad and pointed out how the king could break into the city and take vengeance on his brother.

The artisan led a force along the aqueduct, preceded by a good number of men carrying iron crowbars. The aqueduct had a vent covered by a great stone. Under the direction of the artisan, this was heaved aside by use of the crowbars, and so they entered the city, surprising from the rear those who were firing arrows from the walls. At the sound of a trumpet from the midst of the city, the besiegers seized the gates, opened them up, and crowded in. While the people of the city were caught between two forces and were being cut down on both sides, Godigisel took refuge in the cathedral of the heretics and there he was killed along with the Arian bishop. Next the Franks who had been with Godigisel gathered together in a tower. Gundobad, however, gave orders that none of them should suffer any harm; he had them seized and sent them to King Alaric to be exiled at Toulouse. He killed the senators and Burgundians who had accepted Godigisel.

Gundobad brought back under his authority the whole country now known as Burgundy. He established milder laws among the Burgundians to prevent them dominating the Romans.

Gundobad's Desire to be Converted (II 34)

When Gundobad recognized that there was nothing to the claims of the heretics, he acknowledged that Christ, the Son of God, and the Holy Ghost were both equal to the Father and asked Avitus, the holy bishop of Vienne, to grant him the chrism in secret.

"If you really believe what you say," answered the bishop, "you should follow the teaching of our Lord himself. For He said, 'If anyone acknowledges Me before the world, I will also acknowledge him before my Father, who is in heaven; but whoever denies Me before the world, him I will also deny before my Father, who is in heaven' [cf. Matt. 10:32, 33]. When He was teaching His holy and beloved blessed apostles about the temptations of future persecutions, He urged them, 'Beware of people; for they will deliver you up to councils and will scourge you in their synagogues, and you shall stand before kings and governors for My sake as a witness to them and to the nations' [cf. Matt. 10: 17, 18]. You are a king and have no fear of anyone laying hands on you, but you are frightened of an insurrection among the people and dare not acknowledge in public the Creator of all. Stop being so foolish, and that which you say you believe in your heart, utter with your lips before the people. For as the blessed apostle said, 'With the heart one believes for the sake of righteousness, but with the lips one makes confession for the sake of salvation' [cf. Rom. 10:10].

More scriptural references on the same subject follow.

...This argument confounded Gundobad, but he persisted in this madness to his dying day and would not acknowledge in public the equality of the Trinity.

The blessed Avitus was at this time very eloquent. For at the request of King Gundobad, he wrote against heresy that was arising in Constantinople, both the teaching of Eutyches [ca 440] and of Sabellius [ca 250] that there was nothing divine about our lord Jesus Christ. His splendid letters are extant: once they put down heresy, now they edify the church of God. He wrote one book of homilies, six books in verse on the creation of the world and various other subjects, and nine books of letters, including the ones just mentioned.

He relates in a homily he wrote on the Rogations that these particular services, which we celebrate before the triumph of the Lord's ascension, were established by Mamertus, bishop of Vienne, Avitus's own see, at a time when the city was alarmed by many portents. It was, for example, shaken by frequent earthquakes; also wild stags and wolves entered the gates and, as he says, wandered about the whole city without fear. These signs occurred throughout the course of a year and, as the services of the Easter period approached, the entire community devoutly awaited the mercy of God, so that this day of great commemoration might put an end to this fear. But during the very vigils of that glorious night, while mass was being celebrated, suddenly the royal palace within the city was set ablaze by fire from heaven. While everyone was stricken with fear and rushed from the cathedral, believing that either the whole city would be consumed by this fire or the earth would open up and swallow it, the holy bishop lay prostrate before the altar, begging God's mercy with groans and tears. Why say more? The prayer of the famous bishop reached the heights of heaven; the river of flowing tears quenched the burning palace. When these events had taken place, and as I have said, the day of the Lord's ascension approached, he imposed a fast upon the people, and established the manner of prayer, the times when the fast could be broken, and the joyful disbursement of alms. The alarming events ceased after that; news of the deed spread through all the provinces, causing all the bishops to follow the example of his faith. Down to the present time, these services are held, in Christ's name, with repentant heart and contrite spirit, in all churches.

The Meeting of Clovis and Alaric (II 35)

Then Alaric, king of the Goths, saw that King Clovis kept conquering nations, so he sent envoys to him to say, "If it pleases you, my brother, I am convinced that, by God's grace, we two should meet."

Clovis did not refuse and came to meet him. They got together on an island in the Loire near the village of Amboise in the territory of the city of Tours. They held discussions, ate and drank together and, after swearing mutual friendship, departed in peace. At this time many people in Gaul had by now the most ardent desire to have the Franks as rulers.

Bishop Quintianus (II 36)

As a result it happened that Quintianus, bishop of Rodez, was driven from the city for this offense. "For it is your desire," said his enemies, "that this land fall under the rule of the Franks."

A few days afterward, a quarrel arose between him and the citizens. The Goths who lived in the town became suspicious of him when the citizens accused him of wishing to put them under Frankish rule. They came to a decision to put him to the sword. When news of the plan reached the man of God, he arose in the middle of the night with his most faithful attendants, left Rodez and came to Clermont. There he was welcomed by holy Bishop Eufrasius, successor to the late Aprunculus of Dijon. Eufrasius maintained him, bestowing on him houses, lands, and vineyards.

"The riches of this church are sufficient to support both of us," he said, "provided brotherly love as preached by the blessed apostle persists among the priests of God."

The bishop of Lyons also bestowed upon him some of his church's properties located in the Auvergne.

The rest of the holy Quintianus's story, both the intrigues he endured, and the works the Lord saw fit to perform by his hands, is written in the book of his life [that is Gregory's own *Life of the Fathers*, 4].

War against Alaric (II 37)

Then King Clovis said to his men, "I take it very badly that these Arians hold part of Gaul. With God's help, let's go and conquer them and bring the land under our authority."

Since this talk was to everyone's liking, he mustered his army and brought it to Poitiers. At the time, King Alaric was staying there. Since part of Clovis's forces were crossing the territory of Tours, the Frankish king, out of respect for the blessed Martin, issued an edict that none of his troops were to avail themselves of anything from that district but grass as fodder and water.

A certain soldier, finding hay belonging to a poor man, said, "Has the king not authorized us to take grass and nothing else? Well, this is grass, and we shall certainly not be breaking his order if we take it."

He attacked the poor man, taking his hay by force, but report of his deed reached the king, who, quicker than it takes to say it, had him put to the sword.

"How shall there be hope of victory," asked the king, "if we offend the blessed Martin?"

The army was content to take nothing more from this district. As for the king, he sent a message to the blessed basilica.

"Go now," he said to the messengers, "and perhaps you shall receive a sign of victory from that holy temple."

At this time he gave gifts for them to present to the holy place.

"If you, Lord, are my help," said the king, "and have decreed that this unbelieving nation, which is always jealous of you, is to be delivered into my hands, please disclose for my sake at the entrance to the basilica of holy Martin if you will see fit to favor your servant."

His retainers hurried off and came to Tours as the king had commanded. As they were entering the basilica, the precentor who was leading the singing happened to intone this antiphon: "You have girded me, Lord, with strength for battle. You have subdued under me those rising up against me. You have caused my enemies to show me their backs, and You have destroyed those who hate me" [cf. Ps. 17:40–41].

The messengers, hearing the singing, gave thanks to God and, vowing gifts to the blessed confessor, joyfully brought the news to the king.

Afterwards, when Clovis had reached the Vienne river with his army, he had no idea where to cross it, because the river was swollen by heavy rains. That night he begged the Lord to please show him a ford where he could cross the river. At dawn a hind of marvelous size entered the river in front of them at God's command, and on its fording the river, the troops saw where they could cross.

When the king came to the Poitiers district and was camped some distance from the city, a fiery beacon issuing from the basilica of the holy Hilary seemed as if it reached out over the king; it showed that the king would, with the light of the blessed confessor Hilary, more readily overcome the legions of heretics against whom the saint himself had so often clashed for the sake of the faith. The king called upon the whole army not to despoil travelers or to seize anyone's property in the Poitiers district.

There was in the territory of Poitiers in those days a man praiseworthy for holiness, Abbot Maxentius, who lived as a recluse in his own monastery out of respect for God. I have given no particular name to the monastery, since to our own day the place has been known as the cell of the holy Maxentius. When the monks saw a troop of soldiers drawing near the monastery, they implored the abbot to come out of his cell to help them. When he took his time, they were stricken with fear and, opening the cell door, brought him out. He went fearlessly to meet the soldiers to ask for peace. One of their number drew his sword to take a swing at the abbot's head, but when his hand was raised to his ear it stiffened and the sword fell backwards out of his hand. He fell at the feet of the holy man, begging his pardon. When the rest saw this, fearing they might all perish, they returned to the army terrified. As for the man's arm, the blessed confessor made it better again, applying consecrated oil to it and making the sign of the cross. By his intercession the monastery remained unharmed. He performed many other miracles; anyone who cares to look for them will find them all by reading the abbot's Life.

[This took place] in the twenty-fifth year of Clovis's reign [a. 507].

Meanwhile, King Clovis encountered Alaric, king of the Goths, on the field of Vouillé at the tenth milestone from Poitiers, the Goths engaging at a distance, the Franks holding their ground in close formation. When, as is their habit, the Goths turned in flight, King Clovis himself, by God's aid, obtained the victory. As his ally, he had Chloderic, son of Sigibert the Lame; this Sigibert limped after being wounded in the knee during fighting against the Alamanni around Zülpich. Then, when the Goths had been put to flight, and the king had killed Alaric, two of the enemy suddenly encountered him and struck at him with their spears on each side; but thanks to his body armor and a fast horse, he escaped with his life.

On this field at this time fell a very large contingent of Arvernian troops and their leaders, who were from senatorial families. This force was under the command of Apollinaris.

Amalaric, son of Alaric, fled from this battle into Spain and shrewdly took possession of his father's kingdom.

Clovis sent his own son Theuderic by way of the cities of Albi and Rodez to Clermont. Off he went and subjected to his father's authority those cities from the Gothic to the Burgundian frontiers.

Alaric's reign lasted twenty-two years.

As for Clovis, who spent the winter in Bordeaux, he carried off all Alaric's treasures from Toulouse and came to Angoulême. The Lord showed him such favor that the walls fell down by themselves before his eyes. He drove out the Goths and at that time subjected the city to his own rule.

After that, with victory achieved, he returned to Tours and gave many gifts to the holy basilica of the blessed Martin.

On the Patriciate of King Clovis (II 38)

Then Clovis received from the emperor Anastasius documents conferring the consulate on him, and, in the church of the blessed Martin, having been vested in the purple tunic and chlamys, he set a diadem upon his head. Mounting his horse, he dispersed gold and silver to the people lining the road that runs between the gate of the atrium [of Martin's basilica] and the cathedral church of the city, scattering it with his own hand with a most generous liberality and, from that day, was hailed as consul or Augustus.

He left Tours and came to Paris, where he established the seat of his government. There he was also joined by Theuderic.

Bishop Licinius (II 39)

Then on the death of Eustochius, bishop of Tours, Licinius was consecrated as eighth bishop after Martin. In his time was waged the war which I have described above, and in his time King Clovis came to Tours. Licinius is said to have been to the East, to have visited the holy places, to have even entered Jerusalem itself, and to have often seen the sites of the passion and resurrection of our Lord, which we read about in the Gospels.

The Destruction of the Elder Sigibert and his Son (II 40)

When Clovis was living at Paris, he sent a secret message to the son of Sigibert: "Look, your father has grown old, and limps on a bad leg. If he were to die, his kingdom would by right be yours, together with our friendship."

The prince, led astray by his desire for power, made arrangements to kill his father. One day his father left Cologne and, after crossing the Rhine, decided to take a walk in the forest of Buchau. He was taking a midday nap in his tent when his son, setting assassins upon him, had him killed in order to get possession of the kingdom.

But, by the judgment of God, the son fell into the pit which he had dug to trap his father.

He next sent messengers to King Clovis announcing his father's death and saying, "My father is dead, and I control his kingdom and treasures. Send some of your servants to me and I shall gladly hand over whatever might please you from his treasure."

Clovis answered: "I am grateful for your good will, and I ask that you disclose all the treasure to my messengers, but keep it for yourself."

On the arrival of the envoys, the prince opened his father's treasury.

"In this little chest my father used to keep gold pieces," he said, as they were looking at various items.

"Dip your hands in to the bottom," said the messengers, "and find out how much is there."

So he did, and when he was bent right over, one of them raised his ax and buried it in his brain, and in this way he deservedly met the same death that he had dealt his father.

When Clovis heard that Sigibert and his son were dead, he came to Cologne and called all that people together.

"Hear what has happened," he said. "While I was sailing on the river Scheldt, Chloderic, son of my kinsman, was in pursuit of his father, claiming that I wanted to kill him. When his father fled through the forest of Buchau, he delivered him over to death, setting bandits on him and killing him. He also has been killed, struck down by I don't know who, while opening his father's treasures. I am in no way a party to these deeds; for I couldn't spill the blood of my kinsmen—that would be a criminal act. But since these events have happened, I give you this advice, if it seems agreeable to you: turn to me, and come under my protection."

Those who heard this roared their approval, clashing their shields and shouting; and raising Clovis upon a shield, they made him their king.

Having acquired the kingdom of Sigibert and its treasury, he also received those people under his dominion. For daily the Lord laid his enemies low under his hand and increased his kingdom, because he walked before Him with an upright heart and did what was pleasing in His sight.

The Destruction of Chararic and his Son (II 41)

After this he went against King Chararic. When Clovis had been at war with Syagrius, he had summoned Chararic to aid him, but Chararic kept his distance, helping neither side, but awaiting the outcome of events in order to ally himself with whomever emerged victorious. For this reason Clovis angrily marched against him. He captured Chararic and his son by trickery, bound them and cropped their hair, and even ordered Chararic to be ordained a priest and his son a deacon.

When Chararic lamented his humiliation and wept, it is said that his son replied, "These branches have been cut on green wood. They do not wither at all but shall sprout and grow. May he die just as quickly who did this."

Rumor reached the ears of Clovis that they were threatening to let their hair grow and kill him. He ordered both of them to be executed at the same time. After their death, he took possession of their kingdom, their treasury, and their people.

The Destruction of Ragnachar and his Brother (II 42)

At that time Ragnachar was king in Cambrai, a man whose wantonness was so unbridled that he hardly spared his own near relatives. In this he had a counselor Farro, who was smeared with the same filth. It was said about him that the king, when presented with any food or gift, or anything at all, used to say that it was sufficient for him and his Farro. On this account the Franks were bursting with anger.

For this reason it came to pass that Clovis gave gold armlets and belts to Ragnachar's *leudes* to entice them to call him in against their lord—actually the gifts only looked like gold, everything being copper, gilded to fool them. Afterwards, Clovis mustered his forces against Ragnachar, who frequently sent out scouts to gather information. When they returned with news, Ragnachar would ask them how strong the enemy was.

"For you and your Farro it is a very good supply," was their reply.

Clovis arrived and deployed his forces against him. Ragnachar, on seeing his army defeated, was ready to run for it, but was caught by the army and brought before Clovis with his arms bound behind his back, as was his brother Richar.

"Why," asked Clovis, "have you disgraced our lineage by allowing yourself to be bound? It would have been better for you to die."

Raising his ax, he drove it into Ragnachar's head. Then he turned to Ragnachar's brother.

"If you had given your brother help," he said, "surely he wouldn't have been bound."

With a blow of his ax, he killed him in the same way.

After the death of the brothers, their betrayers recognized that the gold that they had received from Clovis was false.

When they told the king this, he is said to have answered, "Someone who willfully lures his lord to his death deserves to receive gold such as this." He added that to be alive should be enough for them unless they wanted to pay for the wicked betrayal of their lords by being tortured to death.

On hearing this, they decided to earn his favor, claiming that it was enough if they could obtain their lives.

The above mentioned two kings were kinsmen of Clovis. Their brother, whose name was Rignomer, was killed at Le Mans by order of Clovis. With their deaths, Clovis acquired their entire kingdom and treasure. And he killed many other kings and his own near relatives whom he suspected might take away his kingship, and in this way, he extended his authority over all Gaul.

One day, however, when he had gathered together his followers, he is supposed to have said with respect to the kinsmen he had destroyed, "How sad it is for me to be left like a traveler among strangers and to have no kin to help me if trouble comes along."

He said this, not because he felt grief for their deaths, but as a trick, to see if he could still find someone to kill.

The Death of Clovis (II 43)

After these events had taken place, Clovis died at Paris [a. 511] and was buried in the basilica of the Holy Apostles, which he himself had built along with Chlothild his queen. He passed away in the fifth year after the battle of Vouillé. His reign amounted to thirty years in all. His age was forty-five.

From the passing of the holy Martin to the passing of Clovis, which was in the eleventh year of the episcopate of Licinius, bishop of Tours, amounts to one hundred and twelve years.

Queen Chlothild came to Tours after the death of her husband and served there in the holy basilica of the blessed Martin, living there with extreme virtue and with kindness all the days of her life, only occasionally visiting Paris.

PART II

THE KINGDOM OF THE FRANKS

A. 511–575

CHAPTER TWO
FROM THE DEATH OF CLOVIS TO THE DEATH
OF CHLOTHAR I, a. 511–561
(BOOKS III–IV)

All I say is, kings is kings, and you got to make allowances. Take them all
around, they are a mighty ornery lot. It's the way they're raised.

Huck, in *Huckleberry Finn*, by Mark Twain

*Gregory continued his account of Gallic affairs after Clovis's death with a history of
the king's successors. This history is the major, if not the only, source for the half century
following Clovis's death.*

*Gregory's sources for this period remain largely unknown, his knowledge is uneven,
and his chronology is still extremely vague and in some cases may telescope or confound
the sequence of events. It is difficult, for instance, to reconcile the order of the large number
of ostensibly interrelated events situated by Gregory in what appears to be the early years
of the 530s. The conquest of Burgundy (a. 534) is placed rather early in the sequence,
and the harrying of Auvergne by Theoderic, which Gregory repeatedly associates with the
episcopacy of Quintianus († 525/26) in his works, appears to belong to at least a decade
earlier. (See II 37 for Theuderic's initial acquisition of Clermont.) The relatively secure
points in the sequence are the death of Chlodomer at the battle of Véseronce in 524, the
death of Theuderic in 533, and the conquest of Burgundy in 534.*

*In the selections below, I have rearranged some of the chapters. This reorganization
is intended only to facilitate reading, not to suggest anything about the relative chronology of events. For the same reason I have added subheadings in boldface, appended
dates where these seem reasonable or the text requires them, and added comments or
brief chapter headings in italics to help readers keep their bearings in the narrative. The
chapter headings always give in parentheses the Book and chapter number of the Latin
edition. Though these headings in italics may sometimes resemble the chapter headings
of the* Histories *itself, they are not translations and have been devised for the present
selections.*

Division of the Kingdom among the Sons of Clovis

(III 1)

On the death of King Clovis [a. 511], his four sons, namely, Theuderic, Chlodomer, Childebert, and Chlothar, received his kingdom and divided it equally
among themselves. At that time Theuderic already had a fine and accomplished

son named Theudebert. Since the brothers were endowed with great courage and well provided with strong military forces, Amalaric [a. 511–31], son of Alaric [II, a. 484–507], king of Spain, asked to marry their sister. They graciously granted his request and sent her into the country of Spain with a mass of valuable treasure.

A Danish Raid

(III 3)

The Danish king of this chapter appears to be the same as the Hygelac of the famous Anglo-Saxon poem Beowulf.

Danes under their king Chlochilaich set sail and attacked Gaul from the sea. They landed, devastated one region of Theuderic's kingdom, and took prisoners. When they had loaded their ships with captives and other spoils, they were ready to return home, but their king had stayed on shore until the ships reached the open sea, intending to follow right behind.

When news was brought to Theuderic that his land had been ravaged by foreigners, he sent his son Theudebert into those parts with a strong force thoroughly outfitted for war. He killed the Danish king, defeated the enemy in a sea battle, and brought the plunder back to shore.

War against the Thuringians

Kings of the Thuringians (III 4)

At this time three brothers held royal power over the Thuringians: Baderic, Hermanfred, and Berthar. Hermanfred violently overcame his brother Berthar and killed him. At his death, he left an orphan daughter, Radegund; he left sons as well, about whom I shall write later.

Hermanfred's wife, a wicked and cruel woman named Amalaberg, sowed the seeds of civil war between the brothers. For instance, one day her lord came to dinner to find half the table unlaid. He asked his wife what she meant by this.

"Anyone who has half his kingdom taken from him," she replied, "should have half his table bare."

Egged on by this and similar provocations, he turned against his brother, sending secret messages inviting King Theuderic to attack Baderic.

"If you kill him," said Hermanfred, "we will divide his kingdom in equal parts."

Theuderic was quite happy to hear this, and came to meet Hermanfred at the head of his army. They joined forces, exchanged pledges of mutual loyalty, and set out to war. They engaged Baderic and destroyed his army, cutting his head off with the sword [ca 525/27?].

Victory won, Theuderic returned home. Hermanfred at once forgot his pledge, regarding the fulfilment of his promise to King Theuderic as of no account. Great enmity arose between them.

Theuderic and Chlothar against Hermanfred, ca 531 (III 7–8)

Theuderic did not forget the false promise of Hermanfred, king of the Thuringians, and made arrangements to march against him, calling on his brother Chlothar to help him. He promised King Chlothar a share of the plunder if heaven should grant them the gift of victory.

Theuderic assembled the Franks and said to them, "Be angry, I beg of you, as much for my wrong as for the death of your kinfolk. Remember that the Thuringians in the past made a brutal attack upon our relations and did them great harm. Our people gave hostages and tried to make peace with them, but the Thuringians put the hostages to death in various ways and, falling upon our kinfolk, took all their property. They hung the boys by the sinews of their thighs to trees. On more than two hundred girls they inflicted a cruel death: they tied their arms to the necks of horses which they set galloping in opposite directions with sharp goads, tearing the girls to pieces. Others they staked out over ruts in the roads and had them run over by loaded wagons; and having broken their bones, they gave them to dogs and birds for food. And now Hermanfred has broken his promise and completely ignores fulfilling it. Look, right is on our side! Let's take them on, with God's help."

When they heard this, they were angry at such wrongs and, with one heart and mind, set out for Thuringia. Theuderic went with the army, taking his brother Chlothar and his son Theudebert to help him. But the Thuringians prepared traps for the Franks' coming. In the plain where the fight was to take place, they dug trenches and covered the openings with thick turfs to look as if the plain were still level. So, when the fight began, many of the Frankish cavalry fell into these pits, and the stratagem seriously hindered them, though after it was discovered, they were on the lookout for it. When finally the Thuringians saw that they were taking severe losses and their king Hermanfred had taken to flight, they retreated to the river Unstrut. There such a slaughter of the Thuringians took place that the bed of the stream was filled with heaps of corpses, and the Franks crossed over them to the further bank as if on a bridge.

Victory won, they took possession of that country and reduced it to their authority. As for Chlothar, he went home, taking with him as a captive Rade-

1. Queen Radegund, having left her husband Chlothar, places the symbols of her worldly rank on the altar and enters the religious life (III 7).

gund, daughter of King Berthar, and married her. Afterwards he wrongfully killed her brother through the agency of evil men. Radegund, however, turned to God and, changing her garments, built a monastery for herself in the city of Poitiers. By her prayers, fasting, and almsgiving, she attained such fame that people considered her a remarkable woman.

When the above mentioned kings were still in Thuringia, Theuderic tried to kill his own brother Chlothar. He called him to his side on the pretext that he wished to discuss something with him privately, but he had secretly put in place armed men ahead of time. In one part of the house, a tent-cloth had been stretched from one wall to the other, and he ordered the men to stand behind it. Since the cloth was too short, their feet were exposed to view. Learning of this, Chlothar came into the house with his own men armed. Theuderic, realizing that Chlothar had learned of his preparations, made up a story and talked about this or that matter. Finally, not knowing how to put a good appearance on his trap, he gave him as a favor a great silver platter. And Chlothar said his farewells, thanked him for the gift, and returned to his quarters. But Theuderic complained to his men that he had lost his dish for no good reason.

"Go to your uncle," he said to his son Theudebert, "and ask him if he will give you the gift I gave him."

Theudebert went and got what he asked for. In this kind of deceit Theuderic was very practiced.

Theuderic returned to his own country and told Hermanfred to come to him, giving him a promise that he would be safe. Theuderic honored him with rich gifts. One day, however, it so happened that they were talking on the walls of the city of Zülpich and Hermanfred was pushed—I do not know by whom—and fell from the top of the wall to the ground, where he breathed his last. We do not know who threw him down from there; still, many claim that the deceit of Theuderic was plainly revealed in the deed.

First War against Burgundy and The Death of Chlodomer

Sigismund of Burgundy Kills his Son, a. 522 (III 5)

The date for Sigeric's death comes from the chronicle of Marius of Avenches.

On Gundobad's death [a. 516], his son Sigismund took up his kingdom and with real expertise constructed the monastery of Agaune, with its buildings and churches.

He had lost his first wife, the daughter of Theoderic [the Great], king of Italy [a. 490–526], by whom he had a son called Sigeric, and took another wife. As stepmothers tend to do, she began to mistreat his son badly and harass him.

As a result, it so happened on a ceremonial occasion that the boy recognized his mother's dress on her and became angry.

"You don't deserve to wear those clothes," he said to her. "Everyone knows they belonged to your mistress, my mother."

Inflamed with anger, she cleverly incited her husband.

"This devil wants to get his hands on your kingdom," she said. "And when he has killed you, he plans to extend it as far as Italy. It's obvious he wants to possess the kingdom which his grandfather Theoderic [the Great] held in Italy. He knows perfectly well that while you are alive he cannot accomplish this. Unless you fall, he will not rise."

Driven by these words and others like them, Sigismund took the advice of his wicked wife and ended up an evil killer of his own flesh and blood. One afternoon he told his son, who had drunk himself into a stupor, to sleep it off, and while the son slept, two retainers placed a kerchief under his neck, brought it around his throat, and drawing the ends together, strangled him. When it was done the father repented too late and, falling on the lifeless corpse, began to weep bitterly.

A certain old man is supposed to have said to him, "Hereafter weep on your own behalf, now that you have followed wicked advice and become a most cruel child-killer. There is no need to weep for this innocent boy who has been throttled."

Nevertheless the king went off to the monastery of Agaune and prayed for pardon, spending many days weeping and fasting. He established there a service of perpetual chant and returned to Lyons with divine vengeance on his trail.

King Theuderic married his daughter.

Death of Chlodomer, a. 524 (III 6)

The date of Chlodomer's death comes from the chronicle of Marius of Avenches.

Queen Chlothild addressed Chlodomer and her other sons.

"Dear sons," she said, "let me not regret having lovingly nursed you; I beg you, take offense at the outrage inflicted on me and put your energies into avenging the death of my father and mother [see II 28]."

They listened to this and went to Burgundy to attack Sigismund and his brother Godomar, whose armies were defeated. Godomar retreated. But Sigismund was captured by Chlodomer while trying to escape to the monastery of Agaune. He was taken away as a prisoner along with his wife and children and kept under guard in the territory of the city of Orleans.

When the kings were gone, Godomar recovered his strength, gathered the

Burgundians together, and took back his kingdom. Chlodomer made preparations to march against Godomar once again and, at the same time, decided to kill Sigismund. The blessed abbot Avitus, a remarkable priest of that time, spoke to him.

"If, mindful of God, you change your plans and do not have these people killed," said Avitus, "God will be with you. You will go off and win victory. But if you kill them, you will be handed over into the hands of your enemies and die like them. What you do to Sigismund and his wife and children will be done to you and your wife and sons."

Contemptuous of this advice, Chlodomer said, "I think it's a stupid idea to leave enemies at home while I go against the rest of them. If this lot rises up behind me and that one in front of me, I could be caught between two armies. Victory will be achieved better and more easily if they are kept apart; when one is killed, the other can be put to death easily."

He immediately gave orders for Sigismund to be killed along with his wife and children and for them to be thrown down a well in the village of Columna, in the city of Orleans. Setting out for Burgundy, he called upon King Theuderic to help him. Theuderic, having no wish to avenge the wrong done his father-in-law, promised to go along.

When they had joined forces near Véseronce, in the district of Vienne, they clashed with Godomar. Godomar retreated with his army, and Chlodomer, in pursuit of him, became separated a considerable distance from his own men.

The Burgundians, imitating Chlodomer's battle cry, called out to him, "This way, come this way, we are your men."

Taken in by the trick, he advanced and fell into the midst of his enemies. They cut off his head, set it on a lance, and raised it aloft. The Franks saw it and realized that Chlodomer was dead. Rallying their forces, they put Godomar to flight, crushed the Burgundians, and reduced the country to their authority.

Chlothar lost no time in marrying his brother's wife, who was called Guntheuca. As for Chlodomer's sons, Queen Chlothild took them into her keeping after the period of mourning was past. The name of the first was Theudoald, the second was called Gunthar, and the third, Chlodoald.

Godomar recovered his kingdom a second time.

Harrying of Auvergne, an Invasion of Spain, and the Conquest of Burgundy, ca 531–34

(III 9–12)

Arcadius was the son of Apollinaris, who fought at Vouillé (see II 37), and grandson of Sidonius Apollinaris. Childebert's invasion of Spain is mentioned by the chronicle of

Saragossa, s.a. 531. According to the chronicle of Marius of Avenches, Theudebert, son of Theuderic, participated with his uncles, Chlothar and Childebert, in the invasion and division of Burgundy; Marius dates the conquest to 534. Theuderic died in 533 (below, III 23).

While Theuderic was still in Thuringia [see above III 4, 7–8], Auvergne resounded with news of his death. Arcadius, one of the senators of the Arvernians, called upon Childebert to take possession of the region, and the king wasted no time in coming to Auvergne. On that day the fog was so thick that he could see no more than a few dozen yards ahead of himself.

The king used to say, "I would like to see the Limagne of Auvergne with my own eyes. It is supposed to exude such charm."

But God did not grant him the pleasure.

Though the gates of the city were barred, and there was no way to get in, Arcadius cut through the bar of one of the gates and brought him into the city. While this was happening, news arrived that Theuderic had returned from Thuringia alive.

When Childebert was sure of this, he went to Spain for the sake of his sister Chlothild [a. 531]. She had to endure a lot of miserable treatment from her husband, Amalaric, on account of her Catholic faith. Often, for example, as she made her way to holy church, he ordered shit and all kinds of stinking stuff thrown on her. In the end he is said to have beaten her so cruelly that she sent her brother a kerchief stained with her own blood. Childebert was extremely upset by this and set out for Spain.

When Amalaric heard, he got ships ready so he could flee. Then as Childebert drew near, Amalaric, when he should have been boarding ship, suddenly remembered that he had left behind in his treasury a great many precious stones. He returned to the city to get them but was cut off from the harbor by the army. Seeing that he could not get away, he tried to take refuge in the church of the [Catholic] Christians. But before he could set foot on the holy threshold, someone threw a spear, giving him a mortal wound. He collapsed there and died.

Childebert then received his sister and was anxious to take her with him along with the great treasure. She died upon the journey, from what cause I know not, and her body was afterwards taken to Paris and buried near her father Clovis. Among other treasures, Childebert carried off very valuable services of church plate. For instance he took sixty chalices, fifteen patens, and twenty Gospel covers, all of pure gold and adorned with precious stones. But he did not allow them to be broken up, for he presented all of them to cathedral churches and basilicas of the saints.

After this Chlothar and Childebert made preparations to attack Burgundy. They summoned Theuderic to their aid, but he refused to go.

The Franks who looked to his authority, however, said to him, "If you refuse to go to Burgundy with your brothers, we shall abandon you and choose instead to follow them."

But figuring that the Arvernians were disloyal to him, he said, "Follow me, and I will take you to a land where you will get as much gold and silver as your greedy hearts can desire, where you can seize herds, slaves, and raiment in abundance. Only don't follow my brothers."

Attracted by these promises, they swore to do as he wished. He arranged to make an expedition to Clermont, promising his army again and again that he would allow them to take back home all the booty to be obtained in that region, including its people.

As for Chlothar and Childebert, they marched into Burgundy, besieged Autun, and took control of all of Burgundy, once Godomar was put to flight [a. 534].

Theuderic, however, came to Auvergne with his forces and ravaged and crushed the whole region. In the meantime, Arcadius, the source of the calamity by whose pointless behavior the region was brought to ruin, fled to the city of Bourges; at the time, the city was in the kingdom of Childebert. Arcadius's mother, Placidina, and Alchima, his father's sister, were arrested in the city of Cahors; their property was confiscated and they were sentenced to exile.

King Theuderic came to Clermont and pitched camp outside its walls. The blessed Quintianus [a. 516–25/26] was bishop at the time…

Theuderic's army then harried the Auvergne (III 12, 13).

Munderic the Pretender

(III 14)

Munderic, who claimed he was a kinsman of kings, got carried away with pride and said, "What do I have to do with King Theuderic? The throne of the kingdom is as much my due as it is his. I shall go and gather my forces and exact an oath from them so Theuderic will know that I am a king just like him."

And so he went and began winning people over, telling them, "I am a prince, follow me and you will benefit."

A peasant host followed him, human weakness being what it is, and gave him an oath of loyalty, honoring him as king.

When Theuderic found out, he sent him a message commanding, "Come to me, and if any portion of our kingdom belongs to you, take it." Theuderic said this as a ruse, however, so Munderic could be killed if he came.

But Munderic refused, saying to the messenger, "Go, return to your king, for I am a king just like him."

Then the king ordered an army to get under way by which Munderic could be overwhelmed by force and punished. Munderic found out about it, and unable to defend himself, sought the protection of the fortress of Vitry [-le-Brûlé], taking his property with him; there he busied himself with its defenses with the help of those he had won over to his side. The army that had set out then invested the fortress and laid seige to it for seven days.

Munderic and his followers fought back.

"Let us be strong," he said, "and together fight to the death without giving in to our enemies."

When the army had cast its missiles from its positions outside the fortress to no avail, they reported the situation to the king.

Theuderic sent one of his men, Aregisil by name, telling him, "Look, this traitor is getting away with his disobedience. Go and swear an oath that he can come out safely. When he comes out, kill him and rid our kingdom of his memory."

Aregisil went away and followed the orders he had been given.

First he established a signal with the troops, telling them, "When I say such and such a thing, rush him immediately and kill him."

Aregisil entered the fortress to see Munderic.

"How long are you going to sit around here like a fool," he said to Munderic. "Can you resist the king for long? Look, your supplies have been taken away. When hunger overwhelms you, you'll come out on your own, be handed over into the hands of your enemies, and die like a dog. Take my advice instead and surrender to the king so you and your children can live."

"If I come out," said Munderic, softened up by these words, "I shall be seized by the king and killed, and along with me, my children and all the friends who have joined me."

"Don't worry," replied Aregisil, "if you'll come out, you shall have an oath excusing you and you'll be safe in the eyes of the king. Don't worry, you will be to him just as you were before."

To this Munderic said, "If only I were sure I would not be killed!"

At that point Aregisil put his hands on the holy altar and swore to Munderic that he could come out safely.

When the oath was taken, Munderic came out through the gate of the fortress, holding the hand of Aregisil. The forces looked on from a distance, staring at him.

Then Aregisil, as a signal, said, "Why, men, are you staring so hard? Have you not seen Munderic before?"

Immediately the troops rushed him.

"I know well that with these words you have given the troops a signal to kill me," said Munderic, understanding the situation. "But I tell you, since you have tricked me with perjury, no one shall see you among the living any longer."

Munderic cast his javelin piercing him between the shoulders and Aregisil fell down dead. Then Munderic drew his sword, and along with his men inflicted a great slaughter on the troops. Until he took his last breath, he tried to kill anyone he could reach.

When he was killed, his property was taken by the fisc.

A Treaty between Theuderic and Childebert: Attalus the Hostage

(III 15)

The Gregory of this story, who was bishop of Langres († ca 539), was Gregory of Tours's great-grandfather.

Theuderic and Childebert made a treaty and swore to each other that neither would attack the other. They exchanged hostages to better secure the terms of the agreement. At that time, many sons of senators were given as hostages, but they were reduced to public servitude when a quarrel arose again between the kings, and those who had taken the hostages to guard now made them their slaves. Though many hostages managed to slip away and escape, returning to their homelands, a good number were kept in servitude. Among these was Attalus, nephew of the blessed Gregory, bishop of Langres. He was assigned to public servitude and set to guarding horses. He was in service to a certain barbarian in the territory of Trier.

The blessed Gregory then sent servants to find him. Find him they did and offered his master remuneration, but he rejected it.

"A fellow of such good birth," he said, "should be bought back for ten pounds of gold."

When they had returned home, a certain Leo, one of the bishop's kitchen staff, said, "If you would give me permission, perhaps I might be able to bring him back from captivity."

His master was pleased with the suggestion. Leo came straight to the place and tried to steal away the boy in secret but could not.

Then he hired a certain man and said to him, "Come with me and sell me into the house of that barbarian. Take my purchase price as your profit. All I want is a better opportunity of carrying out what I have resolved to do."

After taking an oath, the man went away and sold Leo for twelve gold pieces and then went his way.

The purchaser inquired of the new slave what work he could do.

"I'm especially skilled in preparing all kinds of dishes suitable for the tables of lords," he answered, "and I've no worry that my equal can be found in this art. To tell you the truth, should you even want a feast readied for a king, I'm able to prepare royal dishes. No one is better at it than I am."

"It's almost Sunday,"—for this is what the barbarians usually call the Lord's day—"on this day my neighbors and relations will be invited to my house. I ask you to make me a feast that will astonish them and make them say, 'we haven't seen better in the king's palace'."

"Let my master have a large number of pullets rounded up, and I shall do what you command."

What the slave had asked for was made ready, and when the Lord's day dawned, he prepared a great feast crammed with delightful dishes. When they had all feasted and praised the meal, the master's relations went away. The master rewarded his slave, and he received authority over all his master's stores. His master cherished him very much, and the slave used to distribute the bread and meat to all the household.

After the course of a year, when his master was now certain of him, Leo went out to the meadow near the house with the boy Attalus, the keeper of the horses. They reclined on the ground but a distance apart and with their backs turned to each other so no one could see them talking together.

"The time has come to think of home," said Leo to the boy. "Listen to me. Tonight, when you fence in the horses, don't fall asleep, come as soon as I call, and off we go."

Now the barbarian had invited many of his relations to a feast, including his son-in-law. At midnight they rose from the table to retire, and Leo accompanied his master's son-in-law to his quarters, giving him a drink.

"Tell me, if you can, my father-in-law's trusted servant, when do you think you'll decide to take his horses and return to your own country?" The fellow said this to make a joke.

In the same way, Leo jokingly replied with the truth. "Tonight, I think—if it's God's will."

"Well I hope my slaves make sure you take nothing of mine."

They parted laughing.

When all were asleep, Leo called Attalus and, when the horses were saddled, asked him if he had a sword.

"No, I have only a small spear," he said.

Leo entered his master's quarters and grabbed his shield and sword.

When his master asked who it was and what he wanted, Leo answered: "It's me, Leo, your slave. I am waking Attalus so he can get up right away and pasture the horses; he's fast asleep as if he were drunk."

"Do what you want." And saying this, his master fell asleep.

Leo went out and armed the boy and, by divine help, found the gates of the courtyard unbarred (at nightfall Attalus had barred them by driving in wedges with a hammer to keep the horses safe). Giving thanks to God, they took the rest of the horses with them and went off, carrying a single bundle of clothing.

When they came to cross the river Moselle and were prevented from doing so by certain people, they abandoned the horses and clothing and swam the river, supported by their shields. Climbing the further bank, they hid themselves in the woods amid the darkness of the night. This was the third night they had traveled without tasting food. It was then, by God's will, that they found a tree full of the fruit commonly called plums; eating them, they were strengthened somewhat and began the journey through Champagne.

As they were going along, they heard the hoofbeats of galloping horses and said, "Let's get down on the ground so the people coming can't see us."

Look what happened next! Quite unexpectedly, there was a great bramble bush growing nearby. They got behind it and threw themselves on the ground, with their swords drawn; had they been noticed, they would have immediately defended themselves with weapons as if attacked by outlaws. In fact, when the party of horsemen reached the spot, it halted in front of the thorn bush.

And while the horses were pissing, one of the riders said, "It really bothers me that these accursed wretches take off and can't be found; I swear by my own salvation, if they are found, I will have one condemned to the gallows, and the other cut to bits by the sword."

The barbarian who was speaking was their master, coming from the city of Rheims in search of them, and he would certainly have found them on the road if night had not prevented it. The riders then galloped off.

The fugitives reached the city that very night, and going in, they found a man and asked him where the house of the priest Paulellus was. He pointed it out to them. While they were going along the street, the bell was rung for matins—for it was the Lord's day—and knocking at the priest's door they went in. Leo told him who his master was.

"My vision was true then," responded the priest. "For this night I saw two doves fly toward me and settle on my hand. One of them was white, and the other black."

"May the Lord forgive our request on this holy day," said Leo to the priest. "We ask you to give us some food; for the fourth day is dawning since we have tasted bread and meat."

The priest hid the slaves, gave them a meal with bread and wine, and went away to matins.

The barbarian, too, came along behind them, looking for the slaves a second time, but made a fool of by the priest, he went home; for the priest had an old friendship with the blessed Gregory. Then, their strength restored by a good meal, the youths stayed two days in the home of the priest before departing. And so they were brought to the holy Gregory.

The bishop rejoiced at seeing them and wept on the shoulder of Attalus, his nephew. He set Leo free from the yoke of slavery with all his family and gave him land of his own, on which he lived a free man with his wife and children all the days of his life.

Death of Chlodomer's Sons: Childebert and Chlothar Divide Chlodomer's Kingdom

(III 18)

On Arcadius, see III 9–12.

While Queen Chlothild was staying at Paris, Childebert saw that his mother had special love for the sons of Chlodomer, whom I mentioned above [III 6].

Prompted by jealously and fearful that they would get a share in the kingdom because of the favor of the queen, Childebert sent a secret message to his brother King Chlothar saying, "Our mother keeps our brother's sons with her and wants them to be given royal powers. You should come quickly to Paris. We must have a meeting to discuss what ought to be done about them, whether they should have their long hair cut and be made the same as the rest of the common people, or whether they should be killed and our brother's kingdom divided equally between ourselves."

Chlothar was very pleased with these words and came to Paris. Childebert had spread a rumor among the populace that the reason the kings were meeting was to raise the small boys to the throne.

The queen was then staying in the city, and when the kings met, they sent her a message saying, "Send the little fellows to us, so they may be raised up to the kingship."

She was pleased with that, unaware of their treacherous plan. Giving the boys food and drink, she sent them along.

"I shall not consider that I have lost a son," she said, "if I see you take over his kingdom."

They went away and were immediately seized. They were taken away from their retainers and governors, who were put under separate guard in one place, while the little boys were kept in another. Then Childebert and Chlothar sent Arcadius to the queen with a pair of scissors and a naked sword. Arcadius came and showed both to the queen.

"Most glorious queen," he said, "your sons, our masters, wish to know your desire. What do you think ought to be done with the boys? Would you have them live with their hair shorn, or would you have them both killed?"

She was terrified by the message and anguish quite unsettled her, especially when she saw the naked sword and the scissors. Overcome by bitterness, she was unaware of what she was saying in her troubled state of mind.

"If they are not raised to the kingship," she said simply, "I would rather see them dead than shorn."

But Arcadius paid no attention to her depressed condition and returned swiftly with the news without giving her time for fuller reflection.

"You have the queen's approval to finish what you have begun," he said; "she wants you to bring your plans to completion."

There was no delay. Chlothar grabbed the older boy by the arm and pushed him to the ground and cruelly put him to death, stabbing him under the armpit with his knife. While the boy was screaming, his brother fell at Childebert's feet and clasped his knees.

"Help me, most dutiful father," he said crying. "I don't want to die like my brother."

Then Childebert, tears running down his cheeks, said, "I ask you, dear brother, let your generosity grant me the life of this boy. I will pay for his life whatever you say—only don't kill him."

But heaping abuse on his brother, Chlothar said, "Push him away from you, or you will surely die in his place. It is you that is the instigator of this deed. Do you go back on your word this quickly?"

Childebert listened to this and, shoving the boy away, pushed him toward Chlothar, who grabbed him and thrust his knife into his side, killing him in the same way as he had his brother. Then they put the servants and the governors to death.

When they were killed, Chlothar mounted his horse and went off, viewing the killing of his nephews as of little consequence. Childebert retired to the outskirts of the city. As for the queen, she placed their small bodies on a bier and accompanied it to the basilica of Saint Peter amid much psalm singing and endless grieving. She buried them side by side. One of them was ten years old, the other seven. But the third, Chlodoald, they were unable to get hold of, since he was saved by the help of his fighting men. He put aside his earthly kingdom and passed over into the Lord's service; cutting his hair with his own hands, he became a cleric, performing good works, and passed away from this life as a priest.

The two kings divided the kingdom of Chlodomer equally between them. Queen Chlothild acted in such a way as to gain the respect of everyone; she continually gave alms, attended holy vigils the whole night through, and remained pure, living a life of chastity and decency. She was generous and readily handed out estates to churches, monasteries, and other holy places where she saw a need, so that it was thought at the time that a real handmaid of God, not a queen, was busy in His service. Neither the royal power of her sons, nor worldly ambition, nor wealth, carried her off to destruction, but humility carried her forward to grace.

The Young Theudebert and the Death of Theuderic I, a. 533

(III 20–24)

Theuderic betrothed his son Theudebert to Wisigard, daughter of a certain [Lombard] king.

After the death of Clovis, the Goths had overrun much of what Theuderic had acquired. To get it back, Theuderic now sent Theudebert, and Chlothar sent his eldest son Gunthecar. Gunthecar got as far as Rodez but returned, I know not for what reason. But Theudebert went on to the city of Béziers, took the fortress of Dio and sacked it. He then sent envoys to another fortress named Cabrières with a message that the whole place would be burned to the ground and its inhabitants taken captive unless they surrendered to him.

At the time there was a matron there called Deuteria, a very capable and clever woman, whose husband had withdrawn to Béziers.

She sent a message to the king saying, "Most dutiful lord, no one can resist you. We know you are our lord. Come and do what is pleasing in your eyes."

Theudebert came to the fortress, but when he peacefully entered it and saw that the people were subdued, he did no harm there. Deuteria came out to meet him. He saw that she was beautiful, and captivated by love of her, took her to his bed.

In those days Theuderic put his kinsman Sigivald [duke of Auvergne] to the sword and sent a message in secret to Theudebert for him to execute Sigivald's son, [also called] Sigivald, whom he had by his side. But because he had taken him from the sacred font, Theudebert refused to destroy him. In fact, he had him read the letter sent by his father.

"Get away from here," Theudebert said. "I have received my father's order to kill you. After his death when you hear that I am ruling, then return to me in safety."

Sigivald thanked him for the warning, said farewell, and departed. At the time the Goths had occupied the city of Arles, from which Theudebert still had hostages, so Sigivald fled to the city. But seeing that he would get little protection there, he went to Italy and took refuge there.

While these events were taking place, word came to Theudebert that his father was seriously ill, and that, unless he came quickly enough to find his father alive, he himself would be disinherited by his uncles and would never be able to return. At this news, Theudebert put everything else aside and returned home, leaving Deuteria with her daughter at Clermont. Not many days after his departure, Theuderic died, in the twenty-third year of his reign [a. 533]. Childebert and Chlothar turned on Theudebert, trying to take the kingdom from him, but he appeased his *leudes* with gifts, won their support, and was established in his kingdom.

Later he summoned Deuteria from Clermont and married her.

When Childebert saw that he could not overcome Theudebert, he sent an embassy to him, bidding him to come on a visit.

"I do not have sons," he said, "and I want to have you for a son."

Theudebert came and was enriched with so many gifts as to astonish everyone. Childebert gave him three pairs of the various costly items appropriate to a king's rank, whether weapons, clothing, or jewels, as well as horses and bowls.

When Sigivald heard that Theudebert had acquired his father's kingdom, he returned from Italy to the king. Rejoicing with his friend and kissing him, Theudebert conferred upon him a third of the gifts that he had received from his uncle; and everything from the property of the elder Sigivald that Theuderic had assigned to his fisc, Theudebert restored to the son.

The Seige of Saragossa a. 541 and the Kings of the Visigoths to 554

Childebert and Chlothar Besiege Saragossa (III 29)

Gregory places the Siege of Saragossa just after the events described below in III 28, p. 43.

Childebert went to Spain. He invaded with Chlothar, invested the city of Saragossa and laid siege to it.

The city turned to God with such abject humility that the citizens put on hair garments, abstained from food and drink, and circled the walls carrying the tunic of Saint Vincent and singing psalms. The women, wearing black mantles and covered in ashes followed with their hair hanging loose, lamenting as if they were attending the funerals of their husbands. And so the place put all its hope in the mercy of God, so that it could be said that the fasting of the Ninevites [cf. Jonas 3:5] was performed there, except that the divine mercy bowed to their prayers.

The besiegers, not knowing what the besieged were doing when they saw them go round the wall, thought that they were practicing witchcraft. Then they seized a local peasant and asked him what was going on.

"They carry the tunic of Saint Vincent and pray with it for God to take pity on them," he said.

The besiegers became fearful and abandoned the city. Still a great part of Spain was seized and they returned to Gaul with considerable spoil.

The Visigoths and their Kings (III 30)

After Amalaric [see III 10], Theudis was appointed king in Spain [a. 531–48]. He was killed and they raised up Theodisclus as king [a. 548–49]. As he was reclining at dinner with his supporters, and was quite merry, the candles were suddenly snuffed out and his enemies killed him by the stroke of a sword.

After him Agila [I a. 549–54] took the kingdom.

You see the Goths have acquired the abominable habit of putting to the sword any of their kings whom they find disagreeable and making someone else king who is to their liking.

The Reign of Theudebert I, a. 534–548

The Goodness of Theudebert (III 25)

See III 20–24.

When established in his kingdom, Theudebert proved to be a great king and thoroughly distinguished for good qualities. For he ruled his kingdom with justice, respected bishops, endowed churches, relieved the poor, and bestowed favors on many with a pious good will. He mercifully remitted all the taxes that were owed to his treasury from the churches located in Auvergne.

Deuteria and Wisigard (III 26–27)

Deuteria saw that her daughter was quite grown up and was afraid that the king would want her and take her. So Deuteria placed her in a wagon hitched to untamed oxen and sent her off a bridge; the daughter lost her life in the river. This happened in the city of Verdun.

It was now the seventh year since Theudebert had betrothed Wisigard [see III 20] and refused to marry her on account of Deuteria. The Franks assembled and were thoroughly outraged with him for leaving his betrothed in the lurch. This time he was stirred into abandoning Deuteria, by whom he had a little son named Theudebald, and marrying Wisigard. He had not married her for long before she died, and he took another wife. But he no longer had anything to do with Deuteria.

Childebert and Theudebert against Chlothar (III 28)

Childebert and Theudebert mustered their armies and made arrangements to march against Chlothar. On hearing about this, and figuring he could not withstand their forces, Chlothar took refuge in a forest, where he made great barricades in the woods, putting all his hope in God's mercy. Queen Chlothild also heard about it. She went to the tomb of the holy Martin and there prostrated herself in prayer; keeping vigil all night long, she prayed that no civil war should arise between her sons.

Childebert and Theudebert came with their armies and besieged their brother, planing to kill him on the following day. But at dawn a storm arose where they had camped. Their tents were blown down, their gear was scattered, and everything thrown into confusion. Lightning mixed with thunder and hailstones descended on them. They threw themselves on their faces on the hail-strewn ground and were severely pounded by the falling hailstones—for they had no covering left but their shields. Their chief fear was being struck by the lightning from the heavens. Their horses, too, were scattered so far that they could scarcely be recovered several miles away, and many were never found at all.

Then the kings—lashed by hailstones, as I have said, and stretched out on the ground—did penance and begged God for forgiveness for having tried to attack their own blood. On Chlothar not a single drop of rain fell; and in his camp no sound of thunder was heard, and no one felt even a breath of wind. The two kings sent envoys to him seeking peace and good relations. When their request was granted, they returned home. Let no one doubt that this miracle was the blessed Martin's, brought about through the intercession of the queen.

Theudebert in Italy, a. 539 (III 32)

Buccelin's expeditions actually took place in 553–54 under Theudebald I.

Theudebert went off to Italy and acquired a great deal of plunder there. But, as we are told, those areas are disease-ridden, and his army suffered losses, falling victim to fevers of various kinds; many troops died in those regions. Seeing the situation, Theudebert returned, he and his men carrying away much spoil.

It is said that at that time he went as far as the city of Pavia, against which he later sent Buccelin. Buccelin captured Lesser Italy, reduced it to the authority of the aforesaid king, and then attacked Greater Italy. Here he fought Belisarius many times and won the victory. When the emperor saw that Belisarius was being beaten more and more, he removed him and replaced him with Narses. To humiliate him, he made Belisarius count of the stable, a post he had held before. Buccelin, for his part, fought great campaigns against Narses. Capturing all Italy, he extended his conquests to the sea, sending much treasure from Italy to Theudebert. When Narses informed the emperor of this, the emperor hired foreign forces to aid Narses. In a later engagement, Narses was defeated and then departed. Then Buccelin seized Sicily, from which he exacted tribute, which he sent to the king. He enjoyed great success in these circumstances [see IV 9].

Theudebert's Gift to the Citizens of Verdun (III 34)

Desideratus, bishop of Verdun, to whom king Theuderic had done many wrongs, received his freedom again at the Lord's command, after many injuries, losses, and hardships. He took up the office of bishop in the city of Verdun, as I said, and felt sorry for its inhabitants since he saw that they were forsaken and very poor. He had been stripped of his own property by Theuderic and had nothing of his own with which to relieve them, and so, perceiving the goodness of King Theudebert and his kindness towards all, he sent a delegation to the king with a message.

"Your reputation for goodness," said the bishop, "is known over the whole world, since your generosity is such that you help even those who do not seek it. I beg you, kind lord, lend us money, if you can spare it, so that we may be able to relieve our citizens; and when those involved in trade increase business in our city to what it is in other cities, we will repay your money with lawful interest."

Then Theudebert was moved by compassion and furnished seven thousand gold pieces, which the bishop took and disbursed among his citizens. Those doing business were made rich by this and are considered to be important people to the present day.

When Bishop Desideratus offered the king the money that was owed, the king answered, "I've no need to take this sum; it's enough for me if, by your management, the poor who were suffering want have been relieved, thanks to your request and my generosity."

Demanding nothing, the aforesaid king made the citizens rich.

Deaths of Theudebert and Parthenius, a. 548 (III 36, 37)

Theudebert began to grow ill. The physicians lavished a great deal of attention on him, but nothing worked, for the Lord was now calling him. And so when he had grown ill for quite a while, growing weak with the sickness, he gave up the ghost.

Now the Franks went in pursuit of Parthenius, since they hated him profoundly for subjecting them to taxation in the time of the aforesaid king. Parthenius saw the danger he was in and fled the city. He humbly begged two bishops to be his escort to the city of Trier and to quell by their preaching the revolt of the raging populace. One night while they were traveling, as he lay in his bed, he suddenly let loose a loud shout in his sleep.

"Help!" he cried. "Whoever is there come help. Bring assistance to a dying man."

The shouting awakened those nearby, and they asked him what was the matter.

He replied, "Ausanius, my friend, and my wife Papianilla, both of whom I killed long ago, were summoning me to judgment. 'Come and defend yourself,' they were saying, 'for you are going to plead your case along with us in the presence of the Lord.'"

Jealousy had led him to kill his innocent wife and his friend some years before.

Coming to Trier, the bishops were unable to handle the riot of shouting people and they tried to hide Parthenius in the cathedral. What they did was place him in a chest and spread over him vestments that were used in the church. People came in and, after searching every nook and cranny of the church, went out in a rage when they found nothing.

Then one said suspiciously, "Look, there's a chest we haven't looked in for our enemy."

The guards said that it contained nothing but church furnishings, but the crowd demanded the key.

"Unless you are quick about unlocking it," they said, "we will break it open ourselves."

In the end the chest was opened and the linens removed. They found Parthenius and dragged him out.

"God has delivered our enemy into our hands," they shouted, clapping their hands.

Then they beat him with their fists and spat on him. Tying his hands behind his back, they stoned him to death against a column.

He was a great glutton and quickly digested what he ate, taking aloes to feel hungry again quickly. Moreover he used to let loose farts in public, without any consideration for those who could hear him. This is how his life ended.

...Thirty-seven years passed between the death of Clovis and the death of Theudebert, who died in the fourteenth year of his reign. His son Theudebald reigned in his place.

This computation ends Book III.

The Death of Queen Chlothild, a. 544

(IV 1)

Queen Chlothild died at Tours, full of days and rich in good works, in the time of Bishop Injuriosus [ca 530–46]. She was taken to Paris with much singing of psalms and buried by her sons, Kings Childebert and Chlothar, at the side of King Clovis in the sanctuary of the basilica of Saint Peter. She herself had erected this basilica in which the most blessed Genovefa is also interred.

King Chlothar and the Income of the Churches

(IV 2)

King Chlothar had proclaimed that all the churches of his kingdom were to pay a third of their income to the fisc. When all the bishops had unwillingly agreed to this and signed their names, the blessed Injuriosus [bishop of Tours, ca 530–46], manfully rejected doing so and refused to sign.

"If you try to take the things of God," he said, "the Lord will quickly take away your kingdom, for it is wrong for the poor to have to fill your granary, when you should be feeding them from it."

He was angry with the king and left without saying farewell.

The king was unsettled by this and, being afraid also of the power of the blessed Martin, sent after the bishop with gifts, begging pardon, condemning his own actions, and asking also that the bishop intercede with the power of the blessed Martin on his behalf.

Chlothar's Wives and Children

(IV 3)

Now the king had seven sons by various wives; by Ingund he had Gunthecar, Childeric, Charibert, Guntram, and Sigibert, as well as a daughter Chlodoswintha; by Aregund, sister of Ingund, he had Chilperic; and by Chunsina he had Chramn.

I will tell why it was he married his wife's sister. When he had already married Ingund and loved her with special affection, he received a request from her.

She said, "My Lord has done with his servant as he pleased and has admitted me to his bed. Now, to complete the favor you have granted, let my lord king listen to what his servant proposes. I beg you, please provide a rich and accomplished husband for my sister, your slave. That way I shall not be humbled, but rather, by being raised higher, I shall be able to serve you more faithfully."

Hearing this, and being licentious in the extreme, he fell in love with Aregund, went to the villa on which she was living, and married her himself. After the marriage, he returned to Ingund.

"I have taken care of the favor your sweet self asked of me," he said. "Demanding a man rich and shrewd with whom to hook up your sister, I could find no one better than myself. And so you should know that I have married her, which I don't think will make you unhappy."

"Let my lord do whatever seems pleasing in his eyes," she replied. "Just let your servant live in favor with the king."

Now Gunthecar, Chramn and Childeric died during their father's lifetime. Of the death of Chramn I shall write later. Alboin, king of the Lombards, married the king's daughter Chlodoswintha.

Counts of the Bretons

(IV 4)

Chanao, a count of the Bretons, killed three of his brothers.

Still wanting to kill Macliav, he seized him, loaded him with chains, and kept him imprisoned. Macliav was freed from death by Felix, bishop of Nantes. Thereafter Macliav swore to his brother that he would be loyal to him. On an occasion I know nothing about, Macliav tried to break the oath. Chanao was aware of this and pursued him again. When Macliav saw that he could not escape, he fled to the protection of another count of that region, Chonomor by

2. "I have taken care of the favor your sweet self asked of me (IV 3)."
Chlothar announces to Ingund that he has married her sister Aregund.

name. Seeing Macliav's pursuers approaching, Chonomor hid him in a coffin under the earth, piling up a mound in the usual way, but leaving a small vent so he could breath.

"Look, here lies Macliav dead and buried," they said to his pursuers on their arrival.

Hearing this, the pursuers were happy, had a drink over the grave, and reported to his brother that Macliav was dead. At this news Chanao took the whole of his kingdom. Nevertheless, after the death of Clovis the Bretons had always been under the power of the Franks and their counts were not called kings.

Macliav, rising up from under the earth, went to the city of Vannes and there was tonsured and ordained bishop. When Chanao died, Macliav turned apostate, let his hair grow, and took up the wife he abandoned when he became a cleric, and as well, his brother's kingdom. He was, however, excommunicated by the bishops.

The nature of his demise, I will describe later [V 16]....

Reign of Theudebert's Son, Theudebald, a. 548–555

(IV 9)

Now that he had grown, Theudebald married Wuldetrada. This Theudebald, they say, had a bad nature. Once when he grew angry with someone he suspected of taking his property, he recounted a fable.

"A snake," he said, "found a jar full of wine. He went in by its neck and greedily drank what was inside. Enlarged by the wine, he could not get out the way he got in. As the snake was trying to get out, without success, the owner of the wine came along and said to him, 'First spew out what you have swallowed, and then you will be able to get away free.'"

This fable made him greatly feared and hated.

Under him, Buccelin, after reducing all Italy to the rule of the Franks, was slain by Narses [a. 554]; Italy was captured on behalf of the emperor and there was no one to recover it later.

In his time, we saw grapes grow on the tree we call elder, with no connection to a vine, and the blossoms of the same trees, which as you know usually produce black seeds, yielded the seeds of grapes. Then a star coming from the opposite direction was seen to enter the circle of the fifth moon. I believe these signs proclaimed the death of the king.

He became very weak and could not control himself from the waist down. He gradually grew worse and died in the seventh year of his reign. King Chlothar obtained his kingdom and took his wife Wuldetrada to his bed. But Chlothar was criticized by the bishops and left her, giving her to Duke Garivald [of Bavaria].

Chlothar sent his son Chramn to Clermont.

Later Years of Chlothar I, a. 555–561

Expeditions against the Saxons (IV 10, 14)

In this year [a. 555] the Saxons rebelled and King Chlothar sent an army against them and annihilated the major part of them. He traversed all of Thuringia, laying it waste, because the Thuringians had given the Saxons assistance....

When Chlothar had taken up the kingship of Francia after Theudebald's death [a. 555] and was making a progress through it, he heard from his people that a second bout of madness had burst out among the Saxons. They were rebelling against him and disdaining to pay the tribute which they were accustomed to pay every year. Aroused by the news, he marched against them. When he was near their territory, the Saxons then sent envoys to him.

"We mean you no disrespect," they said, "nor do we refuse to make the payments we have customarily rendered to your brothers and nephews. We'll give even more if you ask for it. We ask only one thing—that there be peace and your army and our people not come into conflict."

King Chlothar said to his followers when he heard this, "These men speak well. Let's not attack them in case we sin against God."

"We know they're liars," said his men, "and will never keep their promise. Let's go after them."

The Saxons again offered half their chattels in return for peace.

Chlothar said to his men, "Leave these people alone, I beg of you, so we don't arouse God's anger."

But they would not give in. Again the Saxons made offers of garments, cattle, and all their chattels.

"Take all this together with half of our land," they said, "only let our wives and little children remain free, and let no war come between us."

The Franks would not even agree to this.

King Chlothar said to them, "Give up this idea, I beg of you. Our position is not right. Don't wage a war in which you will be destroyed. If you decide to go off on your own, I will not follow."

At that the Franks became angry with King Chlothar and rushed upon him, tearing his tent in pieces. Heaping abuse on him, they dragged him away by force and were going to kill him unless he would go with them. When Chlothar realized this, he went with them against his will.

The battle began, and they suffered an immense slaughter at the hands of their enemies, and such a host perished on both sides that it was impossible to estimate or count their number. Then Chlothar, greatly confounded, asked for peace, saying that it was not of his own free will that he had come against them. He was granted peace and returned home.

Chlothar, his Son Chramn, and the Death of Childebert (IV 13, 16, 17, 20)

In these days, Chramn lived at Clermont [see IV 9]. He committed many mad acts and for this reason his departure from the world came quickly. He was roundly cursed by people. He loved no one from whom he could get good and useful advice. Instead, he gathered round himself low characters in a youthful and restless stage of their lives. He only had affection for them and listened to their advice, even issuing directives allowing them to carry off daughters of senators by force. He seriously wronged Firminus and drove him from the office of count of the city, replacing him with Salustius son of Euvodius....

Chramn, as I said, was committing evil deeds at Clermont and still holding a grudge against [Bishop] Cautinus [see Appendix]. In this period, he became so seriously ill that his hair fell out because of a high fever. He had with him at the time a citizen of Clermont, Ascovindus, a high official and manifestly a man of good character, who did all in his power to turn the prince from his wickedness but could not. For Chramn also had with him Leo of Poitiers, a man like the lion of his name, most savage in fulfilling all his desires, who viciously spurred him on to every kind of evil deed....

Chramn left Clermont and came to the city of Poitiers. There he stayed, exercising great power, but, led astray by the advice of evil men, he became intent on going over to his uncle Childebert and made arrangements to betray his father. Childebert promised, even though quite deceitfully, to receive Chramn, someone he should have admonished with religious arguments against becoming the enemy of his father. At that time they took oaths to each other through secret emissaries and plotted quite happily together against Chlothar. Yet Childebert forgot that whenever he had acted against his brother, he always went away the worse for it.

After entering into this treaty, Chramn went back to Limoges and subjected to his own rule all the parts of his father's kingdom through which he had earlier passed.... King Chlothar now sent his two sons, Charibert and Guntram, to Chramn. They passed through Auvergne and, on hearing that Chramn was in the territory of Limoges, came to the hill called the black mountain, where they found him.... Chramn cunningly sent a stranger to his brothers to announce the death of their father. The war against the Saxons, of which I have spoken above, was being waged at this time. In alarm they returned as fast as they could to Burgundy. Chramn followed behind them with his army and, coming as far as Chalon, took the town after a siege. From there he pushed on to the fortress of Dijon....

At the time King Chlothar was fighting bravely against the Saxons. Incited by Childebert, so they say, and angry with the Franks for the previous year, they had advanced from their territory into Francia, taking plunder as far as the city of Deutz and inflicting serious damage.

At this point, Chramn, who had now married the daughter of Wilichar, came to Paris to establish bonds of loyalty and friendship with Childebert and swore that he was a most determined enemy of his father. While Chlothar was fighting the Saxons, King Childebert entered the champaign of Rheims and pushed on quickly to the city itself, laying everything waste by pillage and fire. For he had heard that his brother had been killed by the Saxons and, figuring that everything was now to be subjected to his authority, seized every part he could reach....

King Childebert grew ill. After being confined for some time to his bed, he died at Paris [a. 558] and was buried in the basilica of the blessed Vincent [later Saint-Germain-des-Prés], which he had built. King Chlothar took his kingdom and treasures; Ultrogotha and her two daughters he sent into exile. Chramn was brought before his father but later proved to be disloyal. When he saw there was no other choice, he went to Brittany and there with his wife and daughters hid out with Chanao count of the Bretons.

Wilichar, Chramn's father-in-law, fled to the basilica of Saint Martin. It was then that the holy basilica was burned because of the sins of the people and the mockeries that were done in it by Wilichar and his wife. We mention this not without a heavy sigh. Moreover, the city of Tours had already been burned the year before, and all the churches built in it were left abandoned. Immediately, by order of King Chlothar, the basilica of the blessed Martin was roofed with tin and restored to its former beauty. Then two swarms of locusts appeared which, crossing through Auvergne and Limousin, so they say, came to the plain of Romagnac, where a battle broke out between them, and there was a great clash of forces.

Chlothar was in a rage against Chramn and brought his army into Brittany against him [a. 560]. Nor was Chramn afraid of coming out against his father. The armies gathered together on a plain and both sides took up positions. Just when Chramn in company with the Bretons had drawn up his forces facing his father, night fell, and they refrained from fighting.

During the night Chanao, count of the Bretons, said to Chramn, "I don't think it's right for you to go out against your father. Let me fall on him through the night and destroy him with all his army."

3. The sons of Chlothar I accompany the body of their father to the basilica of Saint Medard in Soissons (IV 21).

Chramn would not allow this to be done, prevented, I believe, by the power of God.

In the morning, both sides got under way and rushed into battle.

King Chlothar went like a new David to fight against Absalom his son, loudly lamenting, and exclaiming, "Look down from heaven, Lord, and judge my cause, for I suffer wrongs wickedly inflicted by a son. Look down, Lord, and judge justly, and impose that judgment that you once passed on Absalom and his father David."

When both sides engaged, the count of the Bretons retreated and then was killed. Finally Chramn took to flight. He had ships standing by at sea, but since he tried to save his wife and daughters, he was overpowered by his father's forces, taken captive, and bound. News of this was told to King Chlothar, and he gave orders to burn Chramn together with his wife and daughters. They were shut up in the hut of a poor man; Chramn was stretched on a bench and strangled with a towel, and then the hut was burned over them. This is how he perished with his wife and daughters.

Chlothar's Death, a. 561 (IV 21)

In the fifty-first year of his reign, King Chlothar came to the threshold of the blessed Martin with many gifts. He visited the tomb of the aforesaid bishop at Tours, going over all the actions that he might have taken without due consideration. He prayed with loud sighs for the blessed confessor of God to obtain forgiveness for his faults and, by his intercession with God, to blot out the irrational acts he had committed. He then went home and, in the fifty-first year of his reign, while hunting in the forest of Cuise, was seized with a fever and returned to the villa of Compiègne.

There, when the fever grew worse, he would cry out in agony, "What do you think? What kind of king of heaven is this who kills off such great kings in this way?"

Suffering in this fashion, he breathed his last. His four sons carried him with great honor to Soissons and buried him in the basilica of Saint Medard.

He died one day after the anniversary of the death of Chramn.

CHAPTER THREE

FROM THE DIVISION OF CHLOTHAR'S
KINGDOM TO THE DEATH OF SIGIBERT I

a. 561–575

(BOOK IV)

Get what you can and keep what you have.

Proverb

With the succession of Chlothar's sons in 561, the Histories *begins dealing with kings whose reigns coincide with Gregory's own adult years, if not yet his politically important years as bishop. It is worth noting that this circumstance does not mean that Gregory's history was composed concurrently with the events he describes—far from it. There is sufficient indication in his text to show that Gregory wrote of the years recounted below with ample knowledge of what these events, or more specifically, the persons driving them, would eventually bring upon Gaul. The lengthy treatment of Mummolus's campaigns, for example, is not likely a response to relatively recent events but background for the general's importance in political events of later books. Nor was Gregory's account necessarily first-hand. He continued to use sources, some of which are detectable though not identifiable. Gregory's chronology also remains vague for the decade and a half following Chlothar's death—another sign of the retrospective character of the account. I have added dates where they seem reasonable and, as in Chapter Two, subheadings and chapter headings to facilitate reading.*

Of the sons of Chlothar who inherited their father's kingdom, two in particular dominate much of the later Histories*: Chilperic, who ruled a north-western kingdom later known as Neustria, and Guntram, who ruled the kingdom of Burgundy. The early death of another son, Charibert, in 567, was significant for later quarrels among his brothers over the inheritance of his kingdom. Sigibert, whose checkered career is cut short at the end of Book IV, and his wife Brunhild, approved Gregory's appointment as bishop of Tours in the year 573.*

The First Two Years

Partition of the Kingdom, a. 561 (IV 22)

After the funeral of his father, Chilperic took possession of the treasures that were stored in the royal villa of Berny. He then looked around for the most powerful Franks, softened them up with gifts, and brought them under his

authority. He soon entered Paris and took over the residence of King Childebert, but he was not allowed to hold it for long. His brothers joined forces and
drove him from there. This is how the four kings, that is, Charibert, Guntram,
Chilperic, and Sigibert, came to make a lawful division among themselves.

The partition conferred on Charibert the kingdom of Childebert, with Paris
as the capital; on Guntram, the kingdom of Chlodomer, with the capital being
Orleans; on Chilperic, the kingdom of his father Chlothar, with his throne at
Soissons; on Sigibert, the kingdom of Theuderic, with Rheims as the capital.

Invasion of the Avars. Civil War between Sigibert and Chilperic (IV 23)

*Gregory uses the old term Huns to refer to the Avars, an eastern nomadic people new
to the West. At this time the Avars began to occupy the Hungarian plain and became a
major military power in central Europe.*

After the death of King Chlothar, the Huns attacked Gaul [a. 562]. Sigibert
led his forces against them, and in the campaign, defeated them and put them
to flight. Afterwards, their king sent envoys and gained friendly relations with
Sigibert. But while he was having his troubles with the Huns, his brother Chilperic overran Rheims and took away other cities that belonged to him. What
is worse, civil war broke out between them for this reason.

Returning as victor over the Huns, Sigibert took Soissons, where he discovered Theudebert, King Chilperic's son. He took him into custody and sent him
into exile. He brought his forces against Chilperic, whom he defeated and put
to flight, and re-established his authority over his cities. He ordered Chilperic's
son Theudebert to be kept for a whole year under guard at the villa of Ponthion;
but as he was merciful, he afterwards loaded him with gifts and sent him back
safe and sound to his father. He did this on condition that Theudebert swear
never again to act against him. The oath was afterwards broken, due to sin.

The Kings and Their Wives

Guntram's Wives (IV 25)

Good King Guntram at first took to bed as a concubine Veneranda, a slave of
one of his followers; by her he had a son Gundobad.

Afterwards he married Marcatrude, daughter of Magnachar. He sent his son
Gundobad to Orleans. After Marcatrude had a son, she jealously set out to
bring about Gundobad's death, poisoning him with a doctored drink, so they
say. Following his death, by the judgment of God, she lost the son she had and
incurred the hatred of the king. Sent away by him, she died not long after.

After her Guntram took Austrechild, also named Bobilla. By her he again had two sons; the older of them was called Chlothar and the younger Chlodomer.

Charibert's Wives and his Death (IV 26)

The husband in Kent was King Aethelberht, converted to Christianity by the Roman mission of Augustine in 597.

Next King Charibert married Ingoberga, by whom he had a daughter, who afterwards was taken to Kent to be married. Ingoberga had in her service at the time two girls, the daughters of a poor man. The first of them was called Marcovefa, who wore the religious habit, and the other was Merofled. The king was very much in love with them. They were, as I said, the daughters of a wool worker.

Jealous that they were loved by the king, Ingoberga privately made sure that the father was put to work, supposing that when the king saw this he would take a dislike to the daughters. While the father was working, she called the king, who expected to see something special, but only saw this man at a distance sorting the royal wool. The sight made him angry, so he left Ingoberga and married Merofled.

He also had another girl named Theudogild, the daughter of a shepherd. By her he is said to have had a son, who, as soon as he came forth from the womb, was carried to the grave....

Afterward Charibert married Marcovefa, Merofled's sister. For this reason, they were both excommunicated by the holy bishop Germanus [of Paris]. But since the king would not leave her, she was struck by God's judgment and died. In no time at all the king himself followed her to the grave [a. 567].

After his death, Theudogild, one of his queens, took it upon herself to send messengers to King Guntram, offering to marry him.

The king gave them this response, "Let her have no worry about coming to me with her treasure. For I will marry her and make her a great woman in everyone's eyes. Rest assured she will have greater honor with me than with my brother who has just died."

Very pleased, she gathered up everything and went to him.

When the king saw what she brought, he said, "It's better for this treasure to be in my hands than under the control of this woman who was unworthy to lie in my brother's bed."

Then, having taken away much and left little, he sent her to a monastery at Arles. Theudogild took it ill to be put to fasts and vigils and so she contacted a Goth by secret messengers, promising that she would leave the monastery with her treasure and follow him willingly if he would take her to Spain and marry her. He agreed without hesitation. But when she had gathered her things and bundled them up and was ready to leave the convent, the enterprise of the abbess frustrated her desires. The abbess detected the deceit and had her severely beaten and put her under guard. There she remained to the end of her life in this world, worn down by no slight suffering.

Sigibert Marries Brunhild (IV 27)

Next, when king Sigibert saw that his brothers were marrying unworthy wives, and were themselves so worthless as to even marry slaves, he sent an embassy to Spain with many gifts to ask for Brunhild, daughter of King Athanagild [a. 551–58]. She was a well-mannered, good-looking girl, decent and well behaved, with good judgment and a persuasive manner. Her father did not reject the request for her hand and sent her to Sigibert with great treasure. The king assembled his leading followers, prepared a feast and took her as his wife with immense rejoicing and celebration. She had been a follower of the Arian creed but was converted by the preaching of the bishops and the admonition of the king himself. Having confessed the blessed Trinity in unity, she believed and received the chrism. She continues to be a Catholic, in Christ's name.

Chilperic's Wives (IV 28)

The statement in the text, as we have it, that, after the death of Galswinth, Chilperic's brothers "toppled him from power (regnum)," is difficult to accept at face value. Whatever the brothers may have done fell short of actual expulsion or deposition.

When Chilperic saw this, he asked for Brunhild's sister Galswinth, although he already had several wives, promising through his envoys that he would abandon the others, if only he could win a bride worthy of himself and the offspring of a king. With these assurances, her father sent his daughter, as he had the first, along with a great deal of wealth. Galswinth was older than Brunhild.

When she came to King Chilperic, she was received with great honor and made his wife. Moreover his love for her was considerable, for she had brought great treasure. But because of his love for Fredegund, whom he had before, a disgraceful conflict arose to divide them. Galswinth had already been converted to the Catholic creed and received the chrism. She complained to the king of the wrongs she constantly had to endure and told him that he had no respect for her. Finally she asked him to give her freedom to return to her native land if she left the treasures that she had brought with her. But he made up various excuses and mollified her with sweet words. In the end, he had her strangled by

4. Venantius Fortunatus recites an epithalamium, or wedding oration, before
Sigibert and Brunhild.

5.   "In the end, he had her strangled by a slave, and he himself found the
      corpse on the bed (IV 28)." The death of Galswinth.

a slave, and he himself found the corpse on the bed.

After her death God revealed a great sign of his power. A lamp burned before her tomb, suspended by a cord. Without anyone touching it, the cord broke, and the lamp fell to the pavement. The hard pavement gave way before it, and the lamp, as if it had landed in some kind of soft substance, was buried to the middle and was not at all broken. To those who saw it, this did not happen without a great miracle.

The king wept over the body and then, after a few days, took Fredegund back again as his wife. When he did this, his brothers attributed Galswinth's killing to his orders and toppled him from power.

At the time, Chilperic had three sons by his first wife Audovera, namely Theudebert, whom I mentioned above, Merovech, and Clovis.

But let me return to my task.

War, Plague, and New Neighbors

Sigibert's Second War with the Avars, a. 566 (IV 29)

The Huns tried to get into Gaul a second time. Sigibert brought his army against them, leading a great host of good fighting men. Just when they were about to engage, the Huns, who were well versed in the magic arts, exposed them to apparitions of various kinds and defeated them decisively.

Sigibert's army fled, and he himself was surrounded by the Huns. Sigibert was a cultivated and shrewd man, and he would have been kept a prisoner if he had not overcome by the art of giving those whom he could not overcome by the art of war. He gave gifts and entered into an agreement with the king of the Huns that all the days of their lives they would not start wars with each other. This incident is thought to be more to his credit than otherwise, and justifiably so. Moreover, the king of the Huns gave many gifts to King Sigibert. He was called Gaganus [Khan]. All the kings of that people are called by this name.

Sigibert Orders the Arvernians to take Arles (IV 30)

King Sigibert wanted to take the city of Arles and so he ordered the Arvernians to muster their forces. Firminus was count of the city at the time and marched off at the head of the forces. Moreover Audovar approached with an army from the other direction. They both entered the city and exacted oaths on behalf of King Sigibert. As soon as King Guntram found out, he dispatched an army under the patrician Celsus. On the march, Celsus took the city of Avignon. When he reached Arles, he surrounded the city and began hostilities against the forces of Sigibert within the walls.

At that point Bishop Sabaudus [a. 552–86] said to these forces, "Go out and join battle, for you cannot defend us, nor the territory subject to this city, if you remain penned up within the walls. If God is well disposed to you, and you defeat the enemy, we will stand by the pledge of loyalty that we made. But if they beat you, have no fear, you will find the gates open. Come back in and save your lives."

Taken in by the trick, out they went ready for battle. But they were defeated by the army of Celsus, and retreating they returned to the city where they found the gates barred. The army was stung by javelins from the rear and showered with stones by the townsmen, so the troops made for the river Rhône. There, supporting themselves on their shields, they tried to reach the farther bank. The strength of the current swept many of them away to their deaths, and the Rhône now did to the Arvernians what the Simois is said to have once done to the Trojans:

> It turned over beneath its waves the shields and helmets of men and their strong bodies. Here and there a man appeared, swimming in that vast torrent. [Virgil, *Aeneid*, i. 104 f., 118]

Swimming with difficulty, as I said, and supported by their shields, they were able to reach the flat ground on the other bank.

They regained their country not without considerable insult, having been stripped of their equipment and deprived of their horses. Firminus and Audovar, though, were allowed to withdraw. In this battle, notable Arvernians of the time were not only swept away by the force of the current but also cut down by the blows of their enemies' swords.

And so King Guntram, having recovered Arles, with his usual good will, restored Avignon to his brother's authority.

Plague (IV 31)

For Cato and Cautinus, see Appendix.

…Even before the great [plague] disaster, prodigies brought terror to the region of Auvergne. There appeared frequently around the sun three or four great lights which the farmers called 'suns'.

"Look, there are three of four suns in the sky," they would say.

One time on the Kalends of October [1 October 563], the sun looked so darkened that not even a quarter of it remained shining, appearing hideous and defaced like sackcloth. And a star, which some call a comet, with a beam like a sword, was seen over that region for a whole year and the sky seemed to blaze, and many other portents appeared....

With the coming of the disaster [a. 571], people died in such numbers through the whole district [of Auvergne] that the legions that fell could not be counted. For when the supply of coffins and planks ran out, ten or more people would be buried in a single trench. One Sunday, three hundred dead bodies were counted in the basilica of the blessed Peter alone. Death was sudden. There would appear on the groin or in the armpit a sore in the shape of a serpent, and people would be killed by the poison so quickly that they took their last breath the second or third day after infection. Moreover the power of the poison robbed them of their senses.

It was at this time that the priest Cato died. When many had fled the epidemic, he stayed where he was, courageously burying people and saying mass. He was a priest of considerable humanity and a great lover of the poor. And if he could be proud, these virtues, I believe, made up for it. Bishop Cautinus [of Clermont], after running around from place to place in fear of the disaster, returned to the city. He took sick and died on the Friday before Easter Sunday. At the very same hour, Tetradius his cousin also died. At that time the populations of Lyons, Bourges, Cahors, and Dijon were seriously depleted by the disaster.

In Spain Leovigild Becomes King (IV 38)

Gosuintha was the widow of Athanagild.

...On the death of Athanagild in Spain, Liuva [a. 568–73] received the kingdom along with his brother Leovigild [a. 569–86]. Then on the death of Liuva, the brother Leovigild took over the entire kingdom.

As his wife was deceased, Leovigild married Gosuintha, the mother of Queen Brunhild; from his first wife he had two sons, of which one [Hermenigild] was betrothed to [Ingund] the daughter of Sigibert and the other [Reccared] to [Rigunth] the daughter of Chilperic. Moreover Leovigild divided the kingdom equally between his sons, putting to death all who were in the habit of killing kings, leaving not one among them who could piss against the wall [cf. 1 Kings 25:34; 3 Kings 16:11].

Alboin and the Lombards Invade Italy, a. 568 (IV 41)

Alboin, king of the Lombards, who had married Chlodoswintha, the daughter of King Chlothar, left his country and set out for Italy with all the Lombard people. They mustered their forces and set off with their wives and children, with the intention of settling there. They entered the country and brought the land under their control, spending almost seven years roving about despoiling churches and killing priests.

When his wife Chlodoswintha died, Alboin married another wife, whose father he had killed a short time before. For this reason the woman always hated her husband and waited for a chance to avenge the wrong done her father. And so it happened that she poisoned her husband, after acquiring a passion for one of the household slaves. When Alboin died, she went off with the slave, but they were both captured and put to death.

The Lombards then set another king over themselves [a. 574].

Mummolus the Patrician

His Career and Campaigns against the Saxons and Lombards (IV 42, 44)

Eunius, also called Mummolus, was promoted to the post of patrician by King Guntram. It is necessary, I think, to recollect at greater length certain details about the beginning of his service.

He was a native of the city of Auxerre. His father was Peonius, who held the post of count of this city. Peonius sent his son with gifts to the king to secure reappointment to the office. The son delivered his father's presents, but secured his father's comital office for himself and displaced a father whose interests he should have furthered. Advancing step by step from this start, Mummolus rose to great prominence.

When the Lombards broke into Gaul [a. 570/71], the patrician Amatus, who had lately succeeded Celsus [cf. IV 30], went against them, but after joining battle, retreated and was killed. The Lombards were said to have wreaked such havoc on the Burgundians that the dead could not be counted. Loaded with plunder, the Lombards withdrew to Italy. On their departure, Eunius, also named Mummolus, was summoned by the king and won the high office of the patriciate.

The Lombards made a second inroad into Gaul and reached as far as Mustiae Calmes near the city of Embrun. Mummolus mustered his forces and marched there with the Burgundians. He surrounded the Lombards with his army and also made an abattis. Attacking them in the remoteness of the forest, he killed a good number and captured some, sending them to the king. The king had them kept under guard in various places through the country. A few somehow escaped and brought the news back to their homeland. Present in this battle were Salonius and Sagittarius, brothers and bishops, whose protection was not the heavenly cross; instead they were armed with the helmet and mailcoat of the world and, what is worse, are reported to have killed many with their own hands. This was Mummolus's first victory.

After this, the Saxons who had accompanied the Lombards into Italy again burst into Gaul [ca 572/74], and pitched camp in the territory of Riez, that is, near the villa of Estoublon. Dispersing through the villas of the neighboring towns, they plundered, took captives, and laid everything waste. When Mummolus learned of this, he mustered his forces. Attacking them, he killed many thousands, not stopping the slaughter until evening, when night put an end to it. For he had found men with their guard down, with no thought of what was about to happen.

In the morning, the Saxons drew up their forces and got ready for battle, but messengers passed from one army to the other and they made peace. Giving presents to Mummolus and abandoning all the plunder of the region and the captives, they withdrew, first swearing an oath that they would come back to Gaul so as to be subjects of the Frankish kings and allies of the Franks.

The Saxons returned to Italy and, collecting their wives and children and all their movable goods, made preparations to return to Gaul, in expectation that Sigibert would assemble them and establish them in the district from which they had set out. They formed two columns, as they say, and one came by way of Nice and the other by Embrun, in fact taking the road they had traveled the previous year. They joined up in the territory of Avignon.

This was harvest time. For the most part the crops of the district lay out in the open; the inhabitants had not yet started to store any of them at home. The Saxons arrived and divided the crops among themselves. They gathered the grain up, ground it, and ate it, leaving nothing to those who had done the work. But afterwards, when they had used up the harvest and had arrived on the bank of the Rhône—they had to cross the river to enter the kingdom of King Sigibert—Mummolus met them.

"You will not cross this river," he said. "Look, you have laid waste the land of my lord king. You have gathered crops, plundered herds, put houses to the torch, and cut down the olive groves and vineyards. You will go no further unless you first compensate those you have left poor. Otherwise you will not escape my hands. I shall put you, your wives, and your children to the sword and avenge the wrong done to my lord king Guntram."

Then they were very much afraid, and giving many thousand pieces of gold to save themselves, they were allowed to cross. And so they came to Clermont.

It was then springtime. There they brought out bronze bars stamped as if they were gold. Anyone seeing them would have no doubt that they were anything but gold, proved and tested; for it was colored, by what means I know not. For this reason, some people were deceived by the trick and, giving gold but receiving bronze, were made poor.

The Saxons went on to King Sigibert and were settled in the land from which they had first come.

After this, three Lombard dukes, Amo, Zaban, and Rodan, burst into Gaul [a. 574]. Amo took the route by Embrun and pushed as far as the villa called Macho in the territory of Avignon, which villa Mummolus had obtained as a gift from the king. Here he pitched his tents. Zaban, coming down by the town of Die, reached Valence, where he set up his camp. Rodan advanced to Grenoble, where he pitched his tents. Amo subdued the province of Arles and the towns in its vicinity and, marching as far as the stony plain near Marseilles, stripped it of its herds and inhabitants. He made preparations to besiege Aix, but withdrew when he received twenty-two pounds of silver. Rodan and Zaban did much the same in the towns they came across.

As soon as this was reported to Mummolus, he mustered an army and intercepted Rodan, who had subdued the city of Grenoble. Although Mummolus's forces had difficulty crossing the Isère river, by the will of God, an animal entered the river, revealing a ford, and so the troops readily reached the farther bank. Seeing this, the Lombards without delay drew their swords and attacked them. Battle was joined and the Lombards were cut down so badly that Rodan, wounded by a spear, took refuge high in the mountains. With the five hundred men he had left, Rodan pushed through remote forests and managed to reach Zaban, then besieging Valence. He told him all that had happened. They then gave up all their plunder, and both returned to Embrun. There Mummolus confronted them with a countless host. The Lombard forces were cut down almost to the point of annihilation in the battle, and the dukes returned to Italy with a few men.

When they reached Susa, there was no warm welcome from the inhabitants, especially as Sisinnius, the emperor's master of the soldiers, had his headquarters there. Then someone pretending to be a servant of Mummolus presented a letter to Sisinnius in the presence of Zaban, greeting him in the name of Mummolus.

"Mummolus himself," proclaimed the messenger, "is close at hand!"

At these words, Zaban departed at great speed, passing the city by. When Amo heard the news, he gathered all his booty and headed off down the road. But held up by the snow, he had to abandon his spoil and barely broke clear with a few companions.

They were terrified by the power of Mummolus.

Mummolus goes to Tours (IV 45)

Mummolus conducted many campaigns from which he emerged victorious. When, after the death of Charibert [a. 567], Chilperic had overrun Tours and Poitiers, which by agreement had been allotted to King Sigibert, this king joined up with his brother Guntram, and they chose Mummolus to restore these cities to their rightful authority. Mummolus came to Tours, drove out Clovis, Chilperic's son, exacted from the people oaths of loyalty to King Sigibert, and proceeded to Poitiers. Basilius and Sigar, two citizens of the city, gathered people together and tried to resist; but Mummolus surrounded them from all sides and overpowered, crushed, and destroyed them. This is how he came to Poitiers and exacted oaths of loyalty to Sigibert.

This account of Mummolus is enough for a while. The rest must be told in its proper place at a later point.

Civil War Takes a Serious Turn

Theudebert, Chilperic's Son, Takes the Cities of Sigibert (IV 47–48)

When Clovis, son of Chilperic, was driven from Tours [see IV 45], he went to Bordeaux [a. 573]. He was staying in this city, with no one particularly bothering him, when one of Sigibert's supporters, a certain Sigulf, attacked him. Clovis fled, and Sigulf pursued him with trumpets and horns, as if driving a running deer. Clovis had difficulty finding a clear way back to his father. He managed to get back to him, though, going by way of Angers.

When a dispute arose between King Guntram and King Sigibert, King Guntram assembled all the bishops of his kingdom at Paris for them to pronounce which of the two was in the right. But so that civil war should grow in intensity, the sinfulness of the kings caused them to pay no attention.

In anger Chilperic sent his eldest son Theudebert to overrun Sigibert's cities, Tours, Poitiers, and other places lying on this side of the Loire. Theudebert had once been captured by Sigibert and taken an oath to be loyal to him [cf. IV 23]. Theudebert came to Poitiers and fought against Duke Gundovald. His forces retreated and Theudebert slaughtered a great many people there. He also burned most of the district of Tours, and would have destroyed all of it, had not the inhabitants surrendered in time. Gathering his forces, he overran, laid waste, and demolished the territories of Limoges, Cahors, and other regions round about them. He burned the churches, took away the sacred vessels, killed clerics, drove monks from the monasteries and treated the nuns shamefully, and laid everything waste. At that time, the sorrow in the churches was greater than in the time of Diocletian's persecution.

And to this day we are astonished and wonder why such disasters fell upon them. But let us recall what their predecessors did and what they do. After the preaching of the bishops, their ancestors gave up temples for churches; they daily take plunder from the churches. Their ancestors respected with their whole hearts the bishops of the Lord and listened to them; they not only refuse to listen to them, but even persecute them. Their ancestors enriched the monasteries and churches; they demolish and ruin them....

Sigibert Goes to Paris (IV 49)

While these events were taking place, King Sigibert mustered the peoples who live on the other side of the Rhine and, initiating civil war, made preparations to march against his brother Chilperic [a. 574]. When Chilperic heard, he sent envoys to his brother Guntram. Together the two of them made a treaty that neither brother would allow the other to be destroyed.

Sigibert advanced at the head of those peoples, but Chilperic on his side took up a position with his army. When Sigibert could find no way of crossing the Seine to attack his brother, he sent an ultimatum to Guntram.

"Unless you allow me to cross this river through your kingdom," he said, "I shall march against you with all my forces."

Fearing attack, Guntram made a treaty with him and allowed him to cross. Chilperic obviously got the impression that Guntram had abandoned him and had gone over to Sigibert, and so he moved his camp to Havelu, a place not far from Chartres. Sigibert followed trying to get him to make ready a field of battle. Chilperic was afraid that, if their two armies fought, their rule would collapse. So he sought terms of peace and restored Sigibert's cities that Theudebert had wrongfully occupied. He asked on behalf of the inhabitants of the cities that they in no way be held guilty, for Theudebert by fire and sword had unjustly forced them to change sides.

At this time most of the communities around Paris were destroyed by fire; houses and other properties were plundered by the enemy and even captives led away. King Sigibert tried to protest their doing this, but he could not control the raging madness of the peoples who had come from over the Rhine and calmly endured it all until he could return home. At this time some of them even criticized him for having pulled them back from battle. But Sigibert was a fearless man and, mounting his horse, rode towards them, calming them down with gentle words; many of them he later had stoned to death.

There is no doubt that it was not without the power of blessed Martin that the kings made peace without recourse to arms; on the very day they made peace, the limbs of three paralytics were straightened in the basilica of the saint. I recorded this miracle, with God's aid, in books I later wrote [VM II 5–7].

Treaty between Guntram and Chilperic. Death of Chilperic's son Theudebert,
a. 574–75 (IV 50)

This chapter contains the first mention of Duke Guntram Boso, a prominent figure in later books.

It makes one heart-sick to record these civil wars.

A year later, Chilperic once more sent envoys to his brother Guntram with a message saying, "Let my brother come and we can have a meeting. And when we have made peace, let us march against Sigibert, our common enemy."

When this was done, and they had met and honored one another with gifts, Chilperic mustered his forces and advanced as far as Rheims, burning and devastating everything in his path.

Sigibert heard the news and a second time summoned the peoples whom I mentioned. He came to Paris and made preparations to march against his brother, while sending orders to the people of Châteaudun and Tours for them to march against Theudebert [cf. IV 47, 49]. When they made up excuses, the king sent Dukes Godigisel and Guntram [Boso] to take command. They levied an army and set out against Theudebert. Abandoned by his forces, Theudebert was left with a few men, but he did not hesitate to come out to fight. The two sides met and Theudebert was defeated and cut down on the field; and his lifeless body, sad to say, was despoiled by the enemy. After being taken up by a certain Aunulf, it was washed, clothed in appropriate garments, and then buried in the city of Angoulême.

Chilperic, learning that Guntram and Sigibert had once more come to terms, fortified himself within the walls of Tournai with his wife and his sons.

Death of King Sigibert, a. 575 (IV 51)

In that year a bright light was seen crossing the sky, just as we saw earlier before the death of Chlothar.

Sigibert, having taken the cities around Paris, marched as far as Rouen, intending to turn the cities over to the forces [from across the Rhine]. He was stopped from doing this by his own followers. On his return, he entered Paris, and there Brunhild came to him with her children. Then the Franks who had once followed the elder Childebert [I], sent a delegation to Sigibert to say that, when he reached them, they would abandon Chilperic and make him king over them. Hearing this, he sent troops ahead to besiege his brother in Tournai, intending to go there himself soon.

The holy bishop Germanus said to him, "If you leave without the intention of killing your brother, you will return alive and victorious. But if you have something else in mind, you will die. This is what the Lord spoke through Solomon, 'If you prepare a pit for your brother, you will fall into it [cf. Prov. 26:27].'"

But because of his sins, the king paid no attention.

He came to the villa called Vitry. The entire army gathered about him, placed him on a shield, and made him king over them. At this time two slaves bewitched by Queen Fredegund, carrying sturdy knives, commonly called scramasaxes, smeared with poison, pretended to bring forward a request and stabbed him from both sides. He shouted out and collapsed. He gave up his spirit not long afterwards.

There too fell Charigisel, his chamberlain. And Sigila, who had once come from Gothia, was badly cut up. He was apprehended afterwards by King Chilperic and came to a cruel end: his every joint was burned with hot irons and he was torn limb from limb. Charigisel's character was as weak as his desires were strong. He had risen from mean circumstances and became a great man at the king's court through flattery. He was a seeker after other people's property and a breaker of testaments. The circumstances of his departure from life were such that, with death approaching, he who had so often invalidated the wills of others was not granted the time to finish a will of his own.

Chilperic was caught in a perilous situation, uncertain whether he could escape or would be destroyed, until messengers arrived to inform him of his brother's death. Then he left Tournai with his wife and children, prepared Sigibert's body and buried it in the villa of Lambres. It was later transferred to Soissons to the basilica of Saint Medard, which Sigibert himself had built, and was buried there by the side of his father Chlothar.

Sigibert died in the fourteenth year of his reign, at the age of forty. From the death of the elder Theudebert [I] to that of Sigibert there were twenty-nine years. Eighteen days passed between his death and that of his nephew Theudebert.

Upon the death of Sigibert, his son Childebert reigned in his place.

A Summary of the Years

From the creation to the flood there were 2242 years. From the flood to Abraham, 942 years. From Abraham to the departure of the children of Israel from Egypt, 462 years. From the departure of the children of Israel from Egypt to the building of the temple of Solomon, 480 years. From the building of the temple to its desolation and the exile to Babylon, 390 years. From the exile to the passion of the Lord, 668 years. From the passion of the Lord to the death of Saint Martin, 412 years. From the death of Saint Martin to

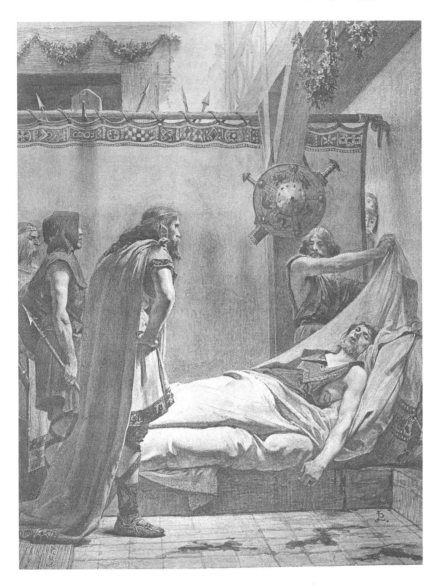

6.   Chilperic views the body of his brother Sigibert (IV 51).

the death of King Clovis, 112 years. From the death of King Clovis to the death of Theudebert, 37 years. From the death of Theudebert to the death of Sigibert, 29 years. Which make a total of 5774 years.

This computation of years ends Book IV.

PART III

THE REIGN OF CHILDEBERT II

A. 576–591

CHAPTER FOUR

SUCCESSION OF CHILDEBERT II AND THE

DEMISE OF ROYAL COUSINS

a. 576–580

(BOOK V)

When beggars die there are no comets seen;
The heavens themselves blaze forth the death of princes.

Calpurnia, in Julius Caesar by William Shakespeare

From Book V onward, Gregory's narrative proceeds year by year, dated according to the regnal years of King Childebert II, the son of Sigibert and, in Gregory's view, the rightful ruler of Tours. Childebert's reign, as Gregory tells us, began on December 25, Christmas day. In giving conventional year dates I treat the year as beginning on January 1 of the following year. The normal year in Gregory's day began in March, which was accordingly the first month and the basis for the numbering of Gregory's months.

Readers should note that the narrative from here on is roughly coterminous with Gregory's years as bishop of Tours. From now on, I give the regnal year of Childebert and its anno domini *equivalent as a subheading.*

Gregory's Prologue to Book V

It is unpleasant for me to record the various civil wars that severely damage the Frankish people and kingdom; worse still, here we now see that time the Lord foretold would be the beginning of sorrows: "Father shall rise against son, son against father, brother against brother, kinsman against kinsman [cf. Matth. 10:12]." They should have been terrified by the examples of former kings: as soon as they were divided, they were destroyed by their enemies. How often have civil wars toppled the very city of cities, the mighty head of the whole earth; when they ceased, it has risen again as if from the ground! Would that you too, kings, were engaged in battles like those in which your fathers sweated, so that foreigners, terrified by the peace you keep amongst yourselves, might be crushed by your strength! Remember what Clovis, the author of your victories, did, he who killed opposing kings, crushed hostile foreigners, subdued their lands, and left to you complete and unimpaired rule over them! And when he did this he had neither silver nor gold such as you now have in your treasuries.

What are you doing? What are you after? What do you not have in abundance? In your residences luxuries are plentiful, in your storehouses wine, grain, and oil abound, in your treasuries gold and silver are piled up. One thing is missing: because you do not maintain peace, you lack the grace of God. Why does one take what belongs to another? Why does each lust after what is not his own? I beg of you, beware this saying of the apostle: "If you bite and devour one another, watch out that you are not both eaten [cf. Gal. 5:15]."

Study carefully the books of the ancients and you shall see what civil wars produce. Look at what Orosius writes about the Carthaginians. When he says that their city and country were destroyed after seven hundred years, he adds: "What preserved this state so long? Concord. What destroyed this state after such a long period of time? Discord." Beware discord, beware civil wars, which destroy you and your people. What else is to be expected but that, when your forces have collapsed, left without help, you shall fall immediately, overwhelmed by enemy nations? And, king, if you take pleasure in civil war, then engage in the one waged, according to the apostle, within the person, so that the spirit may struggle against the flesh and vices fall before virtues. Then you may serve your chief, that is to say Christ, as a free man, you who in shackles once served the root of evil.

Year I of Childebert II, a. 576

Succession of Childebert and Banishment of Brunhild (V 1)

King Sigibert was killed at Vitry while Queen Brunhild was staying with her children in Paris. When she was given the news and, in the distress of her grief and sorrow, did not know what she was doing, Duke Gundovald grabbed Childebert, her little son, and spirited him away, saving him from imminent death. Then he assembled the peoples over which Childebert's father had reigned and proclaimed him king. Childebert was barely five years old. He began his reign on the day of the Lord's birth.

In the first year of Childebert's reign, King Chilperic came to Paris, seized Brunhild and sent her to Rouen in exile. He took away the treasures that she had brought to Paris and ordered her daughters detained at Meaux.

At this time Roccolen came to Tours with troops from Le Mans, took plunder, and committed many crimes. Subsequently I shall tell how he was struck down and killed by the power of the holy Martin for all the evil he did.

Merovech, Chilperic's Son, Marries Brunhild (V 2)

Chilperic sent his son Merovech to Poitiers with an army. But Merovech ignored his father's orders and came instead to Tours, where he spent the holy days of Easter [5 April]. His army did a great deal of damage to the district. Pretending he was going to see his mother, Merovech himself made for Rouen and there met up with Queen Brunhild and married her.

When Chilperic heard that Merovech had married his uncle's widow contrary to divine law and the canons, he became very ill-tempered, and quicker than the time it takes to tell of it he was off to Rouen. When Merovech and Brunhild realized that he was determined to separate them, they took refuge in the basilica of Saint Martin that had been built of wooden planks on the wall of the city. The king arrived and tried many a ruse to get them out, but they refused to trust him, thinking that he was tricking them. Finally he swore an oath to them, declaring that, if it should be God's will, he would not attempt to separate them.

They accepted this oath and came out of the basilica. Chilperic kissed them, received them honorably, and took a meal with them. A few days later he returned to Soissons, taking Merovech with him.

Chilperic's Suspicions of Merovech. Deserters. Duke Rauching (V 3)

While they were in Rouen, there was a gathering of certain men of Champagne who marched on the city of Soissons, drove out Queen Fredegund and Chilperic's son Clovis, and tried to get the city under their control. When Chilperic found out, he brought his army there, sending messages in advance warning them that, if they did no wrong to him, both armies would escape destruction. They paid no heed to the warning and got ready to fight. Chilperic's side won the battle, driving back the other side and killing many good and experienced fighting men. With the remainder put to flight, he entered the city of Soissons.

After these events occurred, the king began to suspect his son Merovech on account of his marriage with Brunhild, saying that this battle was caused by his villainy. Chilperic took Merovech's weapons from him and had him put under guard, though not a close one, all the while pondering what he would do with him in the future.

Godin, who had transfered himself from Sigibert's kingdom to Chilperic and been generously rewarded by him, was the real originator of that fight, though, when defeated in the field, he was the first to run away. Chilperic took away the villas he had granted him from the fisc in the territory of Soissons and conferred them now on the church of Saint Medard. Sudden death caught up with Godin himself not long afterwards.

His widow married Rauching, a man full of every conceit, swollen with pride and shamelessly arrogant. He acted toward those under his control like someone without any awareness of human feelings, committing in his fury unspeakable wrongs against his own people beyond the limits of mere human wickedness and stupidity. For example, when he gave a feast, and a servant, as is customary, stood before him holding a candle, he would have the servant's legs bared and make him hold the candle between his shins until the light went out; when the candle was relit, he would do the same again until the legs of the slave holding the candle were all burned. And if the slave uttered a sound or tried to move from that place to another, he was threatened with a drawn sword so that Rauching could delight in the pleasure of the slave weeping.

Some people said that at this time two of his slaves, a man and a girl, were in love with each other, something that often happens. And when this love had lasted for two years or more, they mated, and both sought the refuge of the church. When Rauching found out, he went to the local bishop; he asked that his slaves be restored to him at once, saying that he had pardoned them.

At the time the bishop said to him, "Make sure you know what respect should be paid to the churches of God; you cannot take these two slaves, unless you promise to acknowledge that their union is lasting and pledge that they shall be spared any physical punishment."

Rauching remained silent for a while, not knowing quite what to think, but at last, turning to the bishop, he placed his hand upon the altar and swore an oath.

"They will never be parted by me," he said, "but I shall see to it that they remain in this union, because, although I am annoyed that this was connived at without my consent, still I am happy with the fact that neither of them has married the slave of another master."

The bishop believed in a simple-hearted fashion the crafty man's promise and restored the slaves, thinking they had been pardoned. Rauching took them, thanked the bishop, and went home. He at once ordered a tree to be felled and limbed, the trunk split with wedges driven in to its ends and hollowed out. He had the hollowed trunk placed in a trench dug in the ground to a depth of three or four feet. He laid the girl out in it as if she were dead and had the male slave thrown in on top. Putting the lid on the tree trunk, he filled in the trench.

"I have not broken my oath that they should never be separated," he said, burying them alive.

When the news reached the bishop, he came quickly and, rebuking Rauching, had trouble getting the slaves uncovered. However he only got the male slave out alive; he found the girl suffocated.

Rauching was utterly depraved in committing deeds like this, having no other talents than derisive laughter, treachery, and every manner of perversity. His departure from life consequently was fitting for the likes of someone who did such deeds when he had the benefits of this life. I intend to relate the events of his death at a later point [IX 9].

Siggo the referendary, who had been the keeper of King Sigibert's signet-ring and had been called upon by King Chilperic to hold the same office he held in the time of his brother, now deserted Chilperic and went over to Childebert, son of Sigibert. The property he had held in Soissons was obtained by Ansovald. Many more of those who transferred themselves from the rule of King Sigibert to Chilperic now came back. The wife of Siggo died not long afterwards; but he married another one.

Roccolen Comes to Tours (V 4)

In these days, Roccolen, who had been sent by Chilperic [see V 1], arrived in Tours with great boasting and pitched his camp beyond the Loire. He sent me a message telling me to drag from the holy basilica [Duke] Guntram [Boso], who was at that time accused in the death of Theudebert [see IV 50]. If I would not do so, he would have the city and all its suburbs burned. I listened and sent a delegation to him to say that what he wanted done had not been done since ancient times. Violation of a holy basilica could not at all be permitted. If it should happen, the outcome would be beneficial neither to him nor to the king who authorized the order. He should stand in greater fear of the holiness of the bishop [Martin] whose power only the day before had straightened paralytic limbs [cf. VM II 27].

This did not frighten him at all. While staying in an establishment belonging to the church on the other side of the river Loire, he tore apart the house itself, which was held together with nails. The troops of Le Mans, who at the time had come with him, carried off the nails by the bagful, destroyed the grain, and laid everything waste.

But as Roccolen did this, he was struck by God, and becoming saffron-colored with the royal disease [jaundice], he sent harsh commands, saying, "If you do not eject Duke Guntram from the basilica today, I will destroy every growing thing around the city, so that the place will be ready for the plow."

Meanwhile the holy day of epiphany came [6 January 576], and he became more and more tormented, at which point, taking the advice of his men, he crossed the river and approached the city. When the clergy came out of the cathedral and headed towards the holy basilica [of Saint Martin] singing psalms, he rode on horseback behind the cross, preceded by standards. When he entered the holy basilica, in fact, his wild threats abated, and when he went back to the cathedral, he could take no food on that day.

Although he was very short of breath, he went off to Poitiers. It was now holy Lent, during which period he often ate baby rabbits. Proceedings in which he would penalize and condemn the citizens of Poitiers were set for the Kalends of March [1 March 576], but he rendered up his life on the day before. And in this way his pride and arrogance were finally stilled.

Conversion of Jews in Clermont (V 11)

On the election of Avitus as bishop of Clermont, see Appendix, Episcopal Election (IV 35). As an archdeacon, Avitus had been charged with the education of the young Gregory. Avitus's prayer for the conversion of the Jews probably refers to a prayer that was part of the Good Friday liturgy on April 3. Venantius Fortunatus dedicated a poem to Gregory commemorating the event described here.

Our God ever sees fit to glorify our bishops, and so I shall disclose what happened this year in Clermont with regard to the Jews.

Although the blessed Bishop Avitus frequently urged them to foresake the veil of the Mosaic law and to interpret their reading in a spiritual sense, noting with pure hearts that Christ in the sacred scriptures is the son of the living God promised by the prophets and the law, there remained in their breast, I would not say that veil that covered the face of Moses [cf. Exod. 34:33–35], but a wall. As the bishop was praying for their conversion to God and for the veil of the letter [of the law] to be removed from them, one of them asked to be baptized at holy Easter [April 5]. Born again in God through the sacrament of baptism, he marched in white robes along with the others. As people went through the gate of the city, one of the Jews, at the instigation of the devil, poured rancid oil on the head of the converted Jew. The whole crowd was shocked and wanted to stone him, but the bishop would not allow that to be done.

On the blessed day [May 14] on which the Lord rose in glory to heaven, having redeemed humankind, as the bishop proceeded from the cathedral to the basilica [of Saint Illidius] singing pslams, the whole host of those following rushed upon the synagogue of the Jews and pulled it down to the ground so that the place looked like a level field.

On another day the bishop sent his representatives to the Jews to say, "I do not compel you by force to confess the son of God, but I preach and bring the salt of knowledge to your understanding. I am a shepherd set over the Lord's sheep, and the true shepherd who suffered for us said with regard to you that He has other sheep not of His fold to which He must lead them so there may be one flock and one shepherd [cf. Joh. 10:16]. If you will believe as I do, be one flock, with me as the keeper. But if you believe otherwise, leave this place."

For some time they fumed and dithered, but on the third day, owing to the intercession of the bishop, as I believe, they joined together as one and sent back to him the message, "We believe in Jesus Christ, the son of the living God, promised to us by the declarations of the prophets, and for that reason we seek to be cleansed by baptism so as not to remain in this transgression."

The bishop rejoiced at the news, celebrated vigils on the holy eve of pentecost [May 23] and went out to the baptistery outside the walls. There the whole crowd humbled itself before him and asked for baptism. Weeping for joy, he washed them all in water, anointed them with the chrism, and gathered them into the bosom of the mother church. Candles flickered, lamps glowed, the whole town became white from the shining flock. Nor was the joy less than that once experienced in Jerusalem when the holy spirit came down upon the apostles.

More than five hundred were baptized. As for those who refused baptism, they left the town and returned to Marseilles.

Clovis Campaigns from Tours. Mummolus Attacks Duke Desiderius (V 13)

King Chilperic sent his son Clovis to Tours. Clovis gathered an army, crossed the regions of Tours and Angers, and advancing as far as Saintes, took the city.

Mummolus, patrician of King Guntram, passed with a great army into the territory of Limoges and engaged Desiderius, Chilperic's duke, in battle. He lost five thousand men in this engagement, but Desiderius lost twenty-four thousand. Desiderius himself barely escaped by flight. The patrician Mummolus then returned through Auvergne, which his army laid waste in places. In this fashion he made his way to Burgundy.

Merovech is Tonsured and Flees to Saint Martin's Basilica at Tours (V 14)

After this, Merovech was tonsured while being kept in custody by his father; changing his clothing for the customary garb of the clergy, he was ordained a priest and sent to the monastery at Le Mans called Aninsola [Saint Calais] to be instructed in the duties of priests. Guntram Boso who, as I said, was living at the time in the basilica of Saint Martin, heard about this and sent the subdeacon Riculf to advise Merovech to try secretly to make it to the basilica of Saint Martin. When Merovech was on his way, Gailen his slave came along from

7.   "Changing his clothing for the customary garb of the clergy, he was ordained a priest and sent to the monastery at Le Mans called Aninsola to be instructed in the duties of priests (V 14)." Merovech's exile.

another direction. And since the force escorting Merovech was small, he was rescued by Gailen on the road, and covering his head and putting on secular clothes, Merovech reached the shrine of the blessed Martin.

I was celebrating mass when, finding the door open, he entered the basilica. After mass, he asked me to give him some blessed bread. With me at that time was Ragnemod, bishop of the see of Paris, who had succeeded the holy Germanus. When I refused the request, Merovech began to shout that I had no right to suspend him from communion without the consent of our brother bishops. When he said this, with the consent of the brother bishop who was present, and without our transgressing canon law, he received the blessed bread from me. My fear was that, by suspending one person from communion, I would end up the killer of many more. For he kept threatening to put to death some of my people if he did not get communion from me. The harm the district of Tours has suffered on this account is considerable.

Around this time, Nicetius, the husband of my niece, went on business of his own to King Chilperic, accompanied by my deacon, who told the king of Merovech's flight.

When Queen Fredegund saw them, she said, "They are spies come to find out what the king is doing and to report it to Merovech."

She immediately had them despoiled and sent into exile, from which they were released in the seventh month [September].

Then Chilperic sent me a message to say, "Drive that apostate from the basilica. If you don't, I'll put the whole region to the torch."

I wrote back that it was impossible that what had not happened in the time of the heretics should be done now in Christian times, but he mustered a force and ordered it to march to Tours.

Year II of Childebert II, a. 577

(V 14 cont'd)

In the second year of King Childebert, when Merovech saw that his father was set in this purpose, he thought about going to Brunhild, taking with him Duke Guntram Boso.

"Far be it from me," said Merovech, "to be the cause of the basilica of lord Martin suffering violence or his country being subjugated."

He entered the basilica during vigils and made an offering of his possessions to the tomb of the blessed Martin. He prayed for the saint to help him and to grant him his favor as he attempted to gain the kingship.

Leudast, who was then count [of Tours] and had set many snares for him out of devotion to Fredegund, at last trapped his servants who had gone out into

8. "Merovech began to shout that I had no right to suspend him from communion without the consent of our brother bishops (V 14)." Merovech
confronts Bishops Gregory and Ragnemod.

the country and put them to the sword. He longed to kill Merovech himself if he could find the right spot.

But Merovech followed Guntram Boso's advice. Wanting to avenge himself, he gave orders for Marileif the chief physician to be seized as he was returning from the king's court. After beating him severely, he took away the gold and silver and other things he had on him and left him naked, and actually would have killed him if the man had not slipped out of the hands of those who were beating him and made his way to the cathedral. I clothed him and later, having managed to get his life spared, sent him back to Poitiers.

Merovech talked about the many crimes of his father and stepmother. Although the crimes were partly true, it was not acceptable to God, I believe, for word of them to be spread by a son, as I learned from subsequent events. One day I happened to dine with him, and while we were sitting together, he humbly asked for something to be read for the instruction of his soul. So I opened the book of Solomon and chose the first verse I came upon. This is what it said: "The eye of him who looks askance at his father, the ravens of the valleys shall pick it out [cf. Prov. 30:17]." He did not understand it, but I regarded this verse as having been revealed by the Lord.

Then Guntram Boso sent a servant to a woman whom he had known from the days of King Charibert; she possessed the spirit of Pytho [i.e., prophecy, cf. Acts 16:16], and he wanted her to tell him what was about to happen. He used to claim, moreover, that she had made known to him before the event, not only the year, but even the day and hour in which King Charibert died.

This is what she told Guntram's servants to tell him: "It will happen that King Chilperic will die this year. And Merovech will exclude his brothers and take the whole kingdom. You will hold the ducal authority over all his kingdom for five years. But in the sixth year, in one of the cities on the river Loire, on its right bank, you will obtain the honor of the episcopal office with the approval of the people, and you will pass from this world old and full of days."

The servants returned and reported this to their master, and he, puffed up with vanity as if he were already sitting on the throne of the cathedral of Tours, immediately related the words to me.

"These questions must be put to God," I said, laughing at his foolishness. "What the devil promises is not to be believed. 'He is a liar from the start and never truthful [cf. John 8:44].'"

He left confounded, and I had a good laugh at a man who thought such things believable.

Then one night, after vigils had been celebrated in the basilica of the holy bishop [Martin], I had gone to bed and fallen asleep when I saw an angel flying through the air.

As it passed by the holy basilica, it cried out woefully in a loud voice, "God has struck down Chilperic and all his sons. No issue of his loins has survived who will forever rule his kingdom." He had at this time four sons by different wives, not to speak of daughters.

When these words were later on fulfilled, I then understood clearly that the promises of soothsayers were false.

Then, while these men were staying in the basilica of Saint Martin, Queen Fredegund, who was already secretly giving Guntram Boso protection for his part in the death of Theudebert, sent him a message saying, "If you can get Merovech out of the basilica so that he can be killed, you shall receive a great reward from me."

Guntram thought the assassins were nearby.

"Why do we hang back like slackers and cowards and skulk about the basilica like half-wits," he said to Merovech. "Have the horses brought round. Let's take our hawks and dogs, go hunting, and enjoy the open countryside."

This was cunning on his part to get Merovech away from the holy basilica. As for Guntram, in other respects he was really a good man, but he was too ready to perjure himself, and truth be told, he never took an oath to any of his friends without disregarding it right away.

And so they went out of the basilica and went as far as Jocundiacus, an establishment quite near the city. But Merovech was harmed by no one.

Guntram was accused at the time of killing Theudebert, as I have said. King Chilperic therefore wrote a letter addressed to the tomb of Saint Martin asking the blessed Martin to write back to him whether it was permissible for Guntram to be dragged from his basilica or not. The deacon Baudegisil, who delivered the letter, put a clean sheet of paper on the holy tomb alongside the one he had brought. After waiting three days, and getting no answer, he returned to Chilperic, who then sent others to exact an oath from Guntram not to leave the church without Chilperic's knowledge. Guntram eagerly took the oath and gave an altarcloth as a pledge that he would not leave there without the king's permission.

As for Merovech, he did not believe the prophetess, but placed three books on the saint's tomb, namely, Psalms, Kings, and the Gospels, and kept a vigil through the whole night, asking the blessed confessor to reveal to him what was going to happen and to let him know by a sign from God whether or not he would obtain royal power. After this, he spent three days in fasts, vigils, and prayer. Going to the blessed tomb a second time, he opened one of the books.

It was the book of Kings, and this was the first verse on the page he opened: "Because you have forsaken the Lord your God and have gone after other gods and have not done right in his sight, therefore the Lord your God has delivered you into the hands of your enemies [cf. I Kings 9:9]."

This was the verse found in the Psalms: "But you have set evils upon them because of their deceitfulness; you have cast them down while they were raised up. How have they been reduced to desolation? They have suddenly failed and perished because of their iniquities [cf. Ps. 73:18, 19]."

And in the Gospels, this was found: "You know that in two days it is the passover and the son of man will be handed over to crucifixion [cf. Matt. 26:2]."

These answers troubled him, and he wept for a long time at the tomb of the blessed bishop. Then, taking Duke Guntram with him, he left with five hundred men or more.

When Merovech had left the holy basilica and was making his way through the territory of Auxerre, he was captured by Erpo, a duke of King Guntram. Although under his custody, he escaped, I do not know how, and entered the basilica of Saint Germanus. When King Guntram heard this, he got angry, fined Erpo seven hundred gold pieces, and removed him from office.

"You held someone who my brother says is his enemy," said Guntram. "Now if you were of a mind to do this, you should first have brought him to me; but otherwise, you should not have touched someone you were not prepared to hold."

King Chilperic's army approached Tours, plundering, burning, and laying the district waste, and it did not spare Saint Martin's property; whatever it touched it stole, neither respecting nor fearing God.

Merovech remained nearly two months in the basilica of Saint Germanus and then fled, going to Queen Brunhild, but he was not accepted by the Austrasians. His father put an army in the field against the people of Champagne, believing that he was hiding there. But it caused no harm, nor could it find Merovech.

War between the Saxons and Suevi (V 15)

This passage picks up events from IV 42. It is not without ambiguities and cruxes. Chlothar I died in 561, seven years before Alboin's invasion of Italy.

In the days when Alboin entered Italy, Chlothar and Sigibert had settled Suevi and other peoples in that district [previously held by the Saxons]. Now those who had returned in the time of Sigibert—namely those who had accompanied Alboin—rose up against them, intending to drive them out of the region or even annihilate them. The Suevi offered the Saxons a third part of the land.

"We can live together without conflict," they said.

But the Saxons were furious with them, because they held this land previously and would not at all be placated.

So the Suevi again offered the Saxons a half, then two thirds, retaining a third for themselves. When the Saxons rejected this, they offered them in addition to the land all their herds, provided they held off from war.

But the Saxons, looking for a fight, did not agree. And before the conflict they discussed among themselves how they would divide the wives of the Suevi and who would get what woman after expelling the men, imagining they had already killed them. God's compassion, which deals out justice, turned back their desire in favor of the other side. For when both sides clashed, of the 26,000 Saxons, the Suevi killed 20,000. There were 6,000 Suevi, of which 480 were killed, and the rest gained the victory. The remnant of the Saxons swore that none of them would cut his beard or hair until he had taken revenge on his enemies. There was a new conflict and the Saxons fell in a greater slaughter.

And thus the hostilities ended.

The Death of Macliav (V 16)

Among the Bretons the following events occurred.

The late Macliav [see IV 4] and Bodic, counts of the Bretons, swore to each other that whichever of them should outlive the other would protect the sons of the deceased as if they were his own. Bodic died and left a son called Theuderic.

Macliav, forgetting his oath, drove Theuderic from his homeland and took his father's kingdom. For a long time Theuderic was a fugitive and a wanderer. At last God took pity on him. Theuderic gathered men from Brittany and attacked Macliav, putting him and his son Jacob to the sword. He took control of the part of the kingdom which his late father held, though Waroch, a son of Macliav, retained the other part.

King Guntram Loses his Sons and Allies himself with Childebert by the Treaty of Stone Bridge (Pompierrre) (V 17)

King Guntram put to the sword two sons of the late Magnachar for making hateful and accursed charges against Queen Austrechild and her children; the king had his fisc confiscate their property. He himself lost two sons, who were suddenly overcome by disease; he was deeply saddened by their death, for he was left bereaved without children....

After [Easter] King Guntram sent envoys to his nephew Childebert, seeking peace and asking for a meeting. It was then that Childebert with his chief officials came to see him. They met at what is called Stone Bridge [Pompierre], greeting one another and exchanging kisses.

King Guntram said, "It has happened that through my sins I have been left without children, and so I ask that this nephew of mine be my son."

And setting him upon his own seat, Guntram handed over to him his whole kingdom.

"Let a single shield protect us," he said, "and a single spear defend us. Should I have sons, I will nevertheless regard you as one of them, so that, God as my witness, you will keep the love I promise you today, sharing it with them."

The chief officials of Childebert likewise made a promise on his behalf.

Eating and drinking together, they honored one another with suitable gifts and departed in peace. They also sent a delegation to King Chilperic, demanding that he restore what he had taken from their kingdom; and if he would not do so, he was to make ready a field of battle.

Chilperic, disdainful of the threat, had circuses put up at Soissons and at Paris as a show for the people.

The Trial of Bishop Praetextatus. Merovech's Death (V 18)

After these events, Chilperic heard that Praetextatus, bishop of Rouen, was giving people gifts contrary to the king's interests and had him summoned to his presence. He examined him and discovered that the bishop was in possession of property entrusted to him by Queen Brunhild. This was confiscated, and the king ordered him kept in exile until the bishops could convene a hearing.

The council met, and Bishop Praetextatus was brought before it. The bishops who attended convened in the basilica of the holy apostle Peter in Paris.

"Bishop," said the king to Praetextatus, "why did you think to join in marriage my enemy Merovech, who ought to have acted as a son, with his aunt, that is, his uncle's wife? Or were you unacquainted with what the canons have established for such a case? Also, not only did you demonstrably go too far in this matter, but you even acted in conjunction with Merovech to give gifts to bring about my assassination. You have made a son an enemy of his father, you have led the people astray with money, so that none of them would maintain the loyalty they had for me, and you have tried to hand my kingdom into the hands of another."

When he said this, the crowd of Franks let out a roar and tried to break open the church doors, intending to drag the bishop out and stone him, but the king stopped this happening.

When Bishop Praetextatus denied having done what the king charged, false witnesses came forward who showed various valuable articles.

"These and these you gave us," they said, "on condition we pledge our loyalty to Merovech."

"You're right that you have often received gifts from me," he said in response to these charges, "but it was not for the purpose of driving the king from the kingdom. Since you furnished me with excellent horses and other things, what else could I do but pay you back at the same value?"

The king returned to his quarters, but we remained seated as a group in the sacristy of the basilica of the blessed Peter. As we were talking together, suddenly Aetius, archdeacon of the bishopric of Paris, came in and greeted us.

"Hear me, bishops of God, gathered here together," he said. "In this hour you shall either exalt your name and show that you deserve a glowing reputation, or instead, if you don't have the sense to stand up for yourselves or if you allow your brother to be destroyed, hereafter no one will take you for bishops of God."

When he said this, none of the bishops said anything in reply. For they feared the savage anger of the queen, at whose instigation these proceedings were being conducted.

As they considered these words, with their fingers on their lips, I said, "Please listen to what I have to say, most holy bishops, especially you who seem to be on quite friendly terms with the king; furnish him with advice as befits holy men and priests, so that he is not destroyed by God's anger, losing his kingdom and reputation in an outburst against a servant of God."

When I said this, all were silent.

Since no one spoke, I added, "My lord bishops, remember the word of the prophet: 'If the watchman sees the iniquity of a person and does not speak, he shall be guilty for a lost soul [cf. Ez. 33:6].' Therefore do not remain silent, but speak out, and set this king's sins before his own eyes, in case some evil comes upon him, and you are held responsible for his soul. Surely you can't be unaware of what has happened in modern times? How Chlodomer captured Sigismund and threw him in prison, and Avitus, God's priest, said to him: 'Do not lay hands on him and when you go to Burgundy you will win the victory.' But he disregarded what was said to him by the priest and went ahead and killed him with his wife and sons. And Chlodomer went to Burgundy and was overcome by the enemy and killed [see III 6]. What about the emperor Maximus? When he forced the blessed Martin to associate with a certain bishop who was a homicide, and Martin gave in to the impious king in order to help free those condemned to death, Maximus was pursued by the judgment of the eternal King and, driven from the imperial throne, was condemned to the vilest death."

When I said this, no one said anything in reply, but all stared in astonishment.

However, two flatterers among them—it is sad to have to say that of bishops—gave a report to the king, telling him that he had no greater opponent of his interests than me. Promptly a court attendant was sent to bring me before him.

When I arrived, the king was standing beside a bower made of branches; on his right stood Bishop Bertram and on his left Ragnemod. There was a table covered with bread and various dishes in front of them.

On seeing me, the king said, "Bishop, you are supposed to confer justice freely on all. But look now, I don't get justice from you. As I see it, you are giving in to iniquity: your actions are an example of the proverb that the crow does not tear out the eye of another crow."

"If any one of us, king, tries to leave the path of justice," I replied, "he can be corrected by you. But if you abandon it, who shall take you to task? We speak to you, but you pay attention only if you wish. And if you refuse to listen, who will pass sentence on you if it is not He who has proclaimed that He is justice?"

He had been inflamed against me by his flatterers and replied, "I have found justice with everyone, but with you I cannot find it. I know what I shall do to disgrace you before the people and reveal to all that you are unjust. I shall assemble the people of Tours and tell them, 'You may cry out against Gregory that he is an unjust man and renders justice to no one.' And to those who shout this, I will reply, 'I who am king cannot get justice from him. Shall you who are less than I find it?'"

"You do not know whether I am unjust," I said. "He to whom the secrets of the heart are revealed knows my conscience. What people falsely cry out when you revile me means nothing, for everyone knows it is your doing. This is why not I but you will be the one disgraced by the outcries. But why go on with this? You have the law and the canons; search them carefully and then you will know that the judgment of God hangs over you if you do not follow their commands."

Thinking that I did not understand his artfulness, he turned to the broth that was set in front of him, as if this would soothe me.

"I had this broth prepared for you," he said. "There is nothing else in it but fowl and a few chickpeas."

Recognizing his flattery, I replied, "My food is doing the will of God, without at all overlooking whatever he commands, not partaking of the pleasures of these delicacies. As for you who find fault with others in matters of justice, promise first that you will not neglect the law and the canons. Then I shall believe that you follow justice."

Then he stretched out his right hand and swore by almighty God that he would in no way overlook the teaching of the law and the canons. After that I took bread and wine and departed.

That night, when the hymns for the night had been sung, I heard heavy knocking on the door of my lodging. From the servant I sent to answer it, I learned that messengers from Queen Fredegund were there. They were brought in, and I received greetings from the queen. Then her servants asked me not to take a position contrary to her interests and, at the same time, promised two hundred pounds of silver if I attacked Praetextatus, and he was convicted.

"We already have the word of all the bishops," they said. "Don't be the only one in opposition."

"Even if you were to give me a thousand pounds of silver and gold," I said to them, "what else can I do but what the Lord tells me to do? I will promise one thing only, that I will follow what the others agree to in accordance with the canons."

Not understanding what I was saying, they thanked me and went away. In the morning some of the bishops came to me bearing a similar message; to them I gave the same answer.

We met in the morning in Saint Peter's basilica, and the king was present.

"The authority of the canons provides that a bishop detected in theft should be removed from the office of bishop," he said.

We asked who the bishop might be against whom the charge of theft was made.

"You saw the articles of value which he stole from me," the king answered.

Three days before the king had shown us two bundles full of costly articles and treasures of different sorts, valued at more than three thousand solidi, as well as a bag of coined gold, the weight of which suggested about two thousand pieces. The king said this had been stolen from him by the bishop.

The bishop answered, "I believe you remember that I came to you when Queen Brunhild left Rouen and told you that I was holding her property in trust, namely, five parcels, and that her servants came to me quite frequently to retrieve them but I would not release them without your advice. And king, you said to me, 'Rid yourself of this stuff and let the woman have her property back, in case hostility arises between me and my nephew Childebert over these goods.' I went back to the city and gave one roll to the servants, as they could carry no more. They returned a second time and asked for the others. I again sought the advice of your magnificence. And you gave me orders, 'Get rid of this stuff, bishop, get rid of it, so it won't be the cause of a quarrel.' I again gave them two bundles and two more remained in my possession. Why now do you make a false charge and accuse me of theft, when this case should be considered one not of theft but of custody?"

"If this property was considered as being in your possession for safekeeping," responded the king, "why did you open one of these bundles, cut in pieces a belt woven of gold thread, and distribute it to men who were to drive me from the kingdom?"

"I told you before," answered Praetextatus, "that I had received their gifts, and as I had nothing at hand to give, I therefore presumed to take this and give it in return for their gifts. It seemed to be my property because it belonged to my son Merovech, whom I received from the baptismal font."

King Chilperic saw that he could not convict him with false charges, and being thoroughly confounded and disturbed by his conscience, he left us and summoned certain of his flatterers.

"I confess," he said to them, "I've been beaten by the bishop's replies and I know that what he says is true. What can I do now if the queen's will is to be done with regards to him?"

Then he said, "Go, approach him and say, as if giving your own advice, 'You know that King Chilperic is pious and tender-hearted and readily moved to mercy; humble yourself before him and say that you are guilty of the charges he laid. Then we will all throw ourselves at his feet and prevail on him to pardon you.'"

Bishop Praetextatus was deceived by them and promised he would do as they suggested.

In the morning we met at the usual place. The king approached the bishop.

"If you conferred gifts on these men in return for gifts," he said, "why did you ask them for oaths that they stay loyal to Merovech?"

"I confess," replied the bishop, "I did seek to gain their friendship for him; and I would have summoned to his aid not just a mere mortal but an angel from heaven, had it been right; for he was my spiritual son from the baptismal font, as I have often said."

When the dispute had gone on for a while, Bishop Praetextatus threw himself on the ground.

"I have sinned against heaven and against you, most merciful king," he said. "I am an unspeakable homicide; I wanted to kill you and raise your son to the throne."

When Praetextatus said this, the king fell at the feet of the bishops and said, "Most holy bishops, listen to the guilty confess his accursed crime."

In tears we raised the king from the ground, and he ordered Praetextatus to leave the basilica.

Chilperic himself went to his quarters and sent a book of canons, into which a new quaternion had been added containing the so-called apostolic canons. The following was among them: "A bishop found to have committed homicide, adultery, or perjury shall be removed from office."

This was read, and while Praetextatus stood there in shock, Bishop Bertram said, "Pay heed, brother and fellow-bishop, that you do not have the king's favor. For that reason you cannot benefit from our friendship until you win the king's pardon."

9. The trial of Praetextatus (V 18).

After these events, the king asked that Praetextatus's robe should be torn off him, or that Psalm 108, which contains the curses against Iscariot, be read over his head, or at the least that judgment be entered against him, excommunicating him forever. These proposals I opposed on grounds that the king had promised that nothing would be done unauthorized by the canons. Then Praetextatus was taken from our sight and placed under guard. He was beaten severely trying to escape custody one night and was sent into exile on an island in the sea off the coast of the city of Coutances.

After this there was news that Merovech was trying to reach the basilica of Saint Martin [in Tours] for the second time. But Chilperic gave orders to guard the church and close every access. The guards left open one door for a few of the clergy to enter for services but kept all the rest closed. This was a cause of considerable inconvenience to people.

When I was staying in Paris signs appeared in the sky, that is twenty rays in the north part, rising in the east and moving to the west; one of these was more extended and rose above the rest and, when it reached a great height, soon faded away, and in the same way, the rest that followed disappeared. I believe they announced Merovech's death.

As for Merovech, he was lurking in the champaign country near Rheims, fearing to entrust himself to the Austrasians openly, and was tricked by the people of Thérouanne, who said they would desert his father Chilperic and submit to him if he would come to them. He took his best fighting men and went quickly to them. They sprung the trap they had prepared: shutting him up in a certain villa, they surrounded him with armed men and sent messengers to his father. On hearing the news, Chilperic got ready to hurry there. But while Merovech was being forced to wait in some lodging-house, he began to fear that he would have to suffer many penalties to satisfy the vengeance of his enemies. He summoned Gailen his confidential servant.

"Up to now," said Merovech, "we have shared the same heart and mind. I ask you not to allow me to fall into the hands of my enemies. Take a sword and run me through."

Without hesitating, Gailen stabbed him with his blade. When the king came, he found his son dead.

There were some at the time who claimed that Merovech's words, which we have just given, were an invention of the queen, and that Merovech had been secretly killed on her orders. As for Gailen, he was seized, his hands, feet, ears, and the end of his nose were cut off and, subjected to many other tortures, he met a very unpleasant death. Grindio they broke on a wheel, which they then raised aloft, and Ciucilo, once count of King Sigibert's palace, they killed by beheading. They also cruelly put to death in various ways many others who had come with Merovech. People even said at the time that Bishop Egidius and Guntram Boso were the chief figures behind the betrayal, because Guntram secretly enjoyed good relations with Fredegund for the killing of Theudebert, and Egidius had been her dear friend for a long time.

Bishops Salonius and Sagittarius (V 20)

Marius of Avenches, a contemporary bishop, describes the pair as brothers.

Then disturbances sprang up against bishops Salonius and Sagittarius.

They had been raised by Saint Nicetius, bishop of Lyons [a. 552–73], and appointed to the diaconate. During his episcopate, Salonius was made bishop of the city of Embrun and Sagittarius bishop of the church of Gap. But once they had received episcopal office, their true wilfulness took over; in a mad fury, they appropriated property and committed beatings, homicides, adulteries, and various crimes. At one point, when Victor, bishop of St-Paul-Trois-Châteaux, was celebrating his birthday, they attacked him, sending a force armed with swords and bows against him. The attackers ripped his clothes, struck down servants and took away vessels and all the utensils of the feast, leaving the bishop grossly insulted.

When King Guntram learned of it, he had a synod assemble at Lyons [ca 570]. The bishops gathered along with the patriarch, blessed Nicetius, and matters were investigated; they found the accused clearly guilty of the crimes with which they were charged and commanded those who could commit such offenses to be deprived of the office of bishop. But since Salonius and Sagittarius knew the king was still well-disposed to them, they approached him, claiming that they had been unjustly removed from office and imploring him to give them permission to take the matter to the pope of Rome. The king granted their request, gave them letters, and allowed them to leave.

Coming before Pope John [III, a. 561–74] they explained how they were removed for no good reason. The pope sent letters to the king ordering them restored to their positions. Without delay, the king brought this about, chastising them first with a long lecture. Worse yet, what resulted was not improvement.

They did, however, seek peace with Bishop Victor, surrendering the men who had been involved in the disturbance. But he, mindful of the Lord's command not to return evil for evil against one's enemies, did nothing to these wicked men and let them go free. For this reason, he was later excommunicated because he had made a public charge but privately spared his enemies without the participation of the brothers before whom he had made the charge. Nevertheless, through the good will of the king, he was restored to communion again.

As for Salonius and Sagittarius, they were daily mixed up in graver crimes; and in the campaigns that I mentioned earlier [IV 42] which Mummolus conducted against the Lombards, they acted as if they were laymen, bearing arms and killing many a man with their own hands. And among their own citizens they grew angry, venting their rage on a good number, beating them with rods even to the point of drawing blood.

And this is how it came about that the outcry of the people for the second time reached the king, who then had them summoned. When they arrived, he refused to look at them, until first a hearing was held and they were found innocent and deserving of a royal audience. But Sagittarius angrily took this procedure badly—he was a flighty, vacuous, senseless babbler. He began to proclaim a great many things touching on the king, saying that his sons would not be able to take up the kingship because their mother was taken for the king's bed from among the household servants of the late Magnachar; he was unaware that the female line is irrelevant and that children born of kings are called kings.

The king was very upset when he heard this and confiscated the horses, servants and whatever else the two bishops had; he had them shut up in monasteries far distant from each other where they could do penance, leaving no more than a single cleric with each; he issued a dire warning to the local judges to guard them with armed men and to allow no access to visitors.

In those days, the king's sons were still alive, though the elder of them had begun to grow sick.

Those close to him approached the king, saying, "His slaves seek to gain the ear of the king, if the king would please be so kind as to listen to their words."

"Say what you wish," he said.

"We hope that those bishops who were exiled were not perhaps innocent nor that the sin of the king to some measure increases, because this could be why the son of our king is dying," they said.

"Go as fast as you can and release the bishops," said the king, "and beg them to pray for our small children."

They went off, and Salonius and Sagittarius were released.

Then they both came forth from the monasteries, met up and exchanged kisses, because they had not seen each other for a time, and then returned to their cities. They were so remorseful that they seemed to be perpetually singing psalms, fasting, and distributing alms; by day they expounded the songs of the books of David and spent the night singing hymns and meditating on scripture.

But not for long did this holiness remain intact. Their conversions were again reversed. They generally spent their nights in eating and drinking, so that while clerics were celebrating matins in the church, they were still asking for cups and pouring out wine. There was no mention at all of God; liturgical prayers were completely forgotten. At daybreak, they would get up from the table, put on soft clothing and doze until the third hour of the day, buried in sleep and wine. Nor were women wanting with whom they could defile themselves. Then getting up and taking a bath, they would recline at a banquet; in the evening they would rise and set themselves to eating until dawn, as I said.

And this is what they did every day until the anger of God destroyed them, but I will get to that later [V 27, VII 39].

Death of Samson, Chilperic's Son (V 22)

Afterwards, Samson, younger son of King Chilperic, came down with dysentery and fever and departed the mortal world. He was born when Chilperic was being besieged by his brother in Tournai; his mother, in fear of death, shoved him away and wanted him destroyed. The king's reproaches prevented her letting this happen, and she gave orders for the child to be baptized. He was baptized, and the bishop himself received him from the water, but the boy died before completing even the first stage of life. His mother Fredegund was grievously ill at the same time, but she recovered.

Guntram Boso Rescues his Daughters and Chilperic Attacks Poitiers (V 24)

Guntram Boso came to Tours with a few armed men and carried off by force his daughters, whom he had left in the holy basilica. He took them to the city of Poitiers, which belonged to King Childebert.

King Chilperic attacked Poitiers and his troops put those of his nephew to flight. They removed Ennodius from the comital office and brought him before the king. He was sentenced to exile and his property confiscated by the fisc, though a year later he was restored to his homeland and property.

Guntram Boso left his daughters in the basilica of the blessed Hilary and joined King Childebert.

Year III of Childebert II, a. 578

Deaths of Dacco and Dracolen (V 25)

In the third year of King Childebert, which was the seventeenth of Chilperic and Guntram, Dacco, son of the late Dagaric, deserted King Chilperic, and while wandering from place to place was treacherously seized by Duke Dracolen, who was known as "the Zealous." Dracolen bound him and, having given him an oath that he would obtain his life for him before the king, brought him to King Chilperic at Berny. But forgetting his oath, Dracolen charged him with abominable crimes and along with the king brought about his death. When Dacco was being kept in bonds and saw that he had no chance of escape, he asked absolution from a priest without the king's knowledge. After receiving it, he was put to death.

At the time when Dracolen was heading home, Guntram Boso was attempting to remove his daughters from Poitiers. As soon as Dracolen heard, he attacked him. But Guntram's men, who were prepared for this, fought back, constantly taking measures to defend themselves. Guntram sent one of his friends to Dracolen.

"Go and give him this message," he said to his friend. "'Since you know that an alliance exists between us, I ask you to stop ambushing my men. I won't stop you taking what you want of my possessions. Just let me go where I want with my daughters, though I be stripped of everything I have.'"

Dracolen, who was boastful and silly, answered, "Look at the rope with which I have led other culprits bound before the king. With this same rope, Guntram shall today be tied up and taken bound to the same king."

When he had said this, he spurred his horse forward and charged Guntram at a swift gallop. The blow he struck was to no effect because his lanceshaft broke, and he dropped his sword. Guntram, when he saw death staring him in the face, called upon the name of the Lord and the great power of the blessed Martin and, raising his lance, struck Dracolen in the throat. As Dracolen was hanging from his horse, one of Guntram's friends thrust a lance into his side and finished him off. Dracolen's party was put to flight, and his body despoiled; Guntram got away scot-free with his daughters.

Some time afterwards, his [that is, Dracolen's?] father-in-law, Severus, had a grave charge brought against him by his sons before the king. When Severus heard about it, he went to see the king, bearing great gifts. He was seized on the road, despoiled and exiled; his life ended with a very miserable death. His two sons, Burgolen and Dodo, were condemned to death on a charge of treason; one of them died in a fight with troops; the other was caught attempting to flee

10.   Guntram Boso, with his daughters, encounters Dracolen (V 25).

and died when his hands and feet were cut off. All their property, like that of their father, was confiscated by the fisc; they had possessed great riches.

Campaign against the Bretons. A Fine Levied on Tours (V 26)

The ban was a fine levied for disobeying a royal command. Saxon settlements on the coast went back to the fifth century (cf. II 18).

Forces of Tours, Poitiers, Bayeux, Le Mans, and Angers, with many others, went off to Brittany at the orders of Chilperic and took up a position on the banks of the Vilaine, threatening Waroch, the son of the late Macliav [see V 16]. But the enemy made a surprise attack at night upon the Saxons of Bayeux and slew the greater part of them. Three days later Waroch made peace with the leaders of King Chilperic's forces, gave his son as a hostage, and bound himself by oath to be loyal to King Chilperic. He also restored the city of Vannes on the condition that he would be entitled to rule it at the king's command and would pay each year the tribute and everything owed from there without a demand having to be made. When this agreement was reached, the army withdrew from that region.

Afterward Chilperic ordered that the ban be extracted from the poor and servants of the cathedral [of Tours] and basilica [of Saint Martin] because they had not served in the army. But it was not the custom for them to carry out any public service.

After these events, Waroch, forgetting about his promise and wishing to break his agreement, sent Eunius, bishop of Vannes, to King Chilperic. But the king became angry and, after scolding the bishop, ordered him to be exiled.

Year IV of Childebert II, a. 579

Removal of Salonius and Sagittarius (V 27)

In the fourth year of Childebert, which was the eighteenth year of Kings Guntram and Chilperic, a synod was held at Chalon by command of prince Guntram.

Various issues were investigated and that ancient fiasco regarding Bishops Salonius and Sagittarius revisited [see V 20]. Criminal charges were laid against them and they were accused not only of adulteries but also of homicides. The bishops agreed that these could be expiated by penance but they added the finding that the two were traitors to the crown and their homeland. For this reason they were stripped of episcopal office and thrust into the basilica of the blessed Marcellus [in Chalon] under guard. From there they escaped and fled, wandering about from place to place, while others were appointed to replace them in their cities.

New Tax Assessments by Chilperic (V 28)

Chilperic ordered new and heavy tax assessments to be made throughout his kingdom. For this reason, many left their cities and personal possessions and went to other kingdoms, thinking it better to emigrate than to run such a danger. For it was decreed that a landlord [*possessor*] render from his own [de-mesne] land one amphora of wine per arpent [of vineyard]. Also many other obligations that could not be fulfilled were imposed on the other lands and dependents.

When the people of Limoges saw they were laden with such a burden, they gathered on the Kalends of March and tried to kill Marcus the referendary, who had been ordered to institute this, and would have done so if Bishop Ferreolus had not delivered him from immediate danger. The mob that assembled also seized the assessment registers and burned them.

The king was very vexed at this and sent people from the court to impose penalties on the populace, to terrify them with tortures, and to inflict the death penalty. They say, too, that at that time abbots and priests were strung up on posts and subjected to various tortures, the royal agents accusing them falsely of having been accomplices in burning the registers during the insurrection of the people. And then they imposed even severer taxes.

Breton Incursions (V 29, 31)

The Bretons severely ravaged the area around Rennes, burning, plundering, and taking captives. They got as far as Corps-Nuds with their devastation.

Bishop Eunius, meanwhile, had been brought back from exile and was assigned to Angers for his maintenance and not permitted to return to his city of Vannes.

Duke Beppolen was sent against the Bretons and overran some areas in Brittany with fire and sword—an action that brought about greater madness....

In this year the Bretons were causing trouble in the area around the cities of Nantes and Rennes. They took away immeasurable spoil, overran fields, stripped the vines of their fruit, and took captives. When Bishop Felix [of Nantes] sent a delegation to them, they promised to make amends without having any intention of doing so.

II.   Marcus the referendary announces new taxes in Limoges (V 28).

12.   The punishment of Limoges (V 28).

Year V of Childebert II, a. 580

Gregory begins the year with a list of natural (and some very unnatural) events and disasters (V 33).

Dysentery and the Death of Chilperic's sons (V 34)

A very serious epidemic followed these portents. For while the kings were quarreling and again making ready for civil war, dysentery affected nearly all of Gaul. Those who suffered it had a high fever with vomiting, extreme pain in the kidneys, and headaches and neck-pains. Their vomit was saffron colored or even green. It was claimed by many that it was a secret poison. Country folk called it internal boils; this is not incredible, because when cupping glasses were placed on the shoulders or legs, tumors formed and broke, the corrupt matter ran out, and many were cured. Also herbs that cure poisons could be taken and brought help to a good many.

This sickness began in the month of August and first affected the little children, carrying them off to their deaths. We lost children, so sweet and dear to us, whom we sat on our laps or carried in our arms and nourished with such care, feeding them with our own hand. But wiping away our tears, we say with the blessed Job: "The Lord has given; the Lord has taken away; what pleases the Lord has been done. Blessed be his name through the ages."

In these days, King Chilperic became seriously ill. As he grew better, his younger son, who was not yet reborn in water and the holy spirit, became sick. When they saw that the end was near, they baptized him. He was doing a little better when his older brother named Chlodobert was stricken by the same disease. Their mother Fredegund saw that they were in danger of death and too late became repentant.

"For a long time the divine goodness has endured our evil doing," she said to the king. "Often it has rebuked us with fevers and other afflictions, and repentance did not follow. Look, now we are losing our sons! The tears of the poor, the laments of widows, and the sighs of orphans are killing them. We are left without a reason for gathering up anything. We pile up riches and do not know for whom we gather it. Our treasury will be left without an owner, full of plunder and curses. Were our storehouses not overflowing with wine? Were our barns not full of grain? Were our treasuries not laden with gold, silver, precious stones, necklaces, and the rest of the trappings of emperors? Look, we are losing what we hold to be even more beautiful! Now please come, let us burn all the unjust registers, and let what was sufficient for your father, King Clothar, be sufficient for our fisc."

13.   The sons of Chilperic and Fredegund are stricken by the epidemic
(V 34).

When the queen had said this, beating her breast with her fists, she ordered brought forward the registers that Marcus had delivered from her cities. She had them thrown in the fire and then turned to the king.

"Why do you delay," she said. "Do what you see me do, so that even if we lose our dear children, we may at least escape eternal punishment."

Then the king, deeply moved, handed all the tax registers over to the fire, and when they were burned, he sent word to stop future assessments.

After this, the younger child wasted away in severe pain until he died. They carried him with immense mourning from the villa of Berny to Paris and had him buried him in the basilica of Saint Dionysius [Denis]. As for Chlodobert, they placed him on a litter and took him to the basilica of Saint Medard in Soissons. They threw themselves down at the holy tomb and made vows on his behalf, but he was already short of breath and weak, and he died in the middle of the night. They buried him in the holy basilica of the martyrs Crispin and Crispinian. There was loud lamentation among the entire population; for men, weeping, and women, wearing mourning clothes, followed his funeral cortege in the fashion of the processions that occur when a spouse dies.

After this, King Chilperic was generous to cathedrals, basilicas, and the poor.

Queen Austrechild (V 35)

Marius of Avenches gives the names of the doctors as Nicolaus and Donatus.

In these days, Austrechild, wife of King Guntram, fell prey to this disease. Before she took her last wicked breath, sighing deeply and realizing she could not survive, she decided that others should share in her demise and arranged for the lamentations of their deaths to accompany her own funeral. She is supposed to have made a request of the king in the fashion of Herod.

"I would still have a chance to live," she said, "if I had not fallen into the hands of wicked physicians. The medicines I have received have robbed me of my life and have caused me to lose strength rapidly. And so, I beg you, don't let my death go unavenged. I want you to take an oath that you will have them put to the sword as soon as I depart from this life. Just as I cannot live longer, they too shall not promote themselves after my death, and our friends and theirs shall share the same grief."

With these words she gave up her unhappy soul. When the usual period of mourning was over, the king, forced by the oath to his wicked wife, complied with her evil instructions. He ordered the two physicians who had attended her to be executed. In the considered opinion of many, this was not done without sin.

Ingund and Hermenigild V 38

Gregory's narrative of Hermenigild's revolt anticipates events that he later gives in their proper sequence (Cf. VI 18, 29, 33, 40, 43).

In this year in Spain there was a persecution of the [Catholic] Christians and many were exiled, deprived of property, reduced by hunger, thrown in prison, beaten, and cut to pieces by various torments. The chief of this criminal undertaking was Goisuinth, who, after her marriage to Athanagild, was married to Leovigild. She impressed the sign of degradation on the servants of God and, with divine vengeance in pursuit, was herself marked in the sight of all people. For a white cloud covered one eye and banished light, which her mind lacked, from her sight.

From another wife Leovigild had two sons, the elder of which had betrothed the daughter of Sigibert and the younger the daughter of Chilperic. Ingund, Sigibert's daughter, was sent with an extensive entourage to Spain and was welcomed by her grandmother [see IV 38] with considerable joy. Goisuinth could not abide her remaining a Catholic for long and tried to persuade her to be re-baptised in the Arian heresy.

"It's good enough for me to have been cleansed once from original sin by the saving power of baptism and have confessed the holy Trinity in a single equality," said Ingund manfully resisting. "I avow that I believe these things with my whole heart, nor shall I ever retreat from this faith."

This response enraged Goisuinth who seized her by the hair of her head, threw her to the ground, and kicked her around for a while; then she ordered her stripped and, still stained with blood, thrown in a pool. But, as many assert, in her heart Ingund never turned from our faith.

Leovigild gave Hermenigild and Ingund one of his cities in which to reside and reign. When they arrived there, Ingund began to preach to her husband to abandon the fallacy of heresy and recognize the truth of the Catholic faith. For a while he rejected it, but at last aroused by her preaching, he was converted to the Catholic faith and took the name John when he received the chrism. When Leovigild heard, he began to look for ways to bring about his son's destruction. Hermenigild saw this and joined himself to the imperial side, establishing ties of friendship with the emperor's prefect who at the time was attacking Spain.

Leovigild sent his son a message saying, "Come to me, for there are matters we should discuss together."

"I shall not come," replied Hermenigild. "For you are hostile to me because I am Catholic."

Leovigild gave the prefect of the emperor 30,000 solidi to remove his support for Hermenigild, mobilized an army, and marched against him. Hermenigild for his part summoned the Greeks and went forth against his father, leaving his wife behind in the city. When Leovigild confronted him, Hermenigild was abandoned by his allies and, seeing he could do nothing to win, entered a church that was nearby.

"Let my father not come against me," he said. "It is wrong for a father to be killed by his son or a son to be killed by his father."

Hearing about this, Leovigild sent Hermenigild's brother [Reccared] to see him.

"Come and throw yourself at the feet of our father and he will forgive you everything," said Reccared, having given oaths that Hermenigild would not be humiliated.

Hermenigild asked for his father to be called, and when he entered, Hermenigild prostrated himself at his father's feet. Leovigild embraced and kissed him, won him over with pleasing words, and took him to the camp. Forgetting about the oath, he nodded to his men who seized Hermenigild. Leovigild had his son stripped of his clothes and put a cheap garment on him. On his return to Toledo, he removed Hermenigild's retainers and sent his son into exile with only one young attendant.

Death of Clovis, Chilperic's Son (V 39)

In the month of October, after the death of his sons, King Chilperic was staying with his wife in the forest of Cuise, still grief stricken. At that time, he sent his son Clovis to Berny at the queen's suggestion; the intention was clearly that Clovis too should suffer the same fate as his brothers. The disease that had killed them was raging there in force in this period. But Clovis suffered no ill effects from his stay.

The king himself went to the villa of Chelles in the territory of Paris. A few days later he ordered Clovis to come to him. It will not be troublesome to tell how he died.

While staying with his father at this villa, he began to boast prematurely, "Look, my brothers are dead. The whole kingdom has been left to me. All Gaul is at my command; the fates have granted me rule over everything. When my enemies have fallen into my hands, I shall do to them whatever I please."

He also disparaged the unseemly qualities of his step-mother Fredegund. When she heard, she became very afraid. A few days later she had a visitor.

The visitor said to the queen, "That you are sitting bereft of your children is the work of Clovis's treachery. He has a passion for the daughter of one of your female slaves and has killed your sons by the magic arts of the girl's mother. So I warn you, you can hope for no better yourself, now that the hope by which you would have ruled has been taken from you."

The queen, overwhelmed now with fear, inflamed with rage and grief-stricken by her recent loss, had the girl on whom Clovis had cast his eyes seized. She had her severely beaten and her hair shorn and gave orders for her to be fastened to a cleft stake and set up before Clovis's quarters. The girl's mother was bound and subjected to torture for some time until Fredegund drew from her a confession confirming that the charges were true. These she brought before the king along with other matters of this kind and asked for vengeance on Clovis.

At the time the king had gone hunting and ordered his son to be brought before him in secret. When Clovis arrived, at the king's command, he was manacled by Dukes Desiderius and Bobo, his weapons and clothing were stripped from him, and he was taken bound and contemptibly dressed to the queen. She ordered him held in custody. She wanted to find out from him whether matters were really as she had heard; whose plan he had followed or by whose prompting he had acted; and especially what friendships he had contracted. He revealed a number of friendships, denying everything else. Three days later the queen had him taken in bonds across the Marne and put under guard in the villa called Noisy. While in custody there, he was stabbed to death, and his body was buried on the spot.

In the meantime messengers reached the king saying the prince had stabbed himself with his own hand; they declared that the knife that struck the blow was still sticking in the wound. Deceived by this account, King Chilperic never shed a tear for the son whom, as I would say, he himself handed over to death at the urging of the queen.

Clovis's servants were dispersed to various places. His mother [Audovera] was put to a cruel death. His sister was tricked and placed in a monastery by the queen's servants, where she assumed the religious habit and where she now remains. All their wealth was handed over to the queen. The woman who informed against Clovis was sentenced to be burned. As she was being led to her death, the wretched woman tried to cry out in protest that she had uttered lies, but her words availed her nothing; she was bound to the stake, and consumed alive in the flames. The treasurer of Clovis was brought back from Bourges by Chuppa, count of the stables, and handed over bound to the queen to undergo various kinds of torture. But, on my intercession, the queen ordered him released from his punishment and from his bonds and allowed him to go free.

Envoys (V 40, 41, 43)

Elafius, bishop of Chalons, was sent to Spain on an embassy to deal with the interests of Queen Brunhild. He came down with a fever and breathed his last....

Miro, king of Galicia, sent envoys to King Guntram. As they were passing through the territory of Poitiers, King Chilperic, then in possession of that region, was informed. He had them brought before him under guard and kept in custody in Paris.... After a year the envoys of the Suebi were released and returned to their own country....

King Leovigild sent as an envoy to Chilperic Agilan, a man of no brains, whose training in logical argument took the form of malevolence against the Catholic faith. His route brought him through Tours, and he tried to challenge my belief and attack the doctrines of the church.

A long debate on the Trinity follows between the Arian Agilan and Gregory.

Afterwards on his return to Spain, weakened by sickness, he was converted to our faith out of necessity.

Chilperic's Writings (V 44)

At the same time King Chilperic issued a circular to the effect that the holy Trinity was to refer not to distinct persons but only God, claiming that it was unseemly for God to be called a person like a mortal of flesh and blood; he also declared that the Father is the same as the Son, and that the Holy Spirit is the same as the Father and the Son.

"This is how it appeared to the prophets and patriarchs," he said, "and this is how the law itself proclaimed Him."

Having had this read out to me, he said, "This is the view I want you and the other teachers of the church to believe."

"Dutiful king," I responded, "give up this false belief. You must observe the doctrines passed on to us by other teachers of the church who followed in the footsteps of the apostles, the teachings furnished by Hilary and Eusebius, and the confession you yourself made at baptism."

The king grew angry at this point.

"It's quite obvious," he said, "that I regard Hilary and Eusebius as my bitterest opponents in this issue."

To which I responded, "It would suit you better to watch out that you do not make God or his saints angry. For you should know that the Father, Son, and Holy Spirit are all distinct in person. It was not the Father who took on a body of flesh and blood, nor the Holy Spirit, but the Son, so that he who was the Son of God would, for the redemption of humankind, be considered the son of a virgin. It was not the Father who suffered, nor the Holy Spirit, but the Son, so that he who had taken on the body of this world was himself made an offering on behalf of this world. As far as persons are concerned, what you say must be understood not in a corporeal but in a spiritual sense. In these three persons there is one glory, one eternity, one power."

Agitated, he said, "I will expound these matters to wiser men than you, and they will agree with me."

"He will be no wise man, but an idiot, who would want to follow what you propose," I replied.

Grinding his teeth at this response, he said no more.

A few days later Salvius, bishop of Albi [a. 574/5–84], visited him. Chilperic had his views read out to him, begging him to be in agreement. On hearing them, Salvius rejected them with such disgust that if he could have laid hands on the paper on which they were written, he would have torn it to shreds. And so the king gave up the project.

The king also wrote other books in verse in imitation of Sedulius. But those poor verses follow no acceptable form of meter at all. He also added letters to our alphabet, namely *w* as in Greek, *ae*, *the*, and *wi*, which are written by the following characters: ω, ψ, Z and Δ. And he sent letters to all the cities of his kingdom, telling them that boys should be taught these letters and that books written in ancient times should be erased with pumice and rewritten.

The Trial of Gregory for Treason and the Fall of Count Leudast (V 47–49)

The following narrative concludes at the end of 580, but it begins much earlier. Leudast's removal, and his replacement by Eunomius, must have occurred in November 579. The Synod of Berny before which Gregory was tried would have been around September 580—prior to the death of Chilperic's young sons, as Gregory notes, and Clovis's execution (see V 34, 39; and V 50).

Chilperic heard all about the harm that Leudast [count of Tours] was doing to the churches of Tours and the entire population, and so the king sent Ansovald there. He came on the festival of Saint Martin, and as the choice of count was granted to me on behalf of the people, Eunomius was raised to the comital office.

Leudast, seeing himself set aside, went to Chilperic.

"Most dutiful king," he said, "up to now I have guarded the city of Tours. But now that I have been removed from office, look how it will be guarded. You should know that Bishop Gregory is preparing to surrender it to the son of Sigibert."

"Not at all," said the king on hearing this, "you bring this up only because you have been removed."

"The bishop speaks of even greater matters that concern you," said Leudast; "for he says that your queen is committing adultery with Bishop Bertram."

At that point the king became angry. He punched and kicked Leudast, ordering him thrown into prison, loaded with chains.

Although this book should come to an end, I would like to tell something of Leudast's career. It seems best to begin with his birth, his homeland, and his character.

Gracina is the name of an island off Poitou, where Leudast was born to Leuchadius, a slave of a vine-dresser of the fisc. From there Leudast was summoned to service and assigned to the royal kitchen. But as his eyes were poor when he was young, and the bitter smoke did not agree with them, he was removed from the pestle and promoted to the baker's basket. Although he pretended to be happy among the fermented dough, he soon ran away and abandoned his service. And when he had been brought back two or three times and could not be prevented from attempting to escape, he was punished by having one of his ears clipped. Then since there was no way for him to conceal the mark imprinted on his body, he fled to Queen Marcovefa, whom King Charibert loved very much and had admitted to his bed in the place of her sister [see IV 26]. She received him willingly, promoted him, and appointed him keeper of her best horses. On this account, now overcome with self-importance and full of arrogance, he canvassed for the office of count of the stables. When he got it, he looked down his nose at everyone, holding them of no account. He was swollen with conceit and undone by the pleasures of the senses; he burned with greed and, as a favorite of his patroness, went here and there on her affairs. After her death, being well provided with plunder, he tried to maintain with King Charibert his former position by giving gifts.

After this, due to the sinfulness of the people, he was sent as count to Tours, and there the prestige of the high office allowed him to be even more arrogant. He showed himself to be a greedy plunderer, a loud-mouthed brawler, and a filthy adulterer. By sowing dissension and bringing false charges, he there amassed no small fortune.

After Charibert's death, when the city became part of Sigibert's share [see IV 45], he went over to Chilperic, and everything that he had unjustly amassed was seized by the adherents of Sigibert. Then King Chilperic, through his son Theudebert, overran Tours [see IV 47]. Since by this time I had arrived in Tours, Theudebert strongly recommended to me that Leudast should hold the office of count, which he had held before. Leudast acted very humbly toward me and was subservient, repeatedly swearing on the tomb of the holy bishop Martin that he would never act unreasonably and that he would be loyal to me in matters affecting my own person as well as in all the needs of the church. For he was afraid that King Sigibert would bring the city back under his authority, as later happened [see IV 50]. On Sigibert's death, Chilperic succeeded to his rule and Leudast again became count. When Merovech came to Tours [see V 14], he plundered all Leudast's property. During the two years that Sigibert held Tours, Leudast took refuge among the Bretons.

When he assumed the office of count, as we have said, his capriciousness reached the point of his entering the cathedral manse wearing body armor and mail, with a bow case slung from a belt, a lance in his hand and a helmet on his head, a man safe from no one because he was the enemy of everyone. If he presided over a trial along with leading members of the clergy and laity and saw someone pursuing justice, he would now immediately go into a rage and belch forth abuse on the citizens; he used to order priests dragged away in fetters and soldiers beaten with staves, and he showed such cruelty as to beggar description.

When Merovech, who had plundered his property, went away, Leudast came forward with false charges against me, claiming that Merovech had followed my advice in taking away his property. But after the injury had been done, he again repeated his oath and offered a covering from the tomb of the blessed Martin as a pledge that he would never be my enemy.

But as it is a long story to follow step by step Leudast's perjuries and other crimes, let me come to his attempt to overthrow me by unjust and execrable calumnies and the divine vengeance wreaked upon him, fulfilling the saying, "Everyone who overthrows shall be overthrown [cf. Jerem. 9:14]," and again, "Whoever digs a pit shall fall therein [cf. Prov. 26:27]."

Note there are two clerics called Riculf to be distinguished in the narrative that follows: the priest Riculf, and the subdeacon Riculf.

After the many wrongs Leudast inflicted on me and mine, and after the many seizures of ecclesiastical property, he joined forces with the priest Riculf, a man as twisted as himself, and blurted out the charge that I had accused Queen Fredegund of a criminal act; he claimed that, should my archdeacon Plato or my friend Galienus be put to torture, they would certainly convict me of having spoken in this way. It was then, as I have said above [V 47], that the king had become angry and, after punching and kicking him and loading him with chains, had him thrown into prison.

Now Leudast said that he had the support of the cleric Riculf, on whose testimony he made these charges. This Riculf was a subdeacon, just as unstable as Leudast. The year before, he had plotted with Leudast on this matter and looked for grounds for going over to him due to my anger. At last he found them and went to him. After preparing all their tricks for four months and having laid their traps, Riculf then came back to me with Leudast and begged me to take him back without penalty. I did it, I confess, and publicly received a secret enemy into my household.

On Leudast's departure, Riculf threw himself at my feet.

"Unless you help me quickly, I am lost," he said. "At the instigation of Leudast, I have said what I should not have said. Send me now to another kingdom;

if you do not, I shall be arrested by the king's men and suffer tortures that will kill me."

"If you have said anything that does not correspond to the truth, your words shall be on your own head," I said. "I will not send you to another kingdom in case I fall under suspicion of the king."

After this Leudast came forward as Riculf's accuser, claiming that he had heard the previously mentioned testimony from Riculf the subdeacon. Riculf was bound and put under guard, while Leudast in turn was released. Riculf claimed that Galienus and the archdeacon Plato were present on the very day the bishop had uttered his charge.

The priest Riculf, who by this time had been promised the episcopal office by Leudast, was so carried away with himself that his pride was the equal to that of Simon Magus. On the sixth day after Easter [April 26], he who had taken an oath to me three or more times on the tomb of Saint Martin spewed out such abuse that he could scarcely keep his hands off me, confident, of course, in the trap that he had laid.

On the next day, that is, the Sabbath after Easter, Leudast came to the city of Tours pretending to have some business to attend to. He arrested Plato the archdeacon and Galienus, tied them up, and ordered them taken to the queen, loaded with chains and stripped of their robes. I heard of this while in my quarters in the cathedral manse and, saddened and disturbed, I entered the oratory and took up the Psalms of David so that some consoling verse might be revealed when I opened them. This is what was found: "He led them away in hope and they were not afraid, and the sea covered their enemies [cf. Ps. 78:53]."

Meanwhile, as they began crossing the river on a ferry whose deck rested on two skiffs, the boat that was supporting Leudast sank, and if he had not escaped by swimming, he might have perished with his comrades. As for the other boat, which was connected to the first and carried the bound prisoners, it was kept above water by God's help.

Then the prisoners were taken to the king and charges that carried a death sentence were immediately laid against them. But the king, on reflection, freed them from their bonds and kept them under guard, unharmed and unshackled.

At Tours, in the meantime, Duke Berulf and Count Eunomius concocted a tale that King Guntram wanted to take the city, and for that reason, to prevent anything going wrong, they said, the city must be provided with a guard. They pretended to set watches at the gates to protect the city, but they were really guarding me. They also sent people to advise me to take valuables from the church and make off secretly to Clermont. But I would not take their advice.

Next the king summoned the bishops of his kingdom and ordered the case carefully investigated.

When the cleric Riculf was repeatedly being examined in secret and, as he often did, was uttering many lies against me and my associates, Modestus, a certain carpenter, said to him, "Unlucky man, who so stubbornly has these designs against his bishop, it would be better for you to be quiet, beg pardon from the bishop, and procure his favor."

At this Riculf began to shout out in a loud voice, "Look at this man who bids me be silent and not pursue the truth. He is an enemy of the queen and will not allow the reasons for the charge against her to be investigated."

These words were immediately reported to the queen. Modestus was arrested, tortured, whipped, put in chains, and kept under guard. He was bound to a post by chains between two guards, but in the middle of the night, when the guards fell asleep, he prayed for the Lord to be so kind as to exert his power on behalf of a wretched man and to let an innocent prisoner in bonds be freed by the visitation of the bishops Martin and Medard. The bonds were broken, the post shattered, the door opened, and soon he entered the basilica of Saint Medard [in Soissons], where I was keeping vigils.

The bishops then assembled at the villa of Berny and were ordered to meet in one building. Next the king arrived and took his seat, after greeting everyone and receiving their blessing. At that point Bertram, bishop of Bordeaux, against whom, along with the queen, this charge had been brought, explained the case and addressed me, saying that the charge had been brought against him and the queen by me. I denied in truth having uttered these things, saying, I heard others say them, but I had not devised them.

Outside the building there was a lot of talk among people, who said, "Why are these charges made against a bishop of God? Why does the king prosecute such charges? How could a bishop have said such things, even about a slave? Lord God, help your servant."

The king said, "The charge against my wife dishonors me. If therefore it is your judgment that witnesses should be presented against the bishop, here they are. But if it seems that this should not be done, and that the matter should be left to the honor of the bishop, speak up. I will gladly pay heed to your command."

All were amazed at the king's wisdom and forbearance.

At that point, when all the bishops said, "The testimony of an inferior cannot be admitted against a bishop," the case came down to this, that I should say three masses at three altars and clear myself of the alleged charges by taking an oath. And though these conditions were contrary to the canons, still they were fulfilled for the sake of the king. Also I cannot be silent about the fact that [the king's daughter] Queen Rigunth, out of sympathy for my suffering, fasted with all her household until a slave reported that I had fulfilled all that had been required of me.

Then the bishops returned to the king.

"All that was imposed upon the bishop has been carried out," they said. "What remains to be done now, king, if not the excommunication of you and Bertram, the accuser of a brother?"

"O no," said the king, "I only reported what I had heard."

They asked who had said this, and he answered that he had heard these things from Leudast. He had already fled owing to the weakness of his plan or his resolution. All the bishops then decided that this sower of discord, traducer of the queen, and accuser of a bishop, should be shut out of all churches, because he had withdrawn from the hearing. To the bishops who were not present, they sent a letter to this effect, bearing their signatures. After this, each of them returned to his own see.

When Leudast heard, he took refuge in the church of Saint Peter in Paris. But on hearing the royal edict prohibiting anyone in Chilperic's kingdom from receiving him, and especially since the son whom he had left at home had died, he came to Tours in secret and carried away his more valuable possessions to Bourges. The king's retainers pursued him, but he escaped by flight. They captured his wife, and she was sent into exile in the district of Tournai.

The subdeacon Riculf was sentenced to death. I managed to obtain his life but I could not free him from torture. Nothing, not even metal, could have endured such beating as was given this wretch. With his hands tied behind his back, he was suspended from a tree from the third hour of the day; at the ninth hour, he was taken down, wracked on pulleys, beaten with staves, rods, and doubled thongs, and not by one or two assailants, but by as many as could reach his wretched limbs. Only at the critical point in the torture did he then reveal the truth and make known the secrets of the plot. This was the explanation he gave for the charge being made against the queen: when she was driven from power, Clovis would obtain the kingdom, once his brothers and father had been killed; Leudast would get a ducal office. As for the priest Riculf, who had been a friend of Clovis from the times of the blessed Bishop Eufronius, he would win appointment to the bishopric of Tours. The subdeacon Riculf was promised the archdiaconate.

I returned to Tours by God's grace and found the church thrown into a turmoil by the priest Riculf. Now this man had been picked out from among the poor under bishop Eufronius and appointed archdeacon. Later he was raised to the priesthood and withdrew to his own property. He was always self-important, arrogant, and impudent. For example, while I was still with the king, he brazenly entered the cathedral manse as if he were already bishop, inventoried the church silver, and brought the rest of the property under his control. He enriched the more important clergy with gifts, granted vineyards, and parceled out meadows; to the lesser clergy, he administered beatings and many blows, even raising his own hand against them.

"Acknowledge your master," he said. "He has gained victory over his enemies, and it is by his devices that Tours has been purged of that crew from Clermont."

The wretched man did not know that, with the exception of five bishops, all the others who have held the bishopric of Tours were descendants of my ancestors. He was accustomed to repeating to his intimates the proverb that no one can expect to trick a wise man without using perjury.

Upon my return, when he continued to hold me in disdain and did not come to greet me as did the other citizens, but rather threatened to kill me, I ordered him taken away to a monastery on the advice of the bishops of my province. While he was closely confined, representatives of Bishop Felix [of Nantes], who had supported the charge against me, intervened. The abbot was taken in by their perjuries; Riculf slipped away and went to Bishop Felix, who received him warmly, though he should have cursed him.

Leudast meanwhile went to Bourges, taking with him all the treasure that he had plundered from the poor. Not long after, forces from Bourges under their count attacked him and carried off all his gold and silver and whatever else he had brought with him, leaving him nothing but what he had on his person; and they would have taken his very life if he had not fled. He regained his strength and in turn led some men from Tours in an attack against his plunderers; killing one of them, he recovered some of his property and returned to the territory of Tours. Duke Berulf heard about this and sent his own retainers outfitted for war to seize him. Leudast realized that he would now be captured, and so he abandoned his property and fled to the church of Saint Hilary in Poitiers. Duke Berulf meanwhile sent the property that he seized to the king.

Leudast would leave the basilica and attack the houses of various people, taking plunder without trying to disguise the fact. He was also repeatedly caught in adultery in the holy confines of the very porch of the basilica. For these reasons, the queen, disturbed that a place consecrated to God was being defiled in such a fashion, ordered him to be expelled from the holy basilica. On being expelled, he went again to his supporters in Bourges, begging them to hide him.

14. "I see the sword of divine wrath unsheathed and hanging over this house
(V 50)." The prediction of Bishop Salvius.

Prediction of the Blessed Salvius about Chilperic (V 50)

I should have mentioned my conversation with the blessed Bishop Salvius earlier, but, as it slipped my mind, I do not consider it unwarranted if it is written later.

When I had said farewell to the king after the council that I mentioned [V 49], and was anxious to return home, I did not want to go without taking leave of Salvius with a kiss. I looked for him and found him in the courtyard of the domain of Berny. I told him that I was about to return home.

We had moved off a little and were speaking of one thing and another when he said to me, "Do you see what I see upon this roof?"

"Why, I see the roof-covering that the king lately had installed," said I.

"Don't you see anything else?"

"I see nothing else." I suspected that he was making some kind of a joke. "Tell me what more do you see?" I added.

Drawing a deep breath, he said, "I see the sword of divine wrath unsheathed and hanging over this house."

Indeed, the bishop's words were not wrong; for twenty days later died the two sons of the king, whose deaths I have already described [V 34].

This chapter concludes Book V.

CHAPTER FIVE

FROM THE TREATY OF NOGENT TO THE

DEATH OF CHILPERIC

a. 581–FALL 584

(BOOK VI)

Woe to thee, O land, when thy king is a child and thy princes eat in the
morning.

Ecclesiastes 10:16

*The new alliance of the Nogent agreements (VI 1, below) cancelled the earlier so-called
treaty of Pompierre (Stone Bridge) between Childebert and Guntram (V 17). Egidius
of Rheims (first mentioned in V 18) hereafter plays an increasingly important role in
diplomatic events.*

Year VI of Childebert II, a. 581

*Alliance of Childebert and Chilperic and the Flight of Mummolus to Childebert's
Kingdom (VI 1)*

In the sixth year of his reign, King Childebert repudiated the peace with King
Guntram and allied himself with King Chilperic. Not long afterwards Gogo
[governor of King Childebert] died; Wandelen was appointed in his place.

Mummolus fled from Guntram's kingdom and shut himself within the walls
of Avignon.

A synod of bishops assembled at Lyons to decide various matters in dispute
and to pass judgment against persons failing in their responsibilities. The king
then presided over the council to deal with many matters arising from the flight
of Duke Mummolus and some arising from the quarreling [of the kings].

Chilperic's Envoys Return from Byzantium (VI 2)

Meanwhile King Chilperic's envoys, who had gone three years before to the
emperor Tiberius, returned, but not without severe loss and hardship. Since
they dared not enter the harbor of Marseilles because of the quarreling of the
kings, they sailed to Agde, located in the kingdom of the Goths. Before they
could land, however, the ship was driven by the wind, dashed on the shore, and
broken into pieces. The legates and their servants saw that they were in danger

and, seizing planks, barely managed to reach the shore; many of the men were lost, but most escaped. The locals took the goods that the waves carried ashore, but the legates did get back the more valuable items and brought them to King Chilperic. The people of Agde, nevertheless, held on to a great deal.

At that time I had gone to the villa of Nogent to meet the king, and there he showed me a great salver, weighing fifty pounds, which he had had fashioned of gold and gems.

"I had this made to honor and ennoble the Frankish people," he said. "Moreover, I shall make many more if things go well."

He also showed me gold pieces, each of a pound's weight, sent by the emperor, having on one side the likeness of the emperor and the inscription in a circle, *Of Tiberius Constantinus, Forever Augustus* and on the other side a four-horse chariot and charioteer with the inscription, *Glory of the Romans*. He showed me many other treasures brought by the envoys.

Childebert's Envoys to Chilperic and the Treaty of Nogent (VI 3)

Then, while Chilperic was residing at Nogent[-sur-Marne], Egidius, bishop of Rheims, came to him on an embassy with leading officials of Childebert. They discussed depriving King Guntram of his kingdom and establishing peace between themselves.

"My sins have grown so great that I have no sons left," said King Chilperic, "and I have no other heir but King Childebert, my brother Sigibert's son. Therefore let him be heir to all that my efforts may win; just let me keep the whole without trouble or dispute for as long as I live."

They thanked him, signed agreements to confirm the terms discussed, and returned to Childebert with expensive gifts. After their departure King Chilperic sent Bishop Leudovald with the leading men of his kingdom. They gave and received oaths of peace, signed agreements, and came back well rewarded.

Lupus, Brunhild's Supporter, Driven from the Kingdom (VI 4)

For some time now, Lupus, duke of Champagne, had been constantly harassed and plundered by various enemies, especially by Ursio and Berthefred. Finally they made an agreement to kill him and raised a force against him. Queen Brunhild found out about it, and distressed at the unjust attacks on her loyal supporter, girded herself like a man and rushed in between the opposing battle lines.

"Men, don't do this evil," she cried. "Don't persecute the innocent; for the sake of one man, don't engage in a battle that will destroy the forces of the region."

This brought a response from Ursio.

"Get back, woman," said he. "It's enough for you to have held power under your husband. Now your son rules. We preserve his kingdom as its guardians, not you. Get back, or our horses' hooves will trample you into the ground."

After many more exchanges of this kind, the queen's determination that they should not fight prevailed.

On leaving the area, however, they burst into dwellings belonging to Lupus, seized all the furnishings and took them home, pretending that they were going to place them in the king's treasury and uttering threats against Lupus.

"He will never escape alive from our hands," they said.

Lupus saw that he was in danger and, placing his wife within the walls of the city of Laon for safety, fled to King Guntram, who welcomed him. He remained with the king in hiding, waiting for Childebert to come of age.

Chilperic Leaves Nogent for Paris. Priscus the Jew (VI 5)

Then Chilperic, while still at the villa of Nogent, had his belongings sent ahead and made preparations to go to Paris. When I went to see him to say farewell, a Jew by the name of Priscus arrived. He was a personal agent charged with making purchases for the king.

Taking Priscus gently by the hair, the king said to me, "Come, bishop of God, and lay your hands on him."

When Priscus struggled, the king said, "O obstinate spirit and ever unbelieving people that does not recognize the Son of God promised to it by the voices of its prophets and the mysteries of the church prefigured in its own sacrifices."

The Jew replied to these words, "God never married, was never blessed with offspring, nor did He ever allow anyone to share his kingdom, for He said by the mouth of Moses, 'Behold, behold, for I am the Lord and without me there is no God. I shall kill and I shall make alive. I shall strike and I shall heal [cf. Deut. 32:39].'"

Arguments of Chilperic and Priscus, and a long discourse by Gregory follow.

… Although I said this and more, the wretched man's conscience showed no signs of believing. When Priscus was silent, and the king saw that my words had had no effect, Chilperic then turned to me and asked to receive my blessing before he departed.

"To you, bishop," he said, "I will say what Jacob said to the angel that was speaking with him, 'I will not let you go unless you bless me [Gen. 32:36].'"

And saying that, he ordered water brought for our hands. After washing and saying a prayer, I received the bread and, giving thanks to God, partook of the bread myself and offered some to the king; taking a draught of wine, I said

15. "Taking Priscus gently by the hair, the king said to me, 'Come, bishop of
God, and lay your hands on him (VI 5).'"

farewell and left. As for the king, he mounted his horse and returned to Paris with his wife and daughter and all his household.

Dynamius and the Struggle for Uzès (VI 7)

Enmity between Albinus and Jovinus went back to the reign of Sigibert (IV 43, omitted here). Dynamius was ostensibly a subject of Childebert.

At this time Ferreolus died, the bishop of Uzès and a man of great sanctity, full of wisdom and understanding. He composed some books of letters in the fashion of Sidonius [Apollinaris, ca 430–80/90].

After his death, Albinus, a former prefect [that is, governor of Provence], took up the bishopric through the influence of Dynamius, the governor of Provence, and without the consent of the king [Childebert]. He held it for no more than three months and died while the question of his removal was still pending. Jovinus, a former governor of Provence, once more obtained a royal directive to take up the episcopacy. But Deacon Marcellus, the son of Felix the senator, forestalled him. He was ordained bishop with the consent of Dynamius at an assembly of the bishops of the province. Still, he was attacked by Jovinus, who was trying to have him removed. Enclosed in the city, Marcellus tried to defend himself by force, but when he could not prevail, he paid to obtain victory.

Dynamius and Theodore, Bishop of Marseilles (VI 11)

At Marseilles, Dynamius, governor of Provence, began to plot heavily against Bishop Theodore. While preparing to make a journey to see King Childebert, the bishop was arrested by the governor and kept prisoner in the middle of the city; he was finally released after enduring severe abuse. The clergy of Marseilles were in on Dynamius's scheme to throw Theodore out of his bishopric.

As Theodore was on his way to King Childebert, he was arrested together with the former prefect Jovinus on the orders of King Guntram. The clergy of Marseilles were filled with great joy on hearing the news, supposing that, now the bishop was in custody, he would be exiled, and that things had now reached a point that he would never return. So they seized the properties of the church, made inventories of the sacred vessels, opened the strong boxes, and pillaged the store-rooms, rummaging through all the property of the church as if the bishop were already dead. All the while, they uttered various criminal charges against him, which, with Christ's help, were afterwards discovered to be false.

As for Childebert, after making a peace agreement with Chilperic, he sent envoys to King Guntram to demand restoration of the half portion of Mar-

seilles that Childebert had given to him after the death of his father Sigibert;
should he refuse, the envoys said, he should know that the holding of this
portion would cost him dear. But Guntram would not restore it and ordered
the roads closed, so that the right to cross through his kingdom would not be
made available to everyone.

When Childebert saw this, he sent to Marseilles Gundulf, a former *domesticus*, who was of senatorial birth and had been appointed duke. Since he did not
dare travel through Guntram's territory, Gundulf came to Tours. I welcomed
him warmly and discovered that he was my mother's uncle. I made him stay
with me for five days and, after providing him with all that he needed, let him
go off. When he reached Marseilles, he was unable to enter the city in face of
the opposition offered by Dynamius. Bishop Theodore, who at this point had
now joined Gundulf, was also not welcomed back to his church. Dynamius and
the clergy barred the city gates, together taunting and heaping abuse on both of
them, the bishop and Gundulf.

Finally, Dynamius was invited to a meeting with the duke and came to the
basilica of the blessed Stephen, next to the city. The doorkeepers guarding the
entrance to the church stood ready to close the doors the moment Dynamius
passed in. When they did this, the crowds of armed men following Dynamius
were locked out and could not get in. Dynamius himself was unaware of what
was happening. As soon as they discussed various matters at the altar, they moved
away from it and passed into the sacristy. Dynamius entered with them, and
they assailed him with terrifying accusations, now that he was deprived of the
support of his men. His followers were driven off—on his removal they began
crowding around noisily with weapons in their hands—and then Gundulf assembled the principal citizens in order to enter the city with the bishop. Seeing
all that had happened, Dynamius now sought pardon. He presented numerous
gifts to the duke, and when he swore an oath that in future he would be loyal
to both the bishop and the king, his equipment was restored to him. The gates
of the town and the doors of the churches were then opened, and the duke and
the bishop both entered the city, with the ringing of bells, acclamations, and
various flags waving in their honor.

Then the clergy involved in this shameful crime—the ringleaders were the
abbot Anastasius and the priest Proculus—fled to the protection of Dynamius's
residence, asking refuge of the man who had put them up to it. Many of them
were released on finding satisfactory sureties and were ordered to proceed to
the king's court. Meanwhile, Gundulf returned to the king, having brought
the city under the authority of King Childebert and restored the bishop to his
see.

But Dynamius paid no attention to the loyalty that he had promised to the king and sent messengers to King Guntram telling him that he would lose the half portion of the city owed to him on account of the bishop, and that he would never hold Marseilles in his power until this fellow was driven from the city. King Guntram became angry and, contrary to divine law, ordered the priest of the most high God to be brought before him in bonds.

"Let the enemy of my kingdom be driven into exile," he said, "so he can't do us any more harm."

Theodore was again seized and carried off to Guntram.

... The bishop was taken before the king but found not guilty; he was allowed to return to his city, where he was welcomed with great honor by the citizens.

Out of this affair bitter enmity arose between King Guntram and his nephew Childebert. They broke the treaty and began to lie in wait for each other.

Chilperic Attacks the Cities of Guntram (VI 12)

King Chilperic saw the dissension arising between his brother and his nephew. He summoned Duke Desiderius and ordered him to inflict some harm on his brother. Desiderius raised a force, drove off Duke Ragnovald, and occupied Périgueux. After exacting oaths, he then went on to Agen. When Ragnovald's wife heard that her husband had fled and that these cities were being brought under King Chilperic's authority, she took refuge in the basilica of the holy martyr Caprasius [in Agen]. But she was brought out, despoiled of her property and the support of her servants, and then, when she had given sureties, sent to Toulouse; there she took up quarters in the basilica of the holy Saturninus. Desiderius took all the cities belonging to King Guntram in the region [of Aquitaine], and subjected them to the authority of King Chilperic.

Duke Berulf, hearing that the people of Bourges were quietly talking about invading the territory of Tours, raised a force and took up a position on their borders. At this time the districts of Yzeures and Barrous in the region of Tours were seriously devastated. Those who were unable to join in this blockade [of Bourges] were later sentenced without mercy.

Duke Bladast went to Gascony where he lost the greater part of his army.

Year VII of Childebert II, a. 582

Gregory begins the seventh year of Childebert's reign again with a list of portents, and an account of a plague (VI 14).

Conversion of Jews by Chilperic (VI 17)

King Chilperic ordered many Jews to be baptized that year and received a number of them from the sacred font [as godfather]. Some of them, however, were purified in body only, not in heart and, lying to God, returned to their former perfidy and could be seen observing the Sabbath as well as honoring the Lord's day.

Priscus [see VI 5] could not be influenced by any argument to recognize the truth. The king became angry with him for that and ordered him put in prison, thinking that, if he could not get him to believe of his own accord, he would make him listen and believe even against his will. But Priscus offered gifts and asked for time until his son could marry a Hebrew girl at Marseilles; he promised falsely that he would then do what the king demanded.

Meanwhile, a quarrel arose between Priscus and Phatir, one of the Jewish converts, who was now a godson of the king. And when on the Sabbath Priscus was retiring to a more out of the way place to fulfill the law of Moses, wearing a shawl and without a weapon in his hand, Phatir suddenly appeared and put him to the sword, together with the companions who were with him. When they were killed, Phatir fled with his men to the church of Saint Julian [in Paris], on a neighboring street. While there, they heard that the king had granted the master his life but ordered his men to be dragged like criminals from the church and put to death. Their master had already been driven away at this point, so one of them drew his sword and killed his comrades. He then left the church armed with his sword, but people attacked him and he was cruelly killed. Phatir obtained permission to return to Guntram's kingdom from where he had come, but he was killed by Priscus's kinsmen not long after his return.

Chilperic's Envoys Return from Spain Where They Were Arranging the Marriage of Chilperic's Daughter (VI 18)

Then Ansovald and Domigisel, King Chilperic's envoys who had been sent to Spain to examine the bridal endowment [promised to Rigunth, Chilperic's daughter], returned home. At this time King Leovigild was accompanying the army sent against his son Hermenigild, from whom he took the city of Merida. I have already explained how the prince had allied himself with the generals of Emperor Tiberius [V 38]. This matter had delayed the envoys' return. When

I saw them, I was anxious to learn whether faith in Christ still burned among the few [Catholic] Christians remaining in that land.

Ansovald gave me this reply: "The Christians now living in Spain preserve the Catholic faith unimpaired. But the king is trying to disturb it with a new scheme, for he pretends to pray at the tombs of the martyrs and in the churches of our faith. And he says, 'Of course I know that Christ is the Son of God and equal to the Father. But I can't believe at all that the Holy Spirit is God, because this isn't written in any of the scriptures.'"...

Ansovald went to Chilperic, followed by an embassy from Spain, which went on from Chilperic to Childebert and then returned home.

Chilperic Loses Men at the River Orge (VI 19)

King Chilperic had placed guards at the bridge over the Orge in the territory of Paris to prevent infiltrators from his brother's kingdom doing any harm. The former duke Asclepius got advance knowledge of this arrangement. In a night attack he killed all the guards and devastated the district near the bridge. When Chilperic got the news, he sent messengers to the counts, dukes, and other officials, ordering them to muster an army and invade his brother's kingdom. But he was dissuaded from so doing by the counsel of good men.

"They have acted wrongly," they told him, "but you should act wisely. Send envoys to your brother; if he will redress the outrage, you will do nothing harmful, but if he refuses, then is the time to consider what course to pursue."

The king accepted their argument, halted the army, and dispatched an embassy to his brother. Guntram made complete amends and sought full reconciliation with his brother.

Portents (VI 21)

In this year the following portents again appeared. There was an eclipse of the moon [18 September]. In the territory of Tours, real blood flowed from bread when it was broken. The walls of Soissons collapsed. In Angers there was an earthquake. Wolves entered within the walls of the city of Bourges and devoured dogs without fear of humans. Fire was seen to course across the heavens. The city of Bazas was burned and the churches and their buildings were devastated. All the church plate, I learned, was saved.

New Counts Appointed. Intercepted Letters of Bishop Charterius (VI 22)

Since King Chilperic had overrun cities belonging to his brother [see VI 12], he appointed new counts and ordered that all taxes of the cities be paid to him. I know this was done as directed.

In these days, two men were arrested by Nonnichius, count of Limoges. They were carrying a letter in the name of Charterius, bishop of Périgueux, that contained many insulting things about the king. In it, in the midst of other matters, was a passage in which the bishop seemed to be complaining that he had fallen from paradise into hell, meaning that he had been transferred from the kingdom of Guntram to the dominion of Chilperic. The count just named sent the letter and the two men under heavy guard to the king. The king calmly had the bishop brought before him to say whether the charges against him were true or not.

The bishop came and the king produced the men and the letter. He asked the bishop if it had been sent by him. He said it had not. The men then were asked from whom they had received that letter. They said from Frontonius the deacon. The bishop was asked about the deacon. He replied that he was his chief enemy and there could be no doubt that this wickedness was his doing since he had often instigated evil accusations against him. The deacon was brought at once and questioned by the king. He testified against the bishop.

"It was I who wrote this letter," he said, "at the bishop's order."

The bishop cried out that this man had often devised clever tricks to cast him out of office. The king took pity, and commending his cause to God, let them both go, interceding with the bishop for the deacon and begging the bishop to pray for the king.

In this way the bishop was sent back to his city with honor. In two months Count Nonnichius, who was the cause of this outrage, died from a stroke. As he was without children, his property was granted to several people by the king.

Son Born to Chilperic (VI 23)

Afterwards a son was born to Chilperic, who had buried so many sons. In honor of the event, the king commanded the gates of the prisons to be opened and those in bonds to be set free and issued instructions not to exact delinquent penalties due to the fisc. But later this infant was the cause of great evil.

Bishop Theodore Again and the Arrival of Gundovald in Gaul (VI 24)

Fresh attacks were now made against Bishop Theodore. For Gundovald, who said he was the son of King Chlothar, returned from Constantinople and landed at Marseilles. I would like to record briefly certain facts about his origin.

He was born in Gaul and brought up very carefully. He wore his hair long down his back, as is the fashion of its kings, and was instructed in letters. His mother presented him to King Childebert [I].

"Here is your nephew, the son of King Chlothar," she told him; "as his father hates him, take him up, for he is your flesh."

Childebert received the child because he had no sons and kept him with him.

This was reported to King Chlothar, who sent messengers to his brother saying, "Let the boy go, so he may come to me."

Without delay Childebert sent the boy to Chlothar, who, when he looked at him, ordered his hair to be shorn.

"I did not produce this one," he said.

Then after the death of King Chlothar, Gundovald was taken in by King Charibert. Sigibert summoned him, once more cut his hair, and sent him to the city of Agrippina, which is now called Cologne. He escaped from there, let his hair grow long again, and made his way to Narses, who governed Italy at the time. There he took a wife, produced sons, and went to Constantinople.

After a long time, he landed at Marseilles, invited by a certain person to return to Gaul, so they say, and was received by Bishop Theodore. He got horses from the bishop and joined Duke Mummolus, who was then at Avignon, as I have said earlier [VI 1].

Duke Guntram Boso arrested Bishop Theodore and imprisoned him on account of this affair, charging him with introducing a foreigner into Gaul and wanting to subject the Frankish kingdom to imperial authorities by this means. It is said that the bishop produced a letter signed by the great men of Childebert's kingdom.

"I did nothing on my own," he said, "but only what our lords and chief officials commanded me."

The bishop was kept under guard in a cell and not allowed to go near a church. One night, while he was earnestly praying to the Lord, the cell shone with a bright light so that the count who was guarding him was thoroughly terror stricken; an immense ball of light was seen above the bishop for a period of two hours. In the morning, the count recounted this event to the others who were with him.

After this, Theodore was taken before King Guntram, as was Bishop Epiphanius, who had fled from the Lombards and was living at Marseilles, because he too was evidently an accessory in this affair. The king examined them, but they were found to have committed no offense. However, he did order them to be kept in confinement, in which Epiphanius died after a great deal of suffering.

As for Gundovald, he withdrew to an island in the sea to await the outcome of events. Duke Guntram Boso divided the property of Gundovald with King Guntram's duke, and carried off with him to Auvergne, so they say, an immense weight of silver and gold and other goods.

Year VIII of Childebert II, a. 583

Guntram Boso and Mummolus (VI 26)

The date of Guntram Boso's visit to Constantinople is generally thought to be 581.

Duke Guntram Boso first returned to Auvergne with the previously mentioned treasures and then went to King Childebert. On his way back, he was arrested along with his wife and sons by King Guntram and detained.

"The invitation that brought Gundovald to Gaul came from you," said the king; "this is why you went to Constantinople a few years ago."

"It was your own duke Mummolus who welcomed him and kept him by his side at Avignon," replied the duke. "Allow me to bring him to you; then I shall be free of the charges brought against me."

"I'm not letting you go anywhere until you pay the penalties that fit the crimes you've committed," replied the king.

Seeing death near, the duke said, "Here is my son. Take him as a hostage for what I promise my lord the king, and if I can't bring Mummolus back to you, let me lose my little boy."

That was when the king allowed him to go, but he kept the child with him.

Duke Guntram Boso took with him troops from Clermont and Velay and went to Avignon. But Mummolus saw to it with one of his tricks that unsafe boats were readied for them at the Rhône. They boarded them without suspicion, and when they reached the middle of the river, the boats filled and sank. In danger of drowning, some swam to safety and a number tore planks from the boats and reached the shore, but a good many who had less presence of mind were drowned in the river. Duke Guntram Boso, nevertheless, reached Avignon.

Before Mummolus's arrival at Avignon, only a small part of the city remained unguarded by the Rhône. Mummolus on entering the city had seen to it that the whole place was protected by a channel into which he led water from the river. He had trenches of great depth dug and the flowing water concealed the traps he had made.

Now along came Guntram Boso. Mummolus cried out from the wall, "If good faith still exists between us, let Guntram come to one bank and I to the other, and let him say what he wants."

When they met, the new channel of the river separated them.

"If it's all right with you," Guntram Boso said from his side, "I'll cross, because we have some things to discuss in greater privacy."

"Come, don't be afraid," said Mummolus.

Guntram Boso entered the water with one of his friends. As the friend was weighed down with a mailcoat, he sank under the water immediately on reaching a trap in the river and did not reappear. But when Guntram Boso sank and was being carried along by the swift current, one of his men nearby reached out a spear to his hand and brought him ashore. After Guntram and Mummolus had hurled insults at one another, they both departed.

As Guntram Boso lay siege to the city with King Guntram's army, news of this was brought to Childebert. He became angry because Guntram Boso was doing this without his orders and dispatched Gundulf, whom I have mentioned before [VI 11], to Avignon. Gundulf put an end to the siege and took Mummolus to Clermont. But a few days later Mummolus returned to Avignon.

Chilperic Enters Paris at Easter. Baptism of Theuderic (VI 27)

Chilperic went to Paris the day before Easter was celebrated. To avoid the curses contained in the agreement between him and his brothers [made following the death of Charibert, a. 567] that none of them should enter Paris without the consent of the others, the relics of many saints were carried before him as he entered the city. He spent Easter with a great deal of revelry and had his son baptized [cf. VI 23]. Ragnemod, bishop of the city, received the child from the holy font. Chilperic gave the boy the name Theuderic.

No News from Spain, Bad News from the Empire (VI 29, 30)

The new emperor was Maurice (a. 582–602).

The envoys returned from Spain and reported nothing definite because Leovigild was campaigning with his forces against his son....

In this year [recte a. 582] the Emperor Tiberius passed from this world, leaving people deeply saddened at his death. He was a man of the greatest goodness, ready to give alms, just in judicial proceedings, most careful in issuing judgment. He disparaged no one but embraced all with good will. Loving all, he in turn was loved by all....

War between Chilperic and Guntram. Mutiny of Childebert's Army (VI 31)

Next King Chilperic received envoys from his nephew Childebert. Their leader was Egidius, bishop of Rheims.

Brought before the king and given an audience, they said, "Our master, your nephew, asks you to keep with special care the peace you have made with him, for he cannot have peace with your brother, who took away half of Marseilles after his father's death and retains fugitives whom he is unwilling to send back. Therefore your nephew Childebert wishes to preserve unbroken the good relations which he now has with you."

"My brother has proven to be guilty of many things," said Chilperic. "If my son Childebert would look for reasonable explanations, he will see at once that his father Sigibert was killed with my brother's connivance."

"If you would join with your nephew, and he with you, and muster an army, speedy vengeance could be inflicted on Guntram as he deserves," responded Bishop Egidius.

When an oath was sworn to that effect and hostages were exchanged, the envoys departed.

Relying on their promises, Chilperic then mustered the army of his kingdom and came to Paris. When residing there, he was the cause of great expense to the inhabitants.

Duke Berulf advanced with the forces of Tours, Poitiers, Angers, and Nantes to the territory of Bourges. Desiderius and Bladast with all the army of the province entrusted to them [that is, southern Aquitaine] hemmed in Bourges from the other side, greatly devastating the country through which they came. Chilperic ordered the army that had gathered at his command to pass through the territory of Paris. As they passed through, he joined them and advanced to the town of Melun, burning and laying everything waste. Although his nephew's army did not join him, Chilperic was accompanied nevertheless by Childebert's dukes and envoys.

At this point, Chilperic sent messengers to Dukes Berulf, Desiderius, and Bladast, saying "Enter the territory of Bourges, advance to the city and extract oaths of loyalty in my name."

The forces of Bourges, however, gathered at the town of Châteaumeillant to the number of fifteen thousand and fought against Duke Desiderius there; great slaughter was done, so that more than seven thousand men from both armies fell. The dukes advanced to the city with the men that were left, plundering and laying everything waste. The devastation inflicted was such as has never been heard of since ancient times, so that no house nor vineyard nor tree was left; but they cut down, burned, and overthrew everything. They even carried off sacred vessels from the churches, which they then set on fire.

King Guntram advanced with an army against his brother [Chilperic], placing all his hope in the judgment of God. One day, towards evening, he loosed his forces and destroyed a greater part of his brother's army. In the morning envoys met and the kings made peace. They promised one another that the party that had exceeded the limits of the law would compensate the other party with whatever the bishops and leaders of the people decided. And in this way they parted peaceably.

When King Chilperic could not keep his army from plundering, he put the count of Rouen to the sword. And so he returned to Paris, leaving all the booty and releasing the captives. The besiegers of Bourges, on getting orders to return home, took with them so much plunder that the entire district they left behind was believed to be emptied of man and beast alike. The army of Desiderius and Bladast entered the territory of Tours, burning, plundering, and killing in the manner usually inflicted on enemies; for they even took captives, most of whom they despoiled and afterwards let go. This disaster was followed by disease among the herds, so that scarcely enough livestock remained to make a new start, and it was strange for anyone to see a bullock or catch sight of a heifer.

During the time these events were happening, King Childebert and his army remained in the same spot. Then one night, when the army had been mobilized, the lesser ranks raised loud complaints against Bishop Egidius and the king's dukes.

They began to shout aloud and openly yelled out, "Get rid of those around the king who sell his kingdom, subject his cities to the dominion of another, and hand over his people to the rule of another prince."

While they continued to shout complaints like this, the morning came. They rushed to the king's tent, weapons in hand; their hope was to get a hold of the bishop and chief officials, overpower them, give them a beating, and cut them up with their swords. When the bishop found out about this, he took flight, mounting a horse and heading for his own city. The troops pursued him in an uproar, hurling stones and spewing forth abuse. The reason he was saved at this time was the fact that they had no horses ready. When the horses of his companions flagged, the bishop continued on alone, so terrified that he did not even bother to collect a boot that slipped off his foot. And this is how he reached his city and shut himself within the walls of Rheims.

The Death of Leudast (VI 32)

A few months earlier, Leudast [see V 47–49] had come to Tours with a royal directive enabling him to get back his wife and to take up residence in the city. He also brought me a letter signed by bishops recommending that he be readmitted to communion. But since I saw no letter from Queen Fredegund, on whose account in particular he had been excommunicated, I refused to admit him.

"When I receive the queen's authorization," I said, "at that time I will not delay admitting him."

In the meantime, I sent her a message, and she wrote back saying, "I was urged by many and had no choice but to let him go. I ask you not to extend peace to him or allow him to receive the holy bread from your hand until I consider more fully what should be done."

When I read the letter, I was afraid he would be killed. I sent for his father-in-law, informed him of the letter, and implored him to tell Leudast to be wary until the queen's animosity was assuaged. But the advice that I gave honestly in the sight of God was received by Leudast with suspicion, and since he was my enemy, he refused to heed any warning that came from me. And so was fulfilled the proverb that I once heard an old man say: "Always give good advice to friend and foe alike because the friend will take it and the foe reject it."

Having spurned this advice, Leudast went to the king, who was staying in the district of Melun with his army, and implored the troops to ask the king to grant him an audience. When all the troops interceded, the king gave him a hearing. Leudast threw himself at his feet and begged for pardon.

"Be careful for a little while yet," said the king, "until I see the queen and arrange how you are to return to her favor, for you still have much to answer for with regard to her."

But Leudast was reckless and foolish and put his confidence in having received an audience with the king. So on the Sunday, when the king returned to Paris, Leudast prostrated himself at the queen's feet in the holy cathedral and asked for pardon. Furious and cursing the sight of him, she drove him away.

"I have no sons left to prosecute wrongs done against me," she said, weeping. "I leave it to you, Lord Jesus, to defend my interests." And throwing herself at the king's feet, she added, "I am heartsick when I see my enemy and can do nothing to overpower him."

At that point Leudast was driven from the holy place, and mass was celebrated.

Then the king and queen came out of the holy church, and Leudast followed them along the street, having no idea what was about to happen to him. He went around the shops of the merchants, grubbing through their costly wares, testing the weight of silver articles, and examining various pieces.

"I'll buy this one and that one," he said, "for I still have lots of gold and silver."

Just as he said this, the queen's retainers arrived suddenly and tried to put him in chains. But he grabbed his sword and struck one of them. This angered them, and grasping their swords and shields, they rushed him. One of them got in a blow that took hair and skin off a great part of his head. When he fled across the bridge of the city, his foot slipped between the planks with which the bridge is made and he broke his leg. He was overpowered and placed in custody with his hands tied behind his back.

The king ordered physicians to attend him, so that, once cured of his wounds, he could be put to death with prolonged torture. He was taken to one of the villas of the fisc, but, when he had reached death's door because his wounds were putrefying, he was stretched out on his back by order of the queen; then a great bar of iron was placed under his neck and they struck his throat with another bar. And in this way a faithless life came to a just end.

Year IX of Childebert II, a. 584

Restoration of Marseilles and Envoys from Spain (VI 33)

In the ninth year of King Childebert, King Guntram himself restored half of Marseilles to his nephew.

Envoys of King Chilperic returned from Spain and reported that the province of Carpetania had been gravely devastated by locusts, so that no tree, vine, or grove, no crop or anything green, was left which the locusts had not ruined. They said the hostilities sprouting up between Leovigild and his son were getting worse....

Reports of plague in Narbonne and Albi. Northern lights.

Marriage Plans and the Death of Chilperic's Son Theuderic (VI 34)

A legation came again from Spain. It brought gifts and received King Chilperic's agreement to the marriage of his daughter to the son of King Leovigild, in keeping with the previous understanding. The agreement made, and all points considered, the envoy started back home.

A new sorrow now afflicted King Chilperic when he left Paris to go to the territory of Soissons. His son, whom the water of holy baptism had cleansed the year before [see VI 23, 27], came down with dysentery and breathed his last. This was the meaning of the bright light descending from the cloud that I recorded above [VI 33].

Utterly grief-stricken, they then returned to Paris and buried the boy. They sent for the envoy to return, hoping that the time the king had set for the wedding might be postponed.

"Look, I have to preserve a period of mourning in my household, so how can I celebrate the nuptials of my daughter?" said Chilperic.

At this point he wanted to send to Spain another daughter, whom he had by Audovera and had placed in the monastery of Poitiers. But she declined and the blessed Radegund especially opposed the project.

"It is unseemly," she said, "that a girl dedicated to Christ should return once again to the pleasures of the world."

Allegations about Theuderic's Death (VI 35)

Mummolus the prefect of this chapter is a different person from Duke Mummolus.

While these events were taking place, the queen was informed that the boy who had died had been taken away by evil arts and spells and that Mummolus the prefect, whom the queen had already hated for some time, was an accessory to this.

It turned out that Mummolus had been having a feast at home when someone from the king's court complained that a boy dear to him had been stricken with dysentery.

"I have an herb all ready," replied the prefect, "so that if a sufferer from dysentery, no matter how hopeless the case, drinks some of it, he will soon be cured."

This was reported to the queen, and she was consumed by even greater rage.

Meanwhile women were arrested in the city of Paris. The queen applied torture to them, forcing them with beatings to confess what they knew. They admitted that they were witches and testified that they had caused many to die, adding something I cannot believe for any reason.

"Queen, we offered your son in exchange for the life of Mummolus the prefect," they said.

Thereupon the queen, after inflicting more severe torments on the women, killed some off by torture, had some burned, and attached others to wheels, breaking their bones over the spokes. And so she retired with the king to the villa of Compiègne and there disclosed to him what she had heard about the prefect.

The king sent his men with orders to fetch the prefect. After interrogating him, they loaded him with chains and subjected him to torture. He was suspended from a beam with his hands tied behind his back and then asked what he knew of evil arts, but he confessed nothing of what we have recorded above. Yet he did admit to one thing: that he had often received ointments and potions from those women to secure for himself the favor of the king and queen.

When he was taken down from the punishment, he called the executioner to him.

"Tell my master the king," he said, "that I feel no ill effect of the tortures inflicted on me."

When the king was told, he said, "Is it not true that he is a sorcerer, if he has not been harmed by these tortures?"

Mummolus was then racked by rope and pulley and beaten with triple thongs until his torturers were tired out. Then they drove splinters under the nails of his fingers and toes. When matters had reached the point that the sword was poised to cut his head off, the queen obtained his life; but the disgrace that followed was not less than death. All his property was taken from him, and he was put on a cart and sent to his birthplace, the city of Bordeaux. On the way he had a stroke and barely managed to reach his destination. Not long after he breathed his last.

After this, the queen took all the boy's effects, both garments and costly articles, either in silk or whatever she could find in fleece, and burned them. They say there were four wagon-loads. She had the items of gold and silver melted down in a furnace and stored so that nothing might remain intact to recall the grief she felt for her son.

Innocentius and Brunhild, Sulpicius and Guntram (VI 37–39)

For Brunhild's claim to Cahors, see IX 11, 20. A likely date for the synod is 587. Sulpicius died in 591.

Lupentus, the abbot of the basilica of Saint Privatus the Martyr in Javols, answered the summons by Brunhild to appear before her. He was accused, so they say, by Innocentius, count of the aforesaid city, of uttering an irreverent remark about the queen. The matter was investigated, and since the abbot was cleared of being a party to anything that smacked of treason, he was dismissed.

But when he took to the road, he was again taken prisoner by the aforesaid count and led to the villa of Ponthion and subjected to many torments. Again he was allowed to go back home. When he pitched camp on the Aisne river, his enemy fell on him again and violently seized him. His head was cut off, placed in a sack weighed down with stones, and thrown in the river; as for the rest of his body, it was tied to a boulder and consigned to the deep. A few days later, it appeared to some herders, and so was dragged from the river and committed for burial. But while the funeral preparations for the body were underway and no one knew who on earth it was, since after all the decapitated head could not be found, unexpectedly an eagle appeared, raised the sack from the bottom of the river and deposited it on the bank. Those who were there were astonished and, taking the sack, carefully investigated its contents and found the severed head, which accordingly was buried with the rest of the body. They say now a light appears there sent from God; and if an invalid prays devoutly at this grave he will go away with his health restored.

Bishop Theodosius of Rodez, who had succeeded Dalmatius, died. In that church, the quarrels about the episopal office and the riots that ensued grew so extreme that it was almost stripped of its liturgical vessels and all its better possessions. Nevertheless the priest Transobadus was rejected and Innocentius, count of Javols, was elected to the episcopacy with the assistance of Brunhild.

When he had assumed office, Innocentius immediately began to harass Ursicinus, bishop of Cahors, claiming that Ursicinus was in possession of parishes that belonged to the church of Rodez. This long lasting dispute grew and so it came about after a few years that the metropolitan met with his suffragan bishops in the city of Clermont and issued a judgment that he should retain the parishes, which no one could recall the church of Rodez ever having possessed. And so it was carried out.

Remigius, bishop of Bourges, died. After his passing the greater part of the city was consumed in a fire, and whatever there had withstood the war [see VI 31] now perished. After this, Sulpicius was the choice for bishop of the city with the support of King Guntram.

When many offered gifts, the king is said to have to have responded to those seeking the episcopal office with the following words: "It is not the custom of our governance to sell the episcopacy at a price nor for you to purchase it with bribes, in case we are branded with the wicked infamy of profit and you are compared to Simon Magus. But you, Sulpicius, shall be be bishop, according to the foreknowledge of God."

And so he was brought into the clerical state and received the episcopal office of the aforementioned church.

He is a man extraordinarily noble and coming from the leading senators of Gaul, well polished in rhetorical composition, second to none in the arts of verse. The synod I mentioned above looking into the matter of the parishes of Cahors met at his urging.

An Envoy from Spain (VI 40)

An envoy, named Oppila, came from Spain, bringing many gifts to King Chilperic. Leovigild, king of Spain, was afraid that King Childebert might muster forces against him to avenge the wrong done to his sister, for when Leovigild had arrested and imprisoned his own son Hermenigild, who had married King Childebert's sister, Hermenigild's wife had been left with the Greeks. When the envoy arrived in Tours on Easter day [2 April] I asked him if he were of our religion....

A theological debate follows between Gregory and Oppila.

Chilperic Retreats to Cambrai. Birth of Chlothar II (VI 41)

When King Chilperic found out that his brother Guntram and his nephew Childebert had made peace [see VI 33] and were planning to take away from him the cities he had seized by force, he withdrew with all his treasure to Cambrai, taking with him everything he could easily move. He sent messengers to the dukes and counts of the cities telling them to repair the walls of their cities and to bring their property, wives, and children within the protection of the walls; if the need arose, they themselves were to offer stout resistance to prevent the enemy doing any harm to the cities.

"And if," he added, "you suffer any loss, you shall get more than was taken from you when we take revenge upon our enemies."

He said this not knowing that achieving victory lies in the hand of the Lord.

Thereafter he several times called up his army, but on each occasion ordered it to stay within his own territory.

At this time, a son was born to him, whom he ordered to be brought up in the villa of Vitry, "in case," he said, "the child suffers harm while being seen in public and dies."

Childebert Invades Italy (VI 42)

King Childebert, however, went to Italy. On news of this, the Lombards submitted to his authority out of fear that they would be slaughtered by his army; they gave him many gifts, promising loyalty and submission to his side. Having achieved all that he wished with them, the king returned to Gaul, and had an army mobilized, which he ordered sent to Spain, but he abandoned the plan.

Some years before, Childebert had received fifty thousand solidi from the emperor Maurice to get rid of the Lombards from Italy. Now the emperor, hearing of the peace just concluded with that people, asked for his money back. But Childebert, sure of his strength, would not even provide a response on the matter.

Death of King Miro (VI 43)

Gregory elsewhere (V 17, omitted here) mentions the miraculous springs of Osser.

Moreover in Galicia there occurred new developments that ought to be recounted from an earlier point.

When Hermenigild, in disfavor with his father as I said above [V 38; cf. VI 18, 29, 33, 40], was staying with his wife in a certain Spanish city and banking on the support of the emperor and Miro, king of Galicia [see V 41], he learned that his father was coming against him with an army. He hatched a plan to drive back or kill his father, little knowing, unhappy man, that divine judgment was threatening him for contemplating such acts against his father, even if he were a heretic. His plan was to select three hundred heavily armed men from his many thousands of troops, put them in the fortress of Osser, in the church of which the springs are made full by God: his father was to be overawed and debilitated by an initial charge of these men and then defeated more readily by a less capable, but much larger force.

His father learned of the stratagem and was thoroughly depressed at the prospect.

"Should I go with the whole army," he said, "it may be brutally rent by the javelins of the enemy if the men are bunched together in one force. And if I go with a few troops, I will not be able to overcome a force of picked fighting men. Nevertheless, I shall go with the whole force."

Reaching the place, he crushed the enemy and burned the fortress as has already been mentioned [cf. V 38].

Victory now achieved, he learned that King Miro was waiting with a hostile force. Surrounding him, Leovigild exacted oaths that he would be loyal to him in the future. And so after exchanging gifts, they both went back home. But Miro, not many days after his return, took to his bed and died. He had been affected by the poor water of Spain and its bad air.

On his death, his son Euric sought good relations with King Leovigild. He gave oaths as his father had done and received the kingdom of Galicia. But in this year, Euric's kinsman, who had betrothed his sister, came with an army. Audica seized Euric, made him a cleric and ordered the office of the diaconate or priesthood forced upon him. And Audica, after marrying the wife of his father-in-law, obtained the kingship of Galicia.

As for Leovigild, he seized Hermenigild, took him along to Toledo, and sentenced him to exile; however, he was unable to get Hermenigild's wife [Ingund] away from the Greeks.

The concluding chapters of Book VI are preceded in VI 44 by a survey of the year's portents and natural afflictions, including locusts, frosts, storms, and drought.

Departure of Rigunth, Daughter of Chilperic, to Spain (VI 45)

The Kalends of September came round and a great embassy of Goths visited King Chilperic [to convey Rigunth to Spain].

Chilperic himself had now returned to Paris and ordered many households to be taken from fiscal properties and placed on the wagons; many who wept and refused to go he ordered imprisoned, to make it easier to send them off with his daughter. They say that many in their anguish hanged themselves, dreading being separated from their relations. Son was taken from father, mother from daughter, and they departed with loud groans and curses. There was such lamentation in the city of Paris that it might be compared with the lamentation of Egypt. Many of the better born who were forced to go made wills and left their property to churches, requesting that, when the girl had entered Spain, the wills should be opened at once as if they were already buried.

Meanwhile envoys arrived in Paris from King Childebert, warning King Chilperic not to take anything from the cities he held belonging to the realm of Childebert's father Sigibert, not to endow his daughter with anything from the late king's treasury, and not to dare touch the dependents or horses or yokes of oxen or anything of that kind belonging to him. One of these legates, they say, was secretly killed, but it is not known by whom; suspicion, however, fell on the king.

King Chilperic promised that he would touch nothing from these cities. Summoning the more important Franks and others who were loyal to him, he celebrated his daughter's marriage. He handed her over to the envoys of the Goths and presented her with a great treasure. Her mother also brought forth a huge quantity of gold and silver and garments, so that when the king saw it he thought he was left with nothing. The queen noticed that he was disturbed and turned to address the Franks.

"Don't think, men, that I have anything here from the treasuries of previous kings," she said. "All that you see has been brought from my own property, for the most glorious king has given me much; and I have gathered a good deal by my own efforts, and have procured most of it from enterprises granted to me, from both revenues and taxes. You also have often enriched me with your gifts, from which come those things you now see before you. But there is nothing here from the public treasury."

And so the concerns of the king were falsely put to rest.

There was so much stuff that it took fifty wagons to carry the gold and silver and other ornaments. The Franks offered many gifts, some giving gold, some silver, many giving horses, and most garments; each as he was able gave a gift.

After tears and kisses, the girl said farewell and was going out the gate when an axle on the carriage broke.

"Evil hour [cf. Fr. *malheur*]," everyone said. Some took it as an omen.

She made her way from Paris and ordered the tents pitched at the eighth milestone from the city. Fifty men rose in the night, took a hundred of the best horses with the same number of golden bridles and two great serving bowls, slipped away, and went to King Childebert. Moreover, along the whole route, when any one could slip away, he took off, carrying whatever he could lay his hands on.

Abundant supplies were gathered largely from the cities along the route. The king ordered that nothing should be supplied from his own fisc but all from the contributions of the poor. And as the king was suspicious that his brother or nephew might prepare an ambush for the girl on the road, he directed that she travel surrounded by an army. Very distinguished officials were with her: Duke Bobo, Mummolen's son, with his wife as attendant to the bride; Domigisel and Ansovald; and the mayor of the palace, Waddo, who had once held the comital office of Saintes; the rest of the crowd numbered over four thousand. Other dukes and chamberlains who had traveled with her turned back at Poitiers, but those continuing the trip went on as best they could. Such spoils and plunder were taken on this journey as can scarcely be described. For they robbed the huts of the poor and ruined the vineyards by cutting off vine-stems with their grapes and carrying them away. Lifting cattle and whatever they could find, they left nothing along the road they traveled. The words that were spoken by Joel the prophet were fulfilled: "What the locust has left, the cankerworm has eaten; and what the cankerworm has left, the caterpillar has eaten; and what the caterpillar has left, the blight has eaten [cf. Joel 1:4]."

That is what happened at this time. What was left by frost the storm leveled, what was left by the storm the drought burned up, and what was left by the drought this host carried away.

The Death of King Chilperic (VI 46)

While they continued on their way with this plunder, Chilperic, the Nero and Herod of our time, went to his villa of Chelles about one hundred stades [11–12 miles] distant from Paris and there went hunting. One day, returning from the hunt after dusk, he was being helped down from his horse and had one hand on a retainer's shoulder, when a man came up and stabbed him with a knife under the armpit and with a second stroke pieced his stomach. As a flood of blood poured from the king's mouth and the open wound, his wicked life at once came to an end.

The text above shows the evil that he did. For he frequently laid waste and burned many districts; and he had no feeling of anguish in doing this but rather joy, like Nero before him, when he recited tragedies as the palace burned. He often punished men unjustly to get their wealth. In his time few clerics were promoted to episcopal office. He was a glutton and his god was his belly. He used to claim that no one was wiser than he. He wrote two books on the model of Sedulius, but their feeble little verses cannot stand on their feet at all, for in his ignorance he put short syllables for long, and long syllables for short. He wrote small pieces also, hymns and masses, which cannot reasonably be used. He hated the interests of the poor. He was constantly blaspheming the priests of the Lord, and when he was in private, he derided and ridiculed no

16.   Gregory reacts to Chilperic's poetry (VI 46).

one more than the bishops of churches. He called this one a lightweight, that one arrogant, another was a spendthrift, and this one a lecher. He would claim that this or that bishop was proud or haughty, because he hated nothing more than churches.

"Look! our fisc has been left poor," he often used to say, "and our wealth has been transfered to the churches. No one rules at all except the bishops; our office will perish and has been ceded to the bishops of the cities."

This being his view, he would constantly invalidate wills made in favor of churches, and he trampled under foot the dispositions of his own father, thinking that no one was left to preserve his wishes. As to lust and debauchery, nothing can be thought of that he did not realize in deed. He was always looking for new means to injure people; at this time, if he found any one guilty, he would order his eyes torn out. In the directions he sent to his judges on matters touching his interests, he would add, "if anyone disregards our orders, let his eyes be torn out as punishment."

He never loved anyone sincerely and was loved by no one, with the result that, when he breathed his last, all his followers abandoned him. Mallulf, bishop of Senlis, who had been sitting in his tent for three days, unable to see him, came when he heard of his death. He washed him and clothed him in better garments. After spending the night singing hymns, he took him by boat to Paris and buried him in the basilica of Saint Vincent.

Queen Fredegund was left in the cathedral church.

CHAPTER SIX
AFTERMATH OF CHILPERIC'S DEATH AND THE
REVOLT OF GUNDOVALD
FALL 584–SPRING 585
(BOOK VII)

> God bless the King—I mean the Faith's defender!
> God bless (no harm in blessing) the Pretender!
> But who pretender is or who is king—
> God bless us all! that's quite another thing.
>
> John Byrom, *To an Officer in the Army*

Book VII covers approximately half a year, from about November 584 through the spring of 585. Gundovald, whose activities dominate much of Book VII, first appears in VI 24, 26, s.a. 582.

Year IX of Childebert II, a. 584 (continued)

Orleans and Blois against Châteaudun and Chartres (VII 2)

After Chilperic died and found the death he had long been asking for [late October/early November 584], troops of Orleans joined those of Blois and attacked the people of Châteaudun, taking them off guard and defeating them. Houses, stores of grain and whatever they could not readily move, they put to the torch; they took herds and carried off anything they could lift. Upon their departure, the forces of Châteaudun with others from Chartres followed their trail and gave as good as they got, leaving nothing in their houses, outside their houses, or belonging to their houses. While they were still raging and inciting quarrels among themselves, and the people of Orleans were marshaling their forces to fight back, the counts intervened and established peace until there could be a hearing and judgment given, at which time the side that had unlawfully ignited the conflict could pay compensation according to the provisions of the law. And in this way the war was brought to an end.

Fredegund Takes Refuge. Treasure Taken to Childebert (VII 4)

Now that Fredegund was a widow, she came to Paris and took refuge in the cathedral along with the treasure she had deposited within the city walls. She was given support by Bishop Ragnemod. The remaining treasure had been left at Chelles and included the large gold salver that Chilperic had recently had made [see VI 4]; it was now removed by officials of the treasury, who at once went off to King Childebert, then staying in Meaux.

Guntram Takes Up Residence in Paris (VII 5)

His return to Chalon is not noted until VII 21.

Queen Fredegund took advice and sent envoys to King Guntram with this message: "Let my lord come and take the kingdom of his brother. I have a small infant, whom I wish to place in his arms; as for myself, I bow to his authority."

When Guntram learned of his brother's passing, he wept quite bitterly, but when his grief subsided, he mustered an army and marched to Paris. He had already been received within the walls when his nephew King Childebert arrived from another direction.

Guntram Tells Off Childebert's Envoys and Takes the Kingdom of Charibert (VII 6)

When the people of Paris refused to admit Childebert, he sent envoys to King Guntram with a message saying, "I know, most dutiful father, that it has not escaped your attention how up to the present time a hostile party has prevented both of us finding the justice that is our due. Therefore, I humbly beg you now to keep the agreements that were reached between us after my father's death [see V 17]."

At this point, King Guntram said to the envoys, "You wretches, ever false, you haven't a speck of truth in you and don't stick to your promises; look, you abandoned every pledge you made to me and wrote a new agreement with King Chilperic to drive me from my kingdom and divide my cities between you [see VI 3]. Here are your very agreements. Here are your signatures by which you confirmed your conniving. Now you have the nerve to ask me to receive my nephew Childebert, whom you tried to make my enemy by your depravity?"

"If you're so overcome with anger that you will not grant your nephew what you have promised," replied the envoys, "at least stop taking what is due to him from Charibert's kingdom."

"Here are the agreements made between us," said the king. "Whoever entered Paris without his brother's consent was to lose his portion, and Polioctus the martyr, along with Hilary and Martin the confessors, were to judge him and take retribution. After this my brother Sigibert entered; he died by the judgment of God and lost his portion [cf. IV 51]. So did Chilperic [cf. VI 5, 27].

Because of these violations, they lost their portions. For this reason, since my brothers have been taken away according to God's judgment and by the curses in the agreement, I will subject all Charibert's kingdom with its treasury to my rule by right of law, and I will not grant anything from it to anyone, except of my own free will. Be off with you, then, you everlasting liars and perjurers, and tell this to your king."

Guntram, Fredegund, and Chlothar II (VII 7)

They departed, but envoys came again to King Guntram with a message from Childebert demanding Queen Fredegund: "Give up that killer who strangled my aunt [cf. IV 28], killed my father [see IV 51] and uncle [cf. VI 46], and put my cousins to the sword [cf. V 18, 39]."

"We shall have a meeting," said Guntram, "and consider what ought to be done and decide all matters there."

For he was supporting Fredegund with his patronage, often inviting her to dinner and promising he would become her strongest advocate. One day, when they were dining at the table together, the queen tried to rise to take her leave but was halted by the king.

"Eat something more," he said.

"Please pardon me, my lord," she replied, "As is the way with women, I happen to be getting up because I am pregnant."

When he heard this, he was astonished, knowing that it was the fourth month since she had borne a son, but he permitted her to rise.

The leading figures of Chilperic's kingdom, such as Ansovald and others, gathered about Chilperic's son, who, as I have said, was four months old and whom they called Chlothar. In the cities that had formerly looked to Chilperic, they exacted oaths of loyalty to King Guntram and his nephew Chlothar.

Guntram, after proper judicial process, restored everything that King Chilperic's followers had wrongfully taken from various sources, and he himself conferred much upon churches. The wills of those who established churches as their heirs when they had died, which Chilperic had suppressed, he restored. He was gracious to many and gave much to the poor.

Guntram and the Parisians (VII 8)

But as he had no trust in the people among whom he had come, he surrounded himself with armed men and never went to church or to the other places he liked to visit without a strong guard. And so it happened one Sunday, when the deacon had called for silence among the congregation so that attention might be paid to the mass, that the king turned and addressed the crowd.

"Men and women present here," he said, "I charge you, please maintain your loyalty to me unbroken and do not kill me as you lately did my brothers. Allow me three years at least to raise my nephews, who have become my adopted sons. For it could happen—and may the eternal Deity not allow it—that if I die while they are infants, you will perish at the same time, for there will be no strong member of our line to protect you."

When he said this, all the people readily said a prayer to the Lord on behalf of the king.

News of Chilperic's Death Reaches Rigunth's Party (VII 9)

While these events were going on, Rigunth, King Chilperic's daughter, reached Toulouse with the treasures described above [VI 45]. And seeing she was now near Gothic territory, she began to make up excuses for delay. Moreover, her own people told her that she ought to remain there for a time, since they were exhausted from the journey, their clothing was shabby, their shoes torn, and the accoutrements for the horses and carriages were not yet assembled, having been transported on the wagons. All these preparations, they said, must be carefully made first, before setting out on the journey and being received in an elegant state by her betrothed; otherwise they might be laughed at by the Goths for appearing among them shabbily outfitted.

While they were delaying for these reasons, news of Chilperic's death reached the ears of Duke Desiderius. He gathered his best men, entered Toulouse, found the treasures, and took them from the queen's control. He put them in a certain house, affixed seals, and posted a guard of capable men. He allowed the queen a scanty living allowance until such time as he should return to the city.

Gundovald Raised to the Kingship. Rigunth at Toulouse (VII 10)

Desiderius hurried off to Mummolus, with whom he had entered into an alliance two years before. Mummolus was at this time staying in the town of Avignon with Gundovald, whom I have mentioned in an earlier book [VI 24, 26]. Gundovald now went in the company of the two dukes to the territory of Limoges and arrived at Brives-la-Gaillarde, where a holy man named Martin, a disciple, as they say, of our own Martin, lies buried. There, placed on a shield, Gundovald was raised up as king. But when they went around with him for the third time, it is said that he fell, so that he was only barely held up by the hands of those standing about him. Then he made a circuit of the neighboring cities.

Rigunth was staying in the basilica of the blessed Mary at Toulouse, where Ragnovald's wife, whom I mentioned previously, had taken refuge out of fear of Chilperic [VI 12]. Ragnovald now returned from Spain, where he had been sent on an embassy by King Guntram, and recovered his wife and property.

At this time the basilica of the above-named Martin at Brives was burned by a threatening enemy so that the altar as well as the columns, made of different kinds of marble, were split by the flames. Later this shrine was so well restored by Bishop Ferreolus that it seemed never to have suffered any damage. The inhabitants devoutly venerate and revere this holy Martin, for they have often proved his miraculous power.

Portents (VII 11)

It was the tenth month of the year [December] when these events took place. At this time fresh shoots with misshapen grapes appeared on the vinestocks, and blossoms were seen on the trees. A great beacon crossed the heavens illuminating the earth far and wide before day dawned. Rays also appeared in the sky. In the north a fiery column was seen for the space of two hours, hanging as it were from the heavens, and above it was a great star. There was an earthquake in Angers, and many other portents appeared, announcing, I believe, the death of Gundovald.

Guntram's Counts Take Cities of Sigibert. Tours and Poitiers Surrender (VII 12, 13)

Then King Guntram sent his counts to take the cities that the late Sigibert had received from the kingdom of his brother Charibert, with orders to exact an oath of loyalty and subject all to his authority.

The people of Tours and Poitiers wanted to go over to Childebert, Sigibert's son, but the forces of Bourges were mustered, made preparations to march against them, and began setting fires in the territory of Tours. At this time they burned down the church of Mareuil in Tours's territory, where relics of the holy Martin were preserved. But the power of the saint was present; for even in so fierce a fire, the altarcloths were not consumed by the flames; and not only these, but even herbs, gathered long ago and placed upon the altar, were not burned at all.

Seeing these fires, the people of Tours sent an embassy to say that it was better for them for the present to submit to King Guntram than for everything to be laid waste by fire and sword.

Immediately on the death of Chilperic, Duke Gararic had come to Limoges and received oaths in the name of Childebert. From there he went to Poitiers, where he was received and where he remained.

When he heard what the people of Tours were suffering, he sent an embassy charging us, if we wished to look after our interests, not to go over to Guntram's side, but rather to remember Sigibert, the late father of Childebert. We, however, sent back this advice to the bishop and citizens of Poitiers, that unless for the time being they submitted to Guntram, they would suffer as we did. We maintained that Guntram now stood in the place of a father over two sons, meaning Sigibert's and Chilperic's, whom he had adopted, and so held the leadership of the kingdom, as his father Chlothar had done before him.

They did not agree with this, and Gararic came out of the town intending to bring forward an army, leaving behind him Ebero, chamberlain of Childebert. Sichar, with the count of Orleans, Willachar, who at that time had received Tours, mustered an army against the people of Poitiers, figuring that forces from Tours and Bourges could lay the whole territory waste from two directions.

When they had approached the territory and had begun to burn houses, the people of Poitiers sent envoys with a message saying, "We ask you to hold off until Kings Guntram and Childebert hold the conference they have arranged. If it is agreed that King Guntram should receive these districts, we shall not resist; if not, we will recognize our lord, to whom we should render service to the full."

"None of this business is our concern, except fulfilling the commands of our prince," was the reply. "If you refuse, we shall finish what we started and lay everything waste."

Since the alternative was complete destruction by fire, pillage or captivity, the Poitevins drove Childebert's men from the city and swore oaths to King Guntram, though they did not keep them long.

Childebert's Envoys before Guntram Again (VII 14)

As the day of the meeting approached, King Childebert sent Bishop Egidius, Guntram Boso, Sigivald, and many others to see King Guntram.

"We give thanks to almighty God," said the bishop, on entering the king's presence; "He has restored you, most dutiful king, to your regions and kingdom after much trouble."

"Due thanks must be given to him who is King of kings and Lord of lords, who in his mercy thought it right to accomplish these things," said the king. "But no thanks are due to you, by whose deceiving counsel and perjuries districts of mine were burned last year [see VI 31]. You've never kept faith with any man; your deceit is spread everywhere; you profess yourself to be, not a priest, but an enemy of my kingdom."

At these words the bishop, though angered, was silent.

But one of the envoys spoke up, "Your nephew Childebert begs you to have the cities that his father held given back to him."

"I have already told you before," said the king in reply to this, "that our agreements confer them on me, and so I refuse to restore them."

Another of the envoys said, "Your nephew asks you to order the witch Fredegund, through whom many kings have been killed, to be turned over so vengeance can be taken for the death of his father, uncle, and cousins [cf. VII 7]."

"She cannot be given into his power," said King Guntram, "because she has a son who is king. Besides, I don't believe what you say against her is true."

Then Guntram Boso approached the king, intending to say something. Since it had been reported that Gundovald had been publicly raised up as king, the king broke in before he could speak.

"Enemy of my country and kingdom, you went a few years ago to the East with the purpose of bringing into my kingdom a certain Ballomer"—that is what the king used to call Gundovald. "You are a perpetual liar and never keep your promises."

"You are lord and king and sit on a royal throne," said Guntram Boso, "and no one dares answer the charges you make. But I declare that I am innocent of this charge. And if there is someone of my rank who pins this crime on me in secret, let him come forward openly and speak. Then, most righteous king, we can put the matter to the judgment of God so He can decide it, when he sees us fighting on the level field of single combat."

At this all were silent.

"This matter [of Gundovald]," added the king, "ought to make everyone eager to drive from our territories an adventurer whose father ran a mill; to tell the truth, his father sat at the loom and wove wool."

And although it is possible for one man to be trained in the two trades, still, one of the envoys answered the king with a rebuke.

"Thus, according to you," he said, "this man had two fathers at the same time, one a woolworker, the other a miller. To speak so poorly, king, hardly becomes you. For it is an unheard of thing that one man should have two fathers at the same time, except in a spiritual sense."

Many of them burst out laughing at this, and another envoy spoke up.

"We say farewell to you, king," he said. "Since you have refused to restore your nephew's cities, we know that the ax is still safe that was driven into the heads of your brothers. Soon it will be driven into your brain."

Thus they went off in anger.

As they left, the king, inflamed at their insults, ordered horseshit, rotten shavings, putrefying chaff and hay, and even the stinking muck of the city to be thrown on their heads. Covered with this filth, they went away, not without immeasurable offense and insult.

Fredegund Misbehaves in the Cathedral (VII 15)

While Queen Fredegund was residing in the cathedral at Paris, Leonard, a former *domesticus*, who had just then arrived from Toulouse, went to see her and began to tell her the instances of abuse and the insults inflicted on her daughter.

"As you commanded, I went with Queen Rigunth," he said, "and I saw her humiliation and how she was robbed of treasure and all her property [see VII 9]. I slipped away and have come to report to my mistress what happened."

On hearing this report, Fredegund became enraged and ordered him despoiled in the very church; she had him stripped of his garments and of the belt that he had as a gift from King Chilperic and ordered him out of her presence. Cooks and bakers, and whoever else she learned had returned from this journey, she left beaten, plundered, and maimed.

She tried to ruin Nectarius, brother of Bishop Baudegisel, by means of unspeakable charges before the king, claiming he had taken a great deal from the treasury of the dead king. In an effort to have him bound and thrown into a dark prison, she also used to say that he had taken hides and large quantities of wine from the storehouses. But the king's forbearance and help from Nectarius's brother Baudegisel prevented this from happening.

She did many foolish things and showed no fear of God in whose church she was seeking help. She had with her at the time a judge, Audo, who had been her accomplice in many misdeeds in the time of the king. For together with Mummolus the prefect, he subjected to public taxation many Franks who in the time of the elder King Childebert were freeborn. After the king's death Audo was despoiled by those he had taxed and stripped, so that he had nothing left except what he had on his person. They burned his house and would surely have taken his very life if he had not fled to the cathedral with the queen.

Bishop Praetextatus Returns from Exile (VII 16)

She received Bishop Praetextatus unwillingly. The citizens of Rouen had recalled the bishop from exile [see V 18] after the king's death and restored him to the city amid loud acclamation. After his return he came to Paris and presented himself to King Guntram, entreating him to make a thorough investigation of his case. The queen maintained that he should not be taken back, since he had been removed from his episcopal office at Rouen by the sentence of forty-five bishops. When the king was going to summon a council to deal with the matter, Ragnemod, bishop of Paris, gave an answer on behalf of all bishops.

"You should know," he said, "that the bishops sentenced him to do penance, but he was by no means removed from his episcopal office."

And so he was received by the king, welcomed to his table, and then returned to his own city.

King Guntram Hears of a Plot against His Life (VII 18)

When the king was staying in Paris, a certain poor man came to him.

"Listen, king, to what I have to say," he said. "You should know that Faraulf, chamberlain of your late brother, is seeking to kill you. I have heard his plan to attack you with a blade or run you through with a spear when you go to church for matins."

The king was astounded, and sent for Faraulf. He made a denial, but the king, fearful of what he had heard, surrounded himself with a strong guard. He never went to the holy places, or anywhere else, except in the company of armed men and guards. Not long afterwards Faraulf died.

Fredegund Sent into Retirement. Chlothar II Taken by the Magnates (VII 19)

A great outcry was raised against those who had been powerful officials under King Chilperic; they were of course accused of having taken villas and other possessions from other people's property. All that had been unjustly taken, the king now ordered restored, as I have previously pointed out [VII 7].

He also ordered Queen Fredegund to go off to the villa of Rueil in the territory of Rouen. All the better born of Chilperic's kingdom attended her and left her there with Bishop Melantius, who had been removed from the see of Rouen. They then went over to her son, promising her that they would bring him up with the very greatest care.

Attempt to Assassinate Brunhild (VII 20)

After Queen Fredegund had gone away to the villa of Rueil, she was very dejected because her power had now partly been taken from her. Considering herself better than Brunhild, she secretly sent a cleric of her household to deceive that queen and kill her. The plan was that he would insinuate himself into her household, obtain her trust, and stab her to death in secret. The cleric came and gained Queen Brunhild's favor by various deceptions.

"I am running from Queen Fredegund," he said, "and ask your help."

He tried to pretend to everyone that he was humble, valuable and obedient, and devoted to the queen. But it was not long before they realized that he had been sent under false pretenses. He was bound and beaten and, once he had

17.   At Reuil, Fredegund contemplates assassinating Brunhild (VII 20).

confessed the secret mission, was permitted to return to his patroness. When he disclosed to her what had happened and told how he could not carry out her orders, he was punished by having his hands and feet cut off.

Eberulf Condemned for Chilperic's Death and Seeks Asylum in Saint Martin's Basilica (VII 21, 22)

After these events, King Guntram, who had now returned to Chalon, was attempting to investigate his brother's death. Fredegund had put the blame on the chamberlain Eberulf. For she had asked him to stay with her after the king's death but could not get her way. As this was a cause of bad feeling, the queen said that the king had been killed by Eberulf and that he had taken a great deal from the treasury and, for this reason, had gone off to Tours; and so, if the king wished to avenge his brother's death, he should know that Eberulf was the leader in this affair.

At that point the king swore to all his magnates that he would destroy not only Eberulf himself but also his family to the ninth generation, so that by their deaths the wicked custom of killing kings might be done away with before more kings were killed.

When Eberulf found out about this, he headed for the basilica of Saint Martin, whose property he had often seized. At this time, given the opportunity of guarding him, troops of Orleans and Blois used to come in turn to keep watch, and at the end of each fifteen-day stint would return home with lots of plunder, leading draught animals, cattle, and whatever else they could take away.

The ones who led off the blessed Martin's draught animals started quarreling, however, and stabbed one another with their spears. Two, who were taking mules, went to a neighboring house and asked for a drink. When the householder said he did not have one, they raised their spears to strike him, but he drew his sword and ran them both through; they both fell down dead. Saint Martin's draught animals were returned. So many offenses were committed at the time by the men of Orleans as to beggar description.

While this was going on, Eberulf's property was being granted to various people; his gold and silver and other valuable items that he had with him were offered for sale. Property he had been granted was confiscated by the state. Herds of horses, swine, and draught animals were also taken. His townhouse, which he had taken from the possession of the church, and which was full of grain, wine, hides, and many other things, was completely cleaned out and nothing left but the bare walls. Because of this he was particularly suspicious of me, although I was running around on his behalf in good faith, and he kept promising that if he ever regained the king's favor he would take vengeance on me for what he had gone through. God, to whom the secrets of the heart are revealed, knows that I helped him honestly as much as I could. And although in former times he had often played me false in order to get Saint Martin's property, still there was a reason why I should forget that—I had taken his son from the holy font.

But I believe that the greatest stumbling block for the unlucky man was that he showed no respect for the holy bishop [Martin]. Continually engaged in excessive drinking and foolishness, Eberulf often resorted to violence within the very atrium, which was close to the saint's feet. When a priest refused to bring him wine, since he was plainly drunk already, Eberulf forced him onto a bench and beat him with his fists and with other blows, so that he looked as if he was about to die; and perhaps he would have died if the cupping-glasses of the physicians had not helped him.

Because of his fear of the king, he had his lodging in the reception chamber of the holy basilica. When the priest who kept the door keys had closed the other doors and gone, Eberulf's female servants, going in with the rest of his attendants by the door of the reception chamber, would look up at the paintings on the walls and grub through the ornaments on the holy tomb, which was quite outrageous in the eyes of the religious. When the priest learned of this he drove nails in the door and fitted bars on the inside. After dinner, when he was drunk, Eberulf noticed this; we were singing in the basilica at the service held at nightfall and he entered in a rage and began to attack me with abuse and curses, accusing me, among other charges, of wanting to keep him away from the holy bishop's tomb cover. I was amazed that such madness possessed the man and tried to calm him with soothing words. But as I could not overcome his rage by gentle words, I decided to keep silent. Finding that I would say nothing, he turned to the priest and spewed out abuse at him. For he assailed both him and me with shameless language and assorted insults. When we saw that he was driven by a demon, so to speak, we left the holy basilica and ended the disgraceful scene and the vigils. We were especially distressed that he had instigated this altercation before the very tomb, without respect for the holy bishop.

In these days I had a dream and told Eberulf about it in the holy basilica.

"I thought that I was celebrating mass in this holy basilica," I said. "When the altar with the offerings was already covered with a silk cloth, I suddenly caught sight of King Guntram entering. He shouted in a loud voice, 'Drag out the enemy of my family, tear this killer away from God's sacred altar.'

"When I heard him, I turned to you and said, 'Take hold of the altarcloth with which the holy gifts are covered, you poor wretch, so you won't be thrown out of here.'

"Although you laid hold of it, your hand was not closed, and you did not hold on tightly. But I stretched out my arms and pressed my chest against the king's chest, saying, 'Don't cast this man out of the holy basilica. You risk your life by being struck down by the power of the holy bishop. Don't kill yourself with your own weapon. If you do this, you will lose your life, for now and eternity.'

"When the king opposed me, you let go of the cloth and came behind me. I was very angry with you. And when you returned to the altar, you took hold of the cloth, but again let go. While you held it feebly and I stoutly resisted the king, I woke up terrified, not knowing what the dream meant.'"

When I had told him these things, he said, "The dream you saw is true, because it very much agrees with my own intention."

"And what was your intention?" I asked.

"I've decided," he said, " that, should the king order me dragged from this place, I will hold the altarcloth with one hand and a drawn sword with the other. I will first kill you and then lay out as many clerics as I can get at. After this, having to die would not be an injustice, as long as I first took vengeance on the clerics of this saint."

I was amazed to hear this and wondered how it was that the devil spoke through his mouth. He never had any fear of God. While he was at liberty his horses and herds were loosed among the crops and vines of the poor. But if those whose labor was being destroyed drove the animals away, they were at once beaten by his men. Even in his present straits, he used to recall repeatedly how he had unjustly taken the property of the blessed bishop. Finally, the year before, he had urged on a certain foolish citizen and had him bring a suit against stewards of church property. At this time, with no regard for the provisions of the law, he took away property once in the possession of the church under the pretense of purchasing it, giving the man a gold portion of his belt. He also acted depraved in many other matters to the end of his life, which I shall recount later.

Year X of Childebert II, a. 585

Poitiers Plundered (VII 24, 25)

In the tenth year of Childebert's reign, King Guntram mustered the peoples of his kingdom and put together a great army. The larger part it, with the forces of Orleans and Bourges, marched on Poitiers. The people there had broken the pledge they had made to the king [see VII 13]. The army sent a delegation before them to discover whether it would be received or not; but Maroveus, bishop of Poitiers, gave the envoys a harsh reception. The troops entered the territory of the city, pillaging, burning, and killing. On their way home with their plunder, they crossed the territory of Tours and, though oaths had already been given, did the same there, even setting the very churches on fire and carrying off everything they could seize. The invasion was repeated until the Poitevins at last were forced to recognize the king. When the army was drawing nearer the city, and the Poitevins realized that the greater part of their territory had already been ravaged, only then did they send messengers declaring their loyalty to King Guntram.

As soon as the troops were admitted within the walls of the town, they rushed upon the bishop, accusing him of disloyalty. But he, seeing himself hard pressed by them, broke up one of the gold chalices used in the service of the altar, had it made into tokens, and so ransomed the people and himself.

The troops eagerly surrounded Marileif, who had been considered the chief physician in King Chilperic's household. He had already been well plundered by Duke Gararic, but he was stripped bare by them a second time, so that he had no property left. They took away his horses, gold, and silver, as well as the more valuable items he had, and reduced him to a dependent of the church. For his father had been obligated to service in the mills of the church, and his brothers and cousins and other relatives were attached to the royal kitchens and bakehouse.

Gundovald in the South (VII 26–28)

Gregory mentions a Sigulf in IV 47, but tells us nothing about the earlier revolt of the Sigulf mentioned here.

Gundovald wanted to come to Poitiers, but was afraid, for he had heard that an army had been mustered against him. In cities that had belonged to King Sigibert, he received oaths sworn in the name of King Childebert; in the others, which had belonged to Guntram or Chilperic, the oath to remain loyal was taken in his own name. After this he went to Angoulême. When he had received oaths there and rewarded the leading citizens, he proceeded to Périgueux. The bishop at the time [Charterius], suffered severely at his hands for not having welcomed him with due honor.

From there he moved on to Toulouse. He sent a message telling Magnulf, bishop of the city, to receive him. But the bishop was mindful of wrongs he once had to endure from Sigulf, who had tried to raise himself to the kingship. He addressed his fellow citizens.

"We know that Guntram and his nephew Childebert are kings," said the bishop, "but as to this man, we don't know where he comes from. Therefore make preparations, and if Duke Desiderius tries to bring this disaster upon us, let him be destroyed in the same way as Sigulf, and let him be an example to all that no outsider should dare to profane the kingship of the Franks."

Though the citizens had no intention of giving in and were preparing to fight, Gundovald arrived with a large army; when they saw that they could not withstand it, they received him into the town.

Later, when seated with Gundovald at the table in the church manse, the bishop said to him, "You claim to be the son of King Chlothar, but we don't know whether that is true or not. And as to your carrying through on your enterprise, to our thinking that is unbelievable."

"I am the son of King Chlothar," said Gundovald, "and I am now about to take possession of part of the kingdom; I shall go quickly to Paris and there establish the capital of the kingdom."

"Is it true then," asked the bishop, "that no one from the line of Frankish kings is left, if you can do what you say?"

Mummolus, hearing the dispute, raised his hand and slapped the bishop around, saying to him, "Isn't it shameful for such a base idiot to answer a great king in this way?"

In fact, when Desiderius found out from the bishop about his comments, he too became enraged and grabbed him. They both hit the bishop with their spears, punched him with their fists, and kicked him. They then bound him with a rope and condemned him to exile and took all his property from him, both personal and that belonging to the church.

Waddo, former mayor of the palace to Queen Rigunth, joined Gundovald's party, but the others who had left Paris with him [see VI 45] slipped away and fled.

Later, the army [see VII 24–25], which had now been moved out of Poitiers, advanced in pursuit of Gundovald. Many people from Tours accompanied it in hope of profit, but the forces of Poitiers fell upon them; some of them were killed, and the greater part returned home despoiled. The troops from Tours who had earlier joined the army now also left. And so the host moved forward to the river Dordogne and waited for news of Gundovald. As I said above, he had been joined by Duke Desiderius and Bladast, as well as by Waddo, mayor of the palace to Queen Rigunth. His chief commanders were Bishop Sagittarius and Mummolus. Sagittarius had already been promised the see of Toulouse.

Death of Eberulf (VII 29)

While these events were taking place, King Guntram entrusted a certain Claudius with a mission.

"If you go and drive Eberulf from the basilica [see VII 22]," said the king, "and put him to the sword or bind him in chains, I will enrich you with great gifts. But above all, I warn you, do no injury to the holy basilica."

Claudius, a foolish and greedy fellow, quickly ran off to Paris, for his wife was a native of Meaux. He began to wonder if he should see Queen Fredegund.

"If I see her," he thought, "I may be able get a reward from her, for I know that she is the enemy of the man against whom I am sent."

He did go to see her and was well rewarded right away. Much was promised him, provided he could get Eberulf out the basilica and kill him, or trap him and bind him in chains, or just cut him down in the atrium itself.

Returning now to Châteaudun, he called upon the count to furnish him with three hundred men to guard the gates of Tours, but actually intending on his arrival there to overpower Eberulf with their assistance. While the count was mustering the men, Claudius himself went to Tours. En route he began to pay attention to auspices, as barbarians have a habit of doing, and to find them unfavorable. At the same time, he made many inquiries whether the power of the holy Martin had shown itself of late against oath-breakers and, especially, whether vengeance had been taken immediately on anyone doing wrong to those who placed their hope in the saint.

Disregarding the men who, as I said, were to have come to help him, he went in person to the basilica. There he at once joined up with the hapless Eberulf, gave him his oath, and swore by everything sacred, by the power of the holy bishop [Saint Martin] there present, that no one who could present his case before the king was more loyal to his interests than himself.

For the wretched man Claudius had said to himself, "Unless I can deceive him by false oaths, I shall not have the better of him."

Indeed, when Eberulf heard him make such promises upon oath within the basilica and in the porticoes and other venerated parts of the atrium, the scoundrel believed the perjurer.

The next day, while I was staying at a villa some thirty miles from the city, Eberulf was invited to a dinner at the holy basilica with Claudius and some other citizens. Claudius would have struck him down with his sword on the spot, if only Eberulf's retainers had been standing further away. But Eberulf in his vanity noticed nothing. When the meal was over, he and Claudius strolled together through the atrium of the manse of the basilica, promising each other loyalty and friendship by exchanging oaths.

While talking in this way, Claudius said to Eberulf, "It would please me to drain a cup at your quarters, if the wine were mixed with spices, or if your lordship could get drink with more kick to it."

Eberulf was delighted with the suggestion and answered that he had wine. "You shall find at my lodging everything you want," he said, "if only my lord will see fit to enter the hovel I am staying in."

He sent his servants, one after the other, to get stronger wines, those of Latium and of Gaza. As soon as Claudius saw that the servants had gone and left their master alone, he lifted up his hand towards the basilica.

"Most blessed Martin," he said, "help me to see my wife and relations soon." For the unhappy man was now at the critical juncture: he was planning to kill Eberulf in the atrium and was fearful of the power of the holy bishop.

At that point one of Claudius's servants who was very strong seized Eberulf from behind, clasped him between his powerful arms, and bent his chest back to receive a fatal blow. Claudius drew his sword from his belt and went for him. But Eberulf, held tight though he was, pulled a dagger from his belt and got ready to strike. As Claudius raised his arm high and thrust his blade into Eberulf's breast, Eberulf quickly drove his dagger under his adversary's armpit, withdrew it, and with a second stroke cut off Claudius's thumb. Then the servants of Claudius gathered round with their swords and wounded Eberulf in several places. He slipped out of their hands, and as he drew his sword and tried to get away, though already near death, they inflicted a deep wound on his head. He fell down dead with his brains spilled out. He did not deserve to be saved by him to whom he never knew how to make an appeal out of faith.

Claudius, filled with terror, made for the abbot's cell, seeking protection from one whose patron he had not had enough sense to respect.

"A great crime has been committed," he said to the abbot, who was in the cell. "Without your help, we'll be destroyed."

As he was saying this, in rushed the servants of Eberulf with swords and spears. Finding the door barred, they broke the glass panes of the cell and threw their spears through the windows in the wall, piercing Claudius, who was already half dead. His followers hid behind doors and under beds. Two of the clergy grabbed the abbot and barely managed to get him out through the swarm of drawn swords alive. The doors were now open, and the crowd of armed men entered. Even some of the registered recipients of alms, along with other poor folk, angered at the crime, tried to pull off the roof of the cell. Moreover, those possessed and various indigents came with stones and clubs to avenge the outrage to the basilica, distressed that it should be the scene of the kind of deeds never done there before. What need is there to say more? The fugitives were dragged from their hiding-places and cruelly cut down; the floor of the cell was stained with gore. Once they were killed, their bodies were then dragged outside and left naked on the cold ground. Their killers took the spoils and slipped away the following night.

God's vengeance was immediate on those who had defiled the blessed atrium with human blood. But the offense of that man cannot be reckoned slight whom the holy bishop [Saint Martin] permitted to endure such things.

The king was very angry at what happened, but when he learned the reason, he calmed down. The property of the hapless Eberulf, movable and real, which he had inherited from his ancestors, the king distributed among his loyal followers. The dead man's wife was left in the holy basilica thoroughly despoiled. The bodies of Claudius and the others were taken away by their next of kin to their own part of the country and buried there.

Gundovald at Bordeaux (VII 30, 31)

Two envoys, in fact clerics, were sent by Gundovald to his friends. One of the envoys, the abbot of Cahors, hid the message he received under the wax in the hollowed out boards of writing tablets. He was arrested by King Guntram's men and, when the message was discovered, brought before the king. He was severely beaten and shoved into prison.

Gundovald was in Bordeaux at this time and highly esteemed by Bishop Bertram. Gundovald was looking for whatever might help his cause, and someone told him that a certain king in the east had taken the thumb of Saint Sergius the martyr and attached it to his own right arm. Whenever the need arose to drive away his enemies, the king would rely on it for help; when he raised his right arm, the enemy host would immediately run away, as though overcome by the power of the martyr. Hearing this, Gundovald began to make careful inquiries whether there might be someone in Bordeaux who had managed to get relics of Sergius the martyr. Bishop Bertram suggested Eufronius, a merchant against whom he bore a grudge. Bertram, craving the man's property, had once had him tonsured against his will, but Eufronius in disdain moved to another city and returned when his hair had grown again.

And so the bishop said, "There is a Syrian here called Eufronius. He has made his house a church and placed relics of this saint in it, and he has observed them work numerous wonders, helped by the power of the martyr. Once when the city of Bordeaux was being consumed by a great fire, his house, though surrounded by flames, was not harmed at all."

At these words, Mummolus at once rushed off to the Syrian's house, accompanied by Bishop Bertram. They stood round the man, and Mummolus ordered him to show the sacred relics. He refused.

But thinking that this was a trap being laid for him out of malice, he added, "Do not trouble an old man or do wrong to the saint, but take a hundred gold pieces from me and go away."

When Mummolus still insisted on seeing the relics, Eufronius offered two hundred pieces, but he could not get Mummolus to leave without the relics being seen. Mummolus then ordered a ladder to be put up against the wall—for the relics were hidden in a casket in the top of the wall facing the altar—and told his deacon to climb it. The deacon went up the ladder step by step and grasped the casket, but was shaken with such trembling that no one thought he would get back down to the ground alive. But, as I have said, having gotten hold of the casket, which was hanging from the wall, he brought it down. The casket was searched and Mummolus found a bone from the saint's finger, which he had no fear of striking with a knife. He struck it first on the upper side, then on the lower. When after many blows he managed to break it with some difficulty, it split into three parts, which vanished in different directions. I think it was unacceptable to the martyr to be treated in this way. Eufronius now started to sob, and all prostrated themselves in prayer, begging God to see fit to reveal what had been removed from mortal sight. After the prayer, the fragments were found. Mummolus took one of them and departed, but not, I believe, with the favor of the martyr, as was made plain in subsequent events.

While Gundovald's party were at Bordeaux, orders were given for the priest Faustian to be consecrated bishop of Dax. The bishop of the city had recently died and Nicetius, count of Dax and brother of Rusticus, bishop of Aire, had obtained a directive from Chilperic for him to be appointed bishop of the town, once he had been tonsured. Gundovald, intent on annulling Chilperic's decrees, convoked the bishops and ordered them to give Faustian the blessing. Bishop Bertram was metropolitan but, wary of the future, charged Palladius of Saintes with giving the blessing. It is true that Bertram's eyes were troubling him at the time. Orestes, bishop of Bazas, was also present at the consecration; he afterwards denied this before the king.

Gundovald's Envoys before Kings Guntram and Childebert (VII 32, 33)

After these events, Gundovald again sent two envoys to the king. They carried consecrated rods according to the custom of the Franks, believing naturally that their persons would not be touched by anyone and that they could return safely with an answer after relating the nature of their mission. But they carelessly revealed to many people what they were after before they entered the king's presence. Word of this reached the king in no time at all, and so they ended up being brought before him in chains.

In no position to deny who sent them, whom they were to see, and what they were to accomplish, they said, "Gundovald, who recently has come from the East, says that he is the son of your father King Chlothar. He sends us to receive the portion of the kingdom that is his due. If you do not restore it, know that he will come into these regions with an army. For all the best fighting men in the part of Gaul beyond the Dordogne have joined him. These are his words: 'When we have joined on the level field of single combat, God will then judge whether I am Chlothar's son or not.'"

The king was furious at this and ordered them racked by rope and pulley and severely beaten, so that they might give clearer proof that they were telling the truth, or, if they were still concealing any information in the secrets of their hearts, the force of the torture might wrench it from them against their will. As the torments were increased, they said that the king's niece, King Chilperic's daughter, had been exiled with Magnulf, bishop of Toulouse; that all her treasure had been taken by Gundovald; and that all King Childebert's well-born followers wanted Gundovald to be king. In particular, they said that Guntram Boso, when he had gone to Constantinople a few years before, had invited Gundovald to come to Gaul [cf. VI 24, VII 14].

After the envoys had been beaten and cast into prison, the king had his nephew Childebert sent for, thinking that both of them together should hear these men. The two kings met and questioned the prisoners, who repeated in the presence of the two kings what previously King Guntram had heard alone. They also remained firm in their statements that the matter, as I have said above, was known to all the chief men in Childebert's kingdom. For this reason some of King Childebert's leading officials at the time who were suspected of being parties to the affair were afraid to attend the present conference.

After this, King Guntram placed a spear in the hand of King Childebert.

"This is a sign," said Guntram, "that I have transfered all my kingdom to you. By virtue of this, go now and subject to the dominion of your authority all my cities as if they were your own. Because of my sins, none of my line remains, except only you who are my brother's son. Succeed as my heir to the entire kingdom, for I have disinherited the others."

Leaving the gathering and taking the boy aside, he spoke with him privately at this time, first earnestly charging him not to reveal the secrets of their conversation to anyone. He now indicated to him the men whose advice he should consider and those whom he should remove from his counsel; those whom he might trust, and those whom he should avoid; those whom he should distinguish by rewards, and those whom he should remove from their offices: all the while enjoining him on no account to trust or have about him Egidius, the bishop [of Rheims], who had always been his enemy and had often sworn falsely both to him and his father.

When they assembled for a banquet, King Guntram then exhorted the entire army.

"Look, men, how my son Childebert has now become a big man," he said. "Look and beware that you do not take him for a child. Now is the time to abandon your disloyalty and the high-handed practices you engage in; for he is a king whom you should now serve."

When the Guntram had spoken these words and others like them, the kings feasted and celebrated together for three days. They separated in peace, exchanging many valuable gifts. It was on this occasion that King Guntram restored to his nephew all that had belonged to Sigibert his father, calling upon him not to visit his mother in case this gave her an opportunity to write to Gundovald or to receive letters from him in return.

Siege of Convenae and the Death of Gundovald (VII 34–38)

The commander of Guntram's forces in this campaign was Duke Leudigisl. The Burgundian Boso, who accompanies Count Ollo, is a different person from the Austrasian Guntram Boso.

Gundovald, on hearing that an army was approaching, crossed the Garonne with Bishop Sagittarius, Dukes Mummolus and Bladast, and Waddo and made for Convenae [Saint-Bertrand-de-Comminges]. Duke Desiderius had abandoned him.

The city is on the top of an isolated height. At its foot a spring gushes forth and is surrounded by a most secure tower; the townspeople can come down to the spring through a tunnel and secretly draw water.

Gundovald entered the city at the beginning of Lent [11 February 585] and addressed the citizens.

"You know I have been chosen king with the support of everyone in Childebert's kingdom," he said, "and have with me a not inconsiderable force. But since my brother King Guntram sends a vast army against me, you must place food and supplies of all kinds within the potection of the walls so that you shall not perish from want until divine mercy provides us with help."

They fell for this, bringing whatever they had into the city and got ready to put up a fight.

At the time Guntram sent a letter to Gundovald in the name of Queen Brunhild saying that, were he to leave the army and order it to return to quarters, he himself could withdraw a fair distance away and take up winter quarters in the city of Bordeaux. Guntram wrote this as a trick so he could better learn what Gundovald was up to.

Gundovald remained at Convenae and addressed the population of the city.

"Look, the army approaches," he said. "Go forth and oppose it."

They went out and Gundovald's people, seizing the gates and closing them, shut out the citizenry and their bishop and took control of everything they could find in the city. Such a large quantity of grain and wine was found that if they had stood their ground like men the food supply would not have run out for many a year.

At the time, the generals of King Guntram heard that Gundovald had taken up a position on the bank across the Garonne with a huge force and was holding on to the treasure that he had taken from Rigunth. Thereupon, they launched an attack, swimming their horses across the Garonne, and losing a fair number of troops in the river. The rest advanced from the bank in search of Gundovald and found camels and exhausted horses he had abandoned along the roads; the camels were heavily laden with gold and silver. Then hearing that the enemy was in the city of Convenae, the better fighting men, as they had now crossed the river, left the wagons and various types of baggage with the petty soldiery and set out in pursuit.

In the course of their march they reached the basilica of Saint Vincent in the territory of the city of Agen, where the martyr himself is said to have completed his combat in the name of Christ. They found it crammed with various valuables belonging to the local inhabitants who hoped that the basilica of such a martyr would not be defiled. Its doors had been fastidiously barred. The approaching army, being unable to open them wasted no time setting them on fire. When the doors were burnt, the troops took all the belongings and goods they could find along with the sacred utensils. But God's vengeance destroyed many men. The hands of a good number were burned by divine intervention, giving off smoke as if from a fire. Some, seized by a demon and driven into a fury, shouted out the name of the martyr. Most, aroused by the commotion, wounded themselves with their own javelins. The remainder of the mob advanced not without considerable trepidation.

Why say more? They convened at Convenae—the name of the city as I said—and the entire force laid out its camp in the fields surrounding the city, and there, having pitched their tents, they waited. They plundered the whole region in the vicinity, but a few, greedier than the rest, wandered quite far from the army and were wiped out by the locals.

Many climbed the hill and used to speak with Gundovald, hurling abuse at him.

"Are you that painter-fellow who used to decorate the walls and vaults of oratories in the time of Chlothar?" they asked. "Are you the one the people of Gaul often used to call Ballomer? Are you the one who had often been tonsured by the Frankish kings for the same presumption you now display and sent into exile? Who brought you, poor fellow, to these parts? Tell us. Who gave you the audacity to dare set foot in the kingdom of our lords? If someone really did summon you, speak up clearly. Death is staring you in the face—that pit of destruction which you have long been seeking and into which you will be hurled headlong. Tell us the names of your adherents, reveal who is encouraging you."

Listening to this, and standing not very far away above the gateway, Gundovald would say, "Everyone knows that my father Chlothar hated me; that my hair was cut short, first by him and later by my brothers, is apparent to all. This was why I joined Narses, prefect of Italy, in which country I took a wife and had two sons. On her death, I went to Constantinople, taking my sons with me. I was kindly received by the emperors and lived there down to the present time. Some years ago, Guntram Boso came to Constantinople, and with some concern I carefully inquired how matters stood with my brothers. I learned that our family was seriously diminished and that of our line there remained only Kings Guntram and Childebert, a brother and a brother's son. The sons of King Chilperic had died with him, and only one small child was left. My brother Guntram had no sons; my nephew Childebert was not at all strong.

"At this time, Guntram Boso, after carefully laying out these circumstances, gave me an invitation. 'Come,' he said, 'for all the leaders of King Childebert's realm invite you, and no one has dared mutter a word against you. We all know you are Chlothar's son, and there is no one left in Gaul to rule that kingdom if you do not come.'

"I gave him many gifts, and he assured me under oath in twelve holy places that I might enter this kingdom in safety. I came to Marseilles, where the bishop graciously welcomed me; he possessed letters written by important officials of my nephew's kingdom. Then I went to Avignon, according to the wishes of Mummolus the patrician. Guntram Boso, ignoring his oath and promises, took my treasures and appropriated them as his own [cf. VI 24].

"Can't you see now, I am a king just like my brother Guntram. But if your hearts are filled with too great a hatred, take me to your king, and if he recognizes me as his brother, he can do what he wants with me. If you will not do this, at least let me return to the place from where I first set out. I will go away and do no harm to anyone. If you want to know the truth of what I say, ask Radegund [widow of Chlothar I] at Poitiers and Ingitrude [mother of Bishop Bertram and kinswoman of King Guntram] at Tours, for they will confirm that what I say is right."

While he made this speech, many of the besiegers accompanied his words with abuse and derision.

The fifteenth day of the seige dawned. Leudegisel was making ready new devices for the destruction of the city, namely wheeled vehicles with rams, covered with wickerwork and planks, under which the army could quickly bring down the walls. But when they came near, they were so overwhelmed by stones that all who approached the wall were destroyed. While some defenders threw vats of burning pitch and fat on them others hurled containers of stones. When night put an end to the fighting, the attacking force returned to camp.

With Gundovald was Chariulf, a very rich and powerful citizen; the city was filled with his warehouses and depositories. The defenders were fed mainly from his stores.

Bladast, realizing what was going on, feared that they would be handed over to death in the event of Leudegisel gaining the victory. So he set fire to the church manse, and when the besieged ran to put out the flames, he slipped away and fled.

The day dawned. The army rose ready to fight again. The troops made fascines from branches to fill the deep ditch that was located on the east side. But this device could cause no damage. As for Bishop Sagittarius he constantly ranged round the ramparts throwing stones on the enemy from the wall with his own hand.

Finally, when those who were attacking the city saw they could achieve nothing, they sent messengers to Mummolus in secret.

"Recognize your lord and now at last stop your disobedience," they said. "What madness possesses you to subject yourself to some nobody? Your wife and children have been captured, you may suppose your sons have now been killed. Where are you going to go, what can you expect but destruction?"

Mummolus said in reply to their message, "Our reign comes to an end, I see, and power fails. One thing is left—were I to know my life was secure, I could save you a lot of bother."

The messengers went away and Bishop Sagittarius along with Mummolus, Chariulf, and Waddo went to the church and there gave one another oaths, swearing that in the event they could get assurance of a promise to spare their lives, they would abandon their loyalty to Gundovald and hand him over to his enemies.

The messengers came back with a promise their lives would be spared.

Mummolus, however, said, "I want just one condition: I for my part shall hand over this man into your power, and recognizing my lord the king, I shall hasten to present myself to him."

At that point the messengers promised that if he did this, they would extend to him their good offices, and if they could not get him the king's pardon, they would place him in a church so he would not be punished by the loss of his life. They gave this promise under oath and left.

Mummolus, Bishop Sagittarius, and Waddo went to Gundovald.

"You stand before us and know the value of the oaths of loyalty we have given to you," they said. "Now take sound advice. Go down from this city and be taken before your brother, as you have often demanded. We have talked with the besiegers and they say the king doesn't want to lose your assistance because too few of your generation survive."

"I have come to Gaul at your invitation," said Gundovald, in tears—for he saw through their trick. "Some of my treasure, which contains a tremendous weight of gold and silver and other valuables, is stored in Avignon; some was stolen by Guntram Boso. Next to God, I have placed all my hope in you. I have entrusted you with my plans. I always hoped to rule with your help. Now may

God take up this matter with you, should you have been telling me any lies; let Him judge my cause."

"We are not telling you anything that is untrue," said Mummolus in reply. "Look, the finest fighting men are standing by the gate awaiting your arrival. Now take off that golden baldric of mine you are wearing so you won't seem ostentatious when you advance; strap on your own sword and return mine."

"Your words don't fool me," he said. "You're taking from me those things of yours I wore up to now as marks of affection."

Mummolus gave an oath that nothing would be done to harm him.

Then they exited the gate, and Gundovald was received by Ollo, count of Bourges, and Boso. Mummolus and his followers went back into the town, and firmly barred the gate. Gundovald saw that he had been given over into the hands of his enemies and raised his hands and eyes to heaven.

"Eternal judge and true avenger of the innocent," he said, "God, from whom all justice comes, to whom falsehood is repugnant, in whom no trick or ingenious malice resides, to You I commend my cause, begging you to swiftly take vengeance on those who have handed me over to my enemies with no fault on my part."

Then he made the sign of the Lord's cross upon himself and began to leave in the company of Ollo and Boso. There is a steep depression all around the city, and when they had gone a distance from the gate, Gundovald was given a shove by Ollo and fell.

"Look you people!" shouted Ollo. "Here is your Ballomer, who says he is the brother and son of a king."

Ollo stabbed him with his lance, trying to run him through, but it did no harm, being deflected by the rings of Gundovald's mail coat. Finally, when Gundovald tried to get up the hill, Boso threw a stone and struck him on the head. Gundovald collapsed and died.

Then the whole throng of the soldiery came and drove their lances into his body. They tied ropes around his feet and dragged him through the camp of the army, tearing out his hair and beard, and left him unburied on the spot where he was killed.

That following night the leaders secretly removed all the treasure they could find in the city along with the plate of the cathedral church. In the morning, the city gates were opened and the army was sent in. The rank-and-file locked within the city were all put to the sword; priests of the Lord and their assistants were also slaughtered at the very altars of the churches. After everyone had been killed so that no one was left who could piss against the wall [cf. 1 Kings 25:34; 3 Kings 16:11], the whole town, including churches and other buildings, was set on fire, leaving nothing there but bare earth.

The End of Mummolus and Sagittarius. Rigunth Comes Home (VII 39, 40, 43).

Leudegisel, on his return to camp with Mummolus, Sagittarius, Chariulf, and Waddo, sent messengers secretly to King Guntram to ask what he wanted done with these men. The king ordered the death penalty for them. By that time Waddo and Chariulf had left their children as hostages and departed. The message regarding their death sentence came, and when Mummolus learned of it, he armed himself and went to Leudegisel's hut.

"Why do you come as if you are on the run?" said Leudegisel when he saw him come in.

"Nothing of the promise that was made is to be kept, I see," said Mummolus; "for I know that I'm close to death."

"I shall go outside and settle everything," said Leudegisel.

He went out and immediately ordered the house surrounded so that Mummolus could be killed. Mummolus held out against his attackers for quite some time, but when he came to the door and stepped out two men struck him with lances on each side. This is how he fell and died.

Bishop Sagittarius saw what was happening, and while he was overwhelmed with fear, someone standing by said to him, "Look with your own eyes, bishop, at what is being done. Cover your head so you won't be recognized, make for the woods and hide for a while. When their anger passes you can get away."

He took the advice, but while he was trying to get away with his head covered, a certain man drew his sword and cut off his head, hood and all.

Then everyone returned home, taking much plunder and committing homicides along the way.

In these days Fredegund sent Chuppa to Toulouse to bring out her daughter from there any way he could. Many said he was really sent to entice Gundovald with many promises, in the event he could be found alive, and to bring him to Fredegund. But when Chuppa had been unable to do this, he took Rigunth and brought her back from Toulouse, not without great humiliation and abuse.

Then Duke Leudegisel came to the king with all the treasure [taken from Gundovald's party]. The king later dispersed it to the poor and the churches. He arrested the wife of Mummolus and tried to determine what had become of the treasures that she and her husband had amassed. When she learned that her husband had been killed and that all their arrogance was humbled in the dust, she revealed all, and said that there was still much gold and silver in Avignon that had not come to the king's attention. Immediately the king sent men to get it with a servant whom Mummolus had greatly trusted and into whose charge it had been committed. Off they went and took possession of everything that had been left in that city. It is said that there were two hundred and fifty talents of silver and more than thirty of gold. All this, so they say, Mummolus took from an ancient treasure that had been· found. The king divided the amount with his nephew Childebert and gave away his own share for the most part to the poor. Guntram left the widow with nothing more than what she had inherited from her relations.

An Attempt to Fine Saint Martin (VII 42)

After this an edict was issued by the judges that anyone who was negligent in appearing for this campaign should be fined. The count of Bourges even sent his servants to despoil men in this category who were part of the House of Saint Martin located in the territory of Bourges. But the administrator of the House tried to protest strongly.

"These are the men of Saint Martin," he said. "You may inflict no harm on them. It is not customary for them to come out in instances like this."

"Your Martin is nothing to us," the leader of the count's servants said. "You are always vainly talking about him in these cases. Both you and those men have to pay the price when you ignore the authority of the king."

Saying that, he entered the atrium of the establishment. He was immediately struck with a malady, collapsed, and began to grow ill.

"I ask you to make the sign of the cross over me," he said in a sorrowful voice, turning to the administrator. "Call on the name of blessed Martin. Now I know his great power. On entering the atrium of the house I saw an old man holding in his hand a tree that soon covered the whole atrium with its spreading branches. One of these branches touched me, which caused me to fall down in confusion."

Nodding to his men, he asked to be removed from the atrium. When he was out, he began to invoke the name of blessed Martin conscientiously. In so doing, he started to get better and was cured.

Desiderius, Waddo, and Chariulf (VII 43)

Desiderius looked to secure his person and his possessions behind the walls of fortresses. Waddo, former mayor of the palace to Rigunth, went over to Queen Brunhild; she welcomed him, gave him gifts, and sent him away with her favor. Chariulf headed for the basilica of the holy Martin.

CHAPTER SEVEN

AFTERMATH OF GUNDOVALD'S REVOLT

SUMMER 585–587

(BOOK VIII)

> Kings are no trouble. It's the queens.
>
> Luigi Donzelli, Claridge's Hotel

Most of this book (VIII 1–38) concerns the summer and fall of 585.

Guntram at Orleans, July 585 (VIII 1–7)

Then King Guntram, in the twenty-fourth year of his reign, went from Chalon to the city of Nevers. He had been invited to go to Paris to receive from the holy font of regeneration Chilperic's son, whom they were already calling Chlothar. From Nevers he came to the city of Orleans and at that time made his presence conspicuous to its citizens. For on receiving invitations he went to their homes and ate the meals that were offered to him. They gave him many gifts, and he bestowed many gifts on them with lavish generosity.

The day on which he came to the city of Orleans was the [summer] festival of the blessed Martin, namely the fourth before the Nones of the fifth month [July 4]. A huge throng of people came to meet him, singing his praises and carrying standards and banners. The acclamations reverberated with the diverse sounds of different languages, here that of the Syrians, there that of the Latins, and even that of the Jews.

"Long live the king," was the shout. "May his reign over the peoples last countless years."

The Jews, who could be seen taking part in the cheering, were calling out, "May all peoples honor you, kneel before you, and be subject to you."

And so it happened, when mass had been said and the king was seated at dinner, that he commented, "Woe to the Jewish people, wicked, without faith, always living a life on the edge of deceit. Today they shouted out their flattering praises that all the peoples should honor me as master for this reason: their synagogue was torn down some time ago by Christians; they want me to order it rebuilt at public expense. By God's command, that I shall never do."

King famous for wonderful wisdom! He understood the craft of the heretics so well that he later flatly turned down their petition.

When the meal was already half over, the king said to the bishops present,

"I hope I may obtain your blessing tomorrow in my house; let me receive the spiritual benefit of your coming, so I may be saved from sin when you pour forth upon my low self your words of blessing."

When he said this, all thanked him, and as dinner was finished, we rose.

In the morning, while the king was visiting the holy places to pray, he came to my quarters. These were in the basilica of Saint Avitus the abbot, whom I mention in my book of wonders [GC 97]. I was delighted to get up to meet him, I admit, and after saying a prayer, asked if he would see fit to accept the blessed bread of Saint Martin in my lodging. He did not refuse, and graciously came in, drank a cup, invited me to the dinner, and went away in good humor.

At that time Bertram, bishop of Bordeaux, as well as Palladius of Saintes, were very much in the king's disfavor for having received Gundovald, an event I referred to above [VII 31]. Bishop Palladius, in addition, had particularly offended the king by too often deceiving him. They had been examined a short time before by the other bishops and the magnates as to why they had welcomed Gundovald, and why they had consecrated Faustian bishop of Dax because of an inconsequential order of Gundovald. But Bishop Palladius removed the blame for the consecration from his metropolitan Bertram and shouldered it himself.

"My metropolitan's eyes were shut with severe pain," he said, "and I was robbed, treated with contempt, and dragged to the place against my will. I could do nothing else than obey one who claimed he had received complete authority over Gaul."

When this was told to the king, he was greatly irritated. Only with difficulty could he be prevailed upon to invite to the dinner those bishops whom he had not previously received.

And so when Bertram came in the king asked, "Who is this one?" The king had not seen the bishop for a long time.

"This is Bertram, bishop of Bordeaux," they said.

"We thank you for keeping faith with your own kindred," said the king. "You ought to have known, beloved father, that you are my kinsman on my mother's side, and you should not have brought a plague from abroad on your own kind."

When Bertram had listened to this and more, the king turned to Palladius.

"Not many thanks are due you either, Bishop Palladius," he said. "You perjured yourself to me three times—an evil thing to say of a bishop—sending me messages full of deceit. With one letter you were giving me excuses and with another you were calling in my brother.

"God will judge my cause, since I have always tried to treat you as fathers of the church, and you have always been treacherous to me."

He said to the bishops Nicasius [of Angoulême] and Antidius [of Agen], "Most holy fathers, tell me what you have done for the good of your region or the benefit of our kingdom."

They made no reply, and the king, after washing his hands and receiving a blessing from the bishops, sat down at the table with a smiling face and a cheerful appearance, as if he had said nothing about the poor way he had been treated.

The dinner had reached the half-way point when the king had me tell my deacon to sing; he had sung the responsorium at the mass the day before. As the deacon sang, the king again told me to instruct each of the bishops present to appoint a cleric from his church and to have him sing before the king. And so I made the request at the king's command, and each sang the responsorium before the king to the best of his ability.

When the courses were being served, the king said, "All the silver you see belonged to that perjurer Mummolus, but now, by the help of God's grace, I own it all. I have already had fifteen of his dishes, like the larger one you see there, broken up, and I have kept only this one and one other of a hundred and seventy pounds. Why keep more for daily use? It's too bad I have no other son but Childebert. He has enough treasure from what his father left him and from what I have had sent to him from this wretched man's property found at Avignon. The rest will have to be distributed to the needs of the poor and the churches.

"There is only one thing that I ask of you, priests of the Lord. Pray for the Lord's mercy for my son Childebert. He is a man of sense and ability. It would be hard over a period of many years to find someone as circumspect and energetic as he is. If God sees fit to grant him to Gaul, perhaps there will be hope that by him our lineage, which has almost been consumed, can rise again. This will happen through His mercy, I don't doubt, because this is what the birth of the boy indicated. It was the holy day of Easter and my brother Sigibert was standing in the church while the deacon was reading from the holy book of the Gospels. A messenger came to the king, and the words of the Gospel and the message were uttered at the same time: 'A son has been born to you.' So it happened that at both announcements everyone cried out at the same time, 'Glory to almighty God.' Besides, the boy was baptized on the holy day of Pentecost and raised up as king on the holy day of the Lord's birth no less. And so if your prayers attend him, God willing, he will be able to rule."

When the king had spoken, all said a prayer to the Lord in His mercy to keep both kings safe.

"It's true," the king added, "that his mother Brunhild threatens to kill me, but I have no fear on that account. For the Lord who snatched me from the hands of my enemies will save me from her plots."

At this time he had much to say against Bishop Theodore [of Marseilles, see VI 11, 24], declaring that, if the bishop came to the synod, he would exile him again.

"I know it was for the sake of these people [that is, Gundovald's party]," said the king, "that he had my brother Chilperic killed. And I shouldn't be considered a man, if I cannot avenge his death this year."

"And who killed Chilperic," I responded, "if not his own evil actions and your prayers? He laid many traps against you contrary to justice; these brought about his death. I would say this was the meaning of a dream I had: in it, when I saw him he had previously been tonsured and was being ordained bishop; then I saw him placed on a plain chair covered only in black and being carried along with shining lamps and tapers going before him."

On my recounting this, the king said, "I also had a dream that foretold his death. He was brought into my presence loaded with chains by three bishops. One of them was Tetricus [of Langres], the second was Agricola [of Chalon], and the third was Nicetius of Lyons.

"Two of them were saying: 'Release him, we entreat you, beat him and let him go.'

"Bishop Tetricus on the contrary was bitterly answering them, saying, 'May it not be so; he shall be burned in a fire for his crimes.'

"And while they argued long and hard, as if quarreling, I saw at a distance a cauldron placed on a fire and boiling furiously. Then as I wept, they seized unhappy Chilperic, broke his limbs, and threw him into the cauldron. Without delay he dissolved and melted in the steam from the water so that no trace of him at all remained."

When the king told this story, we were amazed, and the banquet being over, we rose from the table.

The next day [6 July 585] the king went hunting. On his return I brought before him Garachar, count of Bordeaux, and Bladast, for as I said earlier [cf. VII 37], they had taken refuge in the basilica of Saint Martin because they had been allied with Gundovald.

Since I had previously interceded on their behalf to no avail, I now spoke as follows, "Powerful king, listen to my words. You see, I have been sent to you on an embassy by my master. What shall I tell him who sent me, if you will not give me any answer?"

In astonishment, he said, "And who is the master who sent you?"

"The blessed Martin sent me," I said, smiling.

Then he ordered the men brought forward. When they entered his presence, he reproached them for their many acts of disloyalty and perjury, repeatedly calling them tricky foxes, but he restored them to his favor, giving back what he had taken from them.

When Sunday came [8 July 585], the king went to church to attend the celebration of mass. The brethren and fellow-bishops who were there gave Bishop Palladius the honor of conducting it. When he began to read the Prophetia [Luke 1:68–79], the king inquired who he was. When they told him that it was Bishop Palladius who had begun the service, the king immediately became angry.

"Will someone who has always been disloyal and faithless to me now preach to me sacred words," he said. "I will leave this church immediately. I will not listen to my enemy preaching."

With these words, he started to leave the church.

The bishops, now upset by the humiliation of their brother, said to the king, "We saw him attend the banquet you gave and we saw you receive a blessing at his hand. Why does the king reject him now? Had we known he was hateful to you, we would certainly have turned to another to conduct the service. Now, with your permission, let him continue the service he began; if you bring any charge against him tomorrow, the strictures of the holy canons can settle it."

By this time Bishop Palladius had retired to the sacristy greatly humiliated. The king now had him recalled and he finished the service he had begun.

Now when Palladius and Bertram were again summoned to the king's table, they became angry and accused each other of numerous adulteries and fornications [cf. V 47, 49], and not a few perjuries as well. Many laughed at these matters, but a number who had a quicker understanding found it deplorable that the weeds of the devil should so flourish among the bishops of the Lord. And so Palladius and Bertram left the king's presence but pledged bonds and sureties to ensure their appearance at the synod on the tenth day before the Kalends of the ninth month [23 October].

Guntram at Paris (VIII 9)

After these events, the king came to Paris and addressed everyone.

"My brother Chilperic on his death is said to have left a son," he said. "The child's governors, at the mother's request, asked me to receive him from the holy font at the feast of the Lord's Nativity [Christmas 584]; but they never came. They next requested that the infant be baptized at the holy Paschal feast [March 25]; but the child was not brought at this time either. A third time they asked if he might be presented on Saint John's day [June 24], but they didn't come then. And so now they have had me move from my home in the hot season. I've come, and look! the boy is hidden away and not shown to me. This leads me to think that nothing is as promised and to believe that one of our *leudes* is the real father of the boy; if the child had been of our line, surely they would have brought him to me. You had better know, then, that I shall not acknowledge him unless I get clear proof of his birth."

When Queen Fredegund heard this, she assembled the principal leaders of her kingdom, three bishops and three hundred of the best men, and they all took oaths that the boy's father was Chilperic. In this way suspicion was removed from the mind of the king.

The Bodies of Chilperic's Sons (VIII 10)

Guntram went on mourning the death of Merovech and Clovis after their deaths and had no idea where their bodies had been left. Then a man came to the king with information.

"Were I to suffer no untoward consequences," he said, "I should point out to you where Clovis's body was put."

The king swore that nothing bad would be done to him; in fact, he would be well rewarded.

"The events that occurred themselves shall prove that I speak the truth," said the man. "When Clovis was killed he was buried under the eaves of a certain oratory. The queen feared that if he were ever found he might be given a proper burial, so she ordered him tossed to the bottom of the Marne river. Then I found him in the weir which I had constructed on my own for catching fish. But although I had no knowledge of who it was, I recognized it was Clovis from the long hair. I took him on my shoulders and carried him to the bank and there I buried him under the earth. So you see, his body is saved. Do what you wish."

At this news, the king pretended to go hunting, uncovered the grave and found the body whole and unmarred. Only the part of the hair lying underneath was gone. The rest survived with its long locks intact. It was apparent this was the body that the king had been so eagerly looking for.

Then the bishop of the city [of Paris] was summoned, and along with the clergy and people, the king bore the body amidst countless candles to its burial site in the basilica of Saint Vincent [later Saint-Germain-des-Prés], in a state of mourning for his dead nephew no less than when he saw his own sons buried.

After this, he sent Pappolus, bishop of Chartres, to get the body of Merovech [see V 18] and buried him next to the grave of Clovis.

18. "The king bore the body amidst countless candles to its burial site in the basilica of Saint Vincent (VIII 10)." Guntram buries Clovis.

Accusation of an Assassination Plot against Guntram (VIII 11)

A certain doorkeeper said the following about another doorkeeper.

"Lord king, this fellow was bribed so you could be killed."

The doorkeeper he mentioned was seized, beaten, and subjected to severe torture, but revealed nothing about the matters for which he was arrested. Many people said this was done as a result of a jealous plot, because the accused doorkeeper was greatly beloved by the king. Ansovald [see V 3, 47; VI 18; VII 7] fell under suspicion—what kind I know not—and departed the court without saying goodbye.

As for the king, he returned to Cahors and had Boantus, who had always been disloyal to him, put to death. Surrounded in his house, he was taken by the king's men and killed. His property was taken over by the administration of the fisc.

Theodore of Marseilles Arrested Again (VIII 12)

Then, since King Guntram was trying with all his might to bring charges against Bishop Theodore [of Marseilles] again [see VI 11, 24; VIII 5], and since Marseilles had already been restored to King Childebert's rule, Ratharius was sent there as duke by King Childebert to carry out an investigation. Setting aside the duty with which the king had charged him, however, Ratharius surrounded the bishop, demanded sureties, and sent him to King Guntram. The intention was to present him for condemnation before the bishops who were to meet in the synod at Mâcon.

Divine vengeance was taken on Ratharius's household, including his son, who died of disease. No harm came to the bishop at the hands of Guntram. Gregory tells a story confirming Theodore's sanctity.

Gregory, the Envoy Felix, and King Childebert (VIII 13)

Then King Guntram sent envoys to his nephew Childebert, who was staying at the time at the fortress of Coblenz [*castrum Confluentis*]—the place was so called because the Moselle and the Rhine rivers flow together at this spot and are joined. There had been an agreement for an assembly of bishops of both kingdoms to be held at Troyes in Champagne, but the meeting was not suitable to the bishops of Childebert's kingdom. Arrival of the embassy from Guntram was announced, and credentials delivered by the envoy Felix.

"King," said Felix, "your uncle earnestly asks who it is that causes you to withdraw from this promise, so that the bishops of your kingdom refuse to come to the council that you and he had decided upon. Perhaps there are wrongdoers who cause the root of discord to sprout between you two?"

I responded at this point, because the king was silent, "It's hardly surprising if tares are sown among subjects; but none that take root can readily be found between these two kings. As everyone knows, King Childebert has no other father than his uncle, and his uncle wants no other son than Childebert, to go by what we heard him say this year [see VII 33]. Heaven forbid that the root of discord should grow, since they both should love and protect each other."

Childebert called Felix to a private conference and at that time made a request.

"I beg my lord and father to do no harm to Bishop Theodore. There shall be an immediate quarrel between us if he does so. Hampered by dissension, we whose duty it is to maintain the bonds of love and remain at peace shall be disunited."

The envoy received an answer on some other matters and departed.

Childebert and the Empire. Appointment of Counts (VIII 18)

King Childbert, who was being dunned by imperial messengers for the gold he had been given the previous year [cf. VI 42], sent an army into Italy. Word was that his sister Ingund had now been transfered to Constantinople. But his generals quarreled with one another and came home empty handed from their profitless expedition.

Wintrio, duke [of Champagne] was driven out by the population of his district and lost his ducal authority. He would have lost his life too if flight had not provided him with an escape. Afterward, when the population was pacified, he got back his ducal post.

Eulalius was sent to Clermont to be count, and Nicetius removed from office. Nicetius asked for a ducal office from the king, giving innumerable presents for it. And so he was appointed duke for the cities of Clermont, Rodez, and Uzès. He was quite young but smart and brought peace to Auvergne and the other regions under his command....

King Guntram wanted to control the kingdom of his nephew Chlothar, Chilperic's son, and so he appointed Theodulf as count of Angers. When he was brought into the city, he was ignominiously driven out by the citizenry, the leading part being taken by Domigisel [cf. VI 18]. He went back to the king and again received a letter of appointment. He was brought in by Duke Sigiulf and took control of the countship of the city.

Gundovald beat out Werpin for the countship of the city of Meaux. He entered the city and began hearing cases. Then, as he went on tour of the country districts in his official capacity, he was killed by Werpin in a certain villa. Gundovald's kinsmen gathered and attacked Werpin, shutting him up in a chamber of his house and killing him. And thus, through sudden death, both lost the countship.

The Synod at Mâcon, October 585 (VIII 20)

The day of the assembly came round, and by command of King Guntram the bishops gathered in the city of Mâcon. Faustian, who had been consecrated bishop of Dax at the command of Gundovald [see VII 31], was removed from office on condition that Bertram, Orestes, and Palladius, who had given him the blessing, would support him in turn, furnishing him with a hundred pieces of gold a year. Nicetius, a former layman, who had earlier obtained a directive from King Chilperic, now took over the episcopal office in Dax. Ursicinus, bishop of Cahors, was excommunicated because he openly confessed to having received Gundovald. This was the sentence passed on him: that he do penance for three years, not cut his hair or beard, and abstain from meat and wine; he must never presume to celebrate Mass, ordain clergy, bless churches and the holy chrism, or offer blessed bread. The administration of the business of the church was to be conducted entirely under his direction in the usual manner.

At this council there was a certain bishop who was saying that women could not be included in the term 'man' [homo], but he accepted the reasoning of his brethren, and said no more...

Praetextatus, bishop of Rouen, read out before the bishops, prayers he had written while in exile. Some bishops were pleased with them, and others found fault since he had not at all stuck to literary form. The style, however, in places was fit for the church and decent.

A great brawl then broke out between the servants of Bishop Priscus [of Lyons] and Duke Leudegisel. But Bishop Priscus paid over a lot of money to restablish the peace.

In those days also, King Guntram fell gravely ill, so that some believed he could not recover. I believe this was an act of God's providence. For the king was thinking about driving a number of bishops into exile.

And so Bishop Theodore returned to his city and was welcomed with cheers and the applause of all the people.

Childebert's Assembly, October 585. Guntram Boso Defaults (VIII 21)

While this synod was being held, King Childebert met with his men at his villa of Beslingen, which lies in the midst of the forest of the Ardennes. There

Queen Brunhild lodged a complaint before all the leading men on behalf of Ingund her daughter, who was still detained in Africa [see VI 40, VIII 18], but she received little sympathy.

A case against Guntram Boso was brought forward. A few days before, a female relative of his wife died without children and was buried in a basilica at Metz with fine jewelry and a great deal of gold. It so happened that a few days later the festival of the blessed Remigius took place. This is celebrated at the beginning of the eighth month [October]. Many inhabitants accompanied the bishop out of the city, and especially the chief personages and the duke. Servants of Guntram Boso then came to the basilica where this woman was buried. Going inside, they closed the doors behind them and, opening the tomb, removed all the jewelry they could find on the body. The monks serving the basilica heard them and came to the doors, but Guntram's men would not let them in. For this reason, the monks sent messages to the bishop and the duke. Meanwhile the servants had taken the stuff, mounted their horses, and were trying to get away. But fearing that they might be arrested on the road and subjected to various penalties, they returned to the basilica. They laid the stolen jewels on the altar but did not dare go outside.

"Guntram Boso sent us," they cried out.

When Childebert and his leading officials held their assembly at the villa I mentioned, proceedings were taken against Guntram Boso on this matter. But he gave no reply and quietly fled. All the property that he had held in the Auvergne as a grant from the fisc was later taken from him. In the haste of his departure, he also left behind many things which he had unjustly taken from a number of people.

Important Deaths. Brunhild Asserts Control over her Son (VIII 22)

On Bertram and Palladius, see VII 31, VIII 2, 7, 20. On the document called a consensus, see Appendix, Episcopal Appointments IV 11, 15.

Laban, bishop of Eauze, died in this year. Desiderius, a former layman, succeeded him. The king had promised under oath never to appoint a bishop from the laity, but 'is there anything to which the sacred thirst for gold will not compel human hearts' [cf. Jerome, *Vita Pauli* c. 4; Virgil, *Aeneid* 3.56].

Bertram [bishop of Bordeaux] came down with a fever when he returned from the synod. He summoned Waldo the deacon, whose name at baptism was also Bertram, assigned the bishop's post to him and entrusted him with executing all the terms of his will and his charitable bequests. When Waldo left, the bishop died. Waldo came back and then hurried off to the king, bearing gifts and a consensus of the citizens, but got nothing. The king issued a directive requiring Gundegisil, called Dodo, count of Saintes, to be ordained bishop. And so it was done.

And since many of the clerics of Saintes, following Bishop Bertram's wishes, had written some hostile things to humiliate Bishop Palladius, they were seized by the bishop after Bertram's death, severely beaten, and despoiled.

At this time, Wandelen, governor of King Childebert, died [see VI 1], but no one was appointed in his place because the queen-mother wanted to have charge of her son herself. Whatever Wandelen had received from the fisc was now returned to the fisc's administration....

A New Duke for Tours (VIII 26)

Ennodius [see V 24] was made duke for Tours and Poitiers.

Berulf [see V 49; VI 12, 31], who had previously been responsible for these cities, was under suspicion regarding the treasures of King Sigibert which he, and his associate Arnegisil, had secretly removed. While he was angling for the ducal office in these cities, he was tricked by Duke Rauching who bound him and his accomplice. Without delay Rauching sent retainers to strip Berulf's house of everything. Much that was found was personal property, but some belonged to the aforesaid treasure. It was all sent to King Childebert. When the point was reached in these proceedings when the sword was about to descend on their necks, their lives were saved by the intervention of bishops. But they got nothing back of the property that was seized from them.

Desiderius Forgiven (VIII 27)

Duke Desiderius [see VII 27–28, 34, 43] came to see King Guntram along with certain bishops, the abbot Aredius, and Antestius. The king had no inclination to receive him but was overcome by the entreaties of the bishops and received him back into favor. Eulalius [see VIII 18] was there at the time intending to bring a suit on account of his wife, who had left him and taken up with Desiderius; but he was reduced to silence by laughter and humiliation. Desiderius was rewarded by the king and went home with the king's favor.

Death of Ingund and Hermenigild. A Botched Attempt to Conquer Septimania. Fredegund Sends Assassins (VIII 28–30)

Ingund, who, as I have written above [VIII 21], had been left by her husband with the imperial army, died and was buried in Africa while being conducted to the emperor with her little son. Leovigild put to death his own son, her husband, Hermenigild.

King Guntram was distressed at these events and decided to send an army into Spain; it was first supposed to conquer Septimania, which is still considered a part of Gaul, and then go on from there....

During the mobilization of forces, a letter was discovered, purportedly between Leovigild and Fredegund, referring to a plot against Childebert and Brunhild, and implicating Bladast's mother-in-law.

Although this plot was told to King Guntram and brought to the attention of his nephew Childebert, Fredegund still had two iron blades made ready which she also had deeply grooved and smeared with poison. If a mortal stroke failed to destroy vital organs, the effect of the poison could quickly bring on death. She gave the blades to two clerics with the following instructions.

"Take these swords," she said, "and go as quickly as possible to King Childebert pretending you are beggars. Throw yourselves at his feet as if asking for alms and stab him on both sides, so that at last Brunhild, who gets her presumption from him, shall be brought down with his death and set beneath me. But if he is so well guarded by retainers that you cannot approach, then kill Brunhild, my enemy. This shall be the reward for your action: if you die in this enterprise, I shall confer on your relations benefits, and enriching them with gifts, make them pre-eminent in my kingdom. Meanwhile banish every fear and be not concerned about death. You know that this touches all people. Strengthen your hearts like men and reflect that fighting men constantly fall in battle, and as a result their families, made noble and surpassing all with infinite riches, are superior to everyone."

When the woman had spoken, the clerics began to shake, thinking it a difficult matter to carry out this order. Seeing them waver, she drugged them with a potion and instructed them on their mission. Immediately their courage increased and they promised to fulfill all her commands. Nonetheless she ordered them to carry a small container filled with the drug.

"On the morning of the day you carry out my orders," she said, "drink this potion before the task is begun. You will then acquire the resolution you need to carry out your mission."

With these instructions, she sent them away.

They reached the city of Soissons, but were taken by Duke Rauching. They were interrogated, and revealing everything, were kept bound in prison.

A few days later, Fredegund, now sure her commands had been carried out, sent a retainer to pick up rumours or find someone who could tell him that Childebert had now been killed. The retainer left her and came to Soissons. Hearing that the clerics had been imprisoned, he approached the entrance, but in trying to speak with the warders he was arrested and taken into custody.

Then the whole lot of them were sent to King Childebert. Under interrogation, they revealed the truth, confessing that they had been sent by Fredegund to kill the king.

"We got our orders from the queen and were to pretend to be beggars. When we had cast ourselves at your feet seeking alms, we were to try to stab you with those swords. And if the sword stroke failed to pentrate deeply enough, the poison smeared on the blade would bring on death."

When they had spoken, they were subjected to various tortures. Their hands, ears, and noses, were cut off, and they were put to death in diverse ways.

Then King Guntram gave orders for the army to be sent against Spain.

"Earlier the province of Septimania was subject to our control," he said. "It borders on Gaul, and it is unbecoming that the territories of those appalling Goths should reach all the way to Gaul."

The whole army of Guntram's kingdom being mustered, he sent it to Septimania. The peoples dwelling beyond the Saône, Rhône, and Seine joined the Burgundians, seriously despoiling the banks of the Saône and Rhône of produce and herds. They were guilty in their own territory of homicide, arson, and rapine, stripping bare the churches, killing clerics, priests and others, even in front of altars consecrated to God. In this fashion they advanced to Nîmes. The forces of Bourges, Saintes, Périgueux, and Angoulême, and other cities that at the time were under Guntram's authority, committed similar acts all the way to Carcassonne.

The campaigns of the two armies (including the forces of Childebert's duke Nicetius of Auvergne) were complete and humiliating disasters.

On their return, King Guntram was thoroughly heartsick. The leaders of the army took refuge in the basilica of the holy martyr Symphorian [in Autun]. When the king attended services for the saint's feast-day, they were brought before him on condition that a hearing would later be held. Four days later he assembled the bishops and well-born laity and began to investigate the commanders.

"How are we to gain victory in these times," he said, "if we don't preserve the practices of our fathers? They built churches, placing all their hope in God; they honored the martyrs, and respected priests; and so they gained victories, and with God's help subdued hostile peoples with sword and shield. As for us, not only do we not fear God, but we plunder his holy places, kill his servants, and even lay waste and scatter in contempt the very relics of the saints. We cannot win victory when such deeds are done. So our hands are weak, our sword grows soft, our shield no longer defends and protects us as once it did. If therefore this is my fault, let God put the blame on me. But if it is you who scorn the king's orders and fail to carry out my commands, it is time that the ax was buried in your heads. It will be a lesson to the whole army if one of its leaders is executed. Now is the time to determine what is to be done. If anyone is prepared to follow justice, now is the time to do it. If anyone holds it in contempt, let the vengeance of the community hang over his head. It is better that a few obstinate people be destroyed than that the anger of God should be visited upon the whole innocent country."

To this speech, the leaders of the army replied, "It is no easy matter, most excellent king, to describe your generous goodness. You fear God, love the churches, reverence bishops, take pity on the poor, and provide for the needy. But although everything your glorious self utters is judged to be right and true, what can we do when the forces are sunk in vice and love to do harm to their fellow man? No one fears the king, no one respects duke or count; and if a commander thinks this isn't right and tries to correct it in order to further the length of your life, immediately there is mutiny in the ranks and a riot ensues. They all become savagely hostile to their superior to such an extent that he believes that to shut up is the way to escape with his life."

"The man who acts according to law shall live," replied Guntram; "but if anyone rejects the law and our orders, let him henceforth be executed so that this sacrilege will no longer hound us."

When he had spoken, a messenger arrived.

"Reccared, son of Leovigild, has come out of Spain," he said. "He has taken the fortress of Cabaret, ravaged the greater part of the territory of Toulouse, and led off captives. He has stormed the fortress of Beaucaire in the district of Arles, carrying off its people and possessions, and from there has shut himself up within the walls of Nîmes."

On hearing the news, the king appointed Leudegisel duke in place of Calumniosus, called Egilan, putting him in charge of the whole Province of Arles and posting over four thousand men as guards along the frontier. In addition, Nicetius, duke of Auvergne, also brought guards and patrolled the border.

The Assassination of Bishop Praetextatus (VIII 31)

While these events were going on and Fredegund was living at Rouen, she had bitter words with Bishop Praetextatus, telling him that the time would come when he would be back in the exile in which he had once been kept.

"Whether in exile or out of exile," he said, "I was, am now, and always shall be a bishop; but as for you, you won't enjoy royal power forever. By God's grace I have been brought from exile back to the world; but you shall be taken from this kingdom and plunged into the abyss. It would be better for you now to give up your stupid, wicked behavior and turn to better things. Stop this boasting, which always makes you excitable. Even you may strive to attain eternal life and can lead the infant you have borne to his age of majority."

When he had said this, she left his presence seething with anger. The woman took his remarks badly.

On the day of our Lord's Resurrection [that is, Sunday], the bishop went early to the cathedral to conduct the church services and, as is the practice, began the singing of the antiphons in their proper order. As he was resting on the bench during the chanting, a bloody-minded assassin appeared. Drawing a blade from his belt, he stabbed the bishop under the armpit. The bishop called out for help to the clergy who were present, but, of all those standing near, no one came to his aid. As he held out his blood-covered hands over the altar, praying and giving thanks to God, he was carried by his followers to his chamber and laid upon his bed.

Fredegund appeared immediately, along with Dukes Beppolen and Ansovald.

"Holy bishop," she said, "that such a thing should have happened as you were conducting services ill becomes me and the rest of your flock. Let's hope the person who dared do this can be pointed out so he can receive the punishments that suit his crime."

"Who did this," he answered, knowing she was lying, "if not the person who has killed kings, repeatedly shed innocent blood, and committed many crimes in this kingdom?"

"I have skilled doctors in my service who can heal this wound. Let them visit you," said the queen.

"God has now had me called from this world," said the bishop. "But you, who have been found out to be the person behind these crimes, shall be accursed down through the ages, and God shall take vengeance on you for my death."

When she left, the bishop put his house in order and breathed his last.

Romachar, bishop of Coutances, came to bury him. Great grief now overcame all the citizens of Rouen, especially the chief Franks of the city. One of their leaders came to Fredegund.

"You have committed a great deal of evil in this world," he said, "but nothing has been worse than having a bishop of the Lord killed. May God swiftly avenge the innocent blood. We shall all investigate this deed, so you won't be allowed to carry on your bloody work much longer."

When he had said this and left the queen's presence, she sent a messenger after him to invite him to dine. He refused, and she asked that, if he would not dine with her, would he at least drink a cup and not go from the royal residence thirsty. He waited for a cup, and when he received it, drank its mixture of absinthe, wine, and honey, as is the custom of the barbarians. The drink contained poison.

19. "Let's hope the person who dared do this can be pointed out (VIII 31)."
Fredegund, Beppolen, and Ansovald visit Praetextatus.

20.   "He waited for a cup, and when he received it, drank its mixture of
absinthe, wine, and honey (VIII 31)."

As soon as he drank it, he felt a severe pain in his chest, as if his insides were being cut up, and called out to his companions, "Run, you poor devils, run from this evil or you will be destroyed with me."

Refusing the drink, they lost no time getting get away. He immediately became blind, collapsed, and died after riding a distance of three stadia [about a third of a mile].

After this, Leudovald, bishop [of Bayeux], sent letters to all the bishops and, on their advice, closed the churches of Rouen, so that the people should expect no more religious services in them until the author of this crime was found through a general investigation. He arrested some people and wrung from them by torture the truth that these things were done as part of a plot devised by Fredegund. She offered a defense against the charge, and the bishop was unable to take vengeance. It was said that assassins approached Bishop Leudovald because he was resolved to investigate this matter keenly; but he was surrounded by his bodyguard, and the assassins were unable to do him any harm.

When the news was told to King Guntram, and accusations were made against Fredegund, the king sent to the alleged son of Chilperic (who as I have written above [VIII 1] was called Chlothar) three bishops, namely Artemius of Sens, Veranus of Cavaillon, and Agricius of Troyes. The bishops, along with the child's governors, were supposed to search out the author of the crime and deliver that person before the king.

When the bishops told their orders to Chlothar's senior officials, the latter replied, "These deeds are thoroughly distressing to us and we are increasingly anxious to take vengeance for them. But we reject the idea that, if someone among us is found guilty, that person should be brought before your king, since we are capable of putting down the crimes of our own people using royal authority."

At this point the bishops said, "You should know that, if the person who committed this crime is not brought before us, our king will come here with an army and lay waste the entire country with fire and sword; for it is plain that she who had the Frank [of Rouen] killed by witchcraft also had the bishop put to the sword."

With these words, they left without getting a reasonable answer. They nevertheless lodged a protest that Melantius [see VII 19], who had already been appointed to succeed Praetextatus, should never perform in that cathedral the duties of the episcopal office.

Bobolen and Domnola (VIII 32)

Many wicked deeds were done at this time.

Domnola, daughter of Victor, bishop of Rennes, widow of the late Burgolen [see V 25] and afterwards wife of Nectarius [see VII 15], had a dispute with Bobolen, Fredegund's referendary, over vineyards. When he heard she was visiting the vineyards, he sent a message objecting to her daring to enter the property. She disregarded the message, and announcing that the property had belonged to her father, entered it. Thereupon Bobolen caused a commotion, attacking her with armed men. He killed her, claimed the vineyards, and seized property. The men and women with her were put to the sword, with no survivors but those who fled.

Birth of Theudebert II (VIII 37)

A son was born to King Childebert. He was taken up from the sacred font by Magneric, bishop of Trier, and called Theudebert.

Guntram was so pleased that he sent an envoy with many gifts for the boy and with a message saying, "Through this child God will see fit to raise up the kingdom of the Franks by the love of His divine majesty, provided the father lives for the child and the child for the father."

Year XI of Childebert II, a. 586

Childebert's eleventh year receives very little attention from Gregory, taking up a scant five chapters (VIII 38–42).

Leovigild's and Reccared's Peace Overtures (VIII 38)

In the eleventh year of the reign of King Childebert envoys again came from Spain seeking peace but they returned without getting a definite answer.

Reccared, the son of Leovigild, came to Narbonne and took plunder in Gallic territory, but got back without being detected.

Further Investigation of Praetextatus's Murder (VIII 41)

When word that Praetextatus had been killed by Fredegund spread through the whole country, the queen ordered a slave arrested and beaten in an effort to clear herself of the charge.

"You have pinned this slander on me by attacking Praetextatus, bishop of

Rouen, with a sword," she said.

She handed him over to the bishop's nephew, who had him tortured. He clearly disclosed the whole matter.

"From Queen Fredegund I got a hundred pieces of gold to do this," he said, "from Bishop Melantius, fifty, and from the archdeacon of the city, another fifty. I also received a promise that I would be freed along with my wife."

On the slave's saying this, Praetextatus's nephew drew his sword and cut the accused to pieces.

As for Fredegund, she established Melantius in the cathedral church. It was Fredegund who had earlier placed him in the bishopric.

Guntram Again Tries to Control Chlothar's Kingdom (VIII 42)

Duke Beppolen [see V 29, VIII 31] was quite harassed by Fredegund and not given the honor due a person of his stature. He saw that he was held in little regard and went over to King Guntram.

Beppolen received from the king ducal authority over the cities that belonged to Chlothar, the son of King Chilperic. He was not received by the people of Rennes, though he arrived with a mighty force. Coming to Angers, however, he inflicted a good deal of harm, breaking down gates without waiting for keys and plundering grain, hay, wine, or anything else he could find in the establishments of the citizens he happened upon. He subjected many of the locals to beatings and wore them down. He even instilled fear in Domigisel [see VIII 18] but made peace with him.

On reaching the town, he happened to dine with various people in a third-floor room, when the floor of the house suddenly collapsed, and he barely escaped with his life, though many were hurt. However, he continued in the wicked acts that he had been committing earlier. At that time Fredegund brought to ruin much of his property in the kingdom of her son.

Beppolen even returned to Rennes. Trying to subject its citizens to Guntram, he left his son there. It did not take long for the citizens to attack; the son was killed along with many important men.

In this year many portents appeared. In the seventh month [September] the trees appeared to flower and many that had borne fruit earlier now gave a new crop which stayed on the trees until the Christmas season. A light was seen to course across the heavens like a snake.

Year XII of Childebert II, a. 587

Nicetius, Antestius, and Bobolen (VIII 43)

In the twelfth year of King Childebert's reign, Nicetius [see VIII 18, 28] was appointed governor of the province of Marseilles and the other cities that belonged to Childebert's kingdom in those parts.

Antestius was sent to Angers by King Guntram. He imposed many penalties on those who were mixed up in the death of Domnola, the wife of Nectarius [see VIII 32]. Because Bobolen had been the instigator of the crime, his property was confiscated by the fisc.

Antestius came to Nantes and began to challenge Bishop Nonnichius.

"Your son is involved in this offense," he said. "He must suffer the penalties that fit his crimes."

The boy fled, terrified and with a guilty conscience, to Chlothar, the son of Chilperic. As for Antestius, he received sureties from the bishop to ensure the latter's appearance before the king, and then went to Saintes.

A rumor was circulating in those days that Fredegund had covertly sent messengers to Spain and that Palladius, bishop of Saintes [see VIII 22], had secretly welcomed them and helped them on their way. It was the time of holy Lent [16 February 587] and the bishop had retired to an island in the ocean to pray. While the people were waiting for him to return to the church for the festival of Lord's supper [March 27], as was his custom, he was intercepted on the road by Antestius.

"Do not enter the city," Antestius said, without asking if the rumor was true. "I am going to sentence you to exile for receiving messengers of an enemy of our lord king."

"I don't know what you are talking about," said the bishop. "But since the holy days are at hand, let me go to the city. When the holy celebrations of the feast are over, allege whatever you want; you'll get an explanation from me because there's nothing in your charges."

"Absolutely not," said Antestius. "You shall not touch the threshhold of your church, for you've shown yourself unfaithful to our lord the king."

What more is there to say? The bishop was detained on the road. The manse of the church was inventoried and property removed. The citizens were unable to persuade Antestius at least to question the bishop after the services were conducted. With them pleading and him refusing, at last 'he revealed the wound concealed in his breast' [cf. Virgil, *Aeneid* XI 40].

"If he will sell me the establishment that he has in the territory of Bourges, I will fulfill your requests," said Antestius. "If not, he will not escape my hands but shall be exiled."

The bishop was afraid to say no. He made out the bill of sale, signed it, and handed over the farm, and so, having given sureties to vouch for his appearance before the king, he was allowed to enter the city.

The days passed and he went to the king. Antestius was present but he could not prove any of his allegations against the bishop. The bishop was ordered back to his city to await a future synod in case any of the allegations could be clearly proven.

Nonnichius was also in attendance, but he went away after giving many gifts.

Another Attempt by Fredegund on Guntram's Life (VIII 44)

Fredegund sent envoys in the name of her son to King Guntram. The request was presented, and the envoys, receiving a reply, bade the king farewell and left. But I know not for what reason, they remained behind for a little while at their lodging.

Day dawned, and the king went to morning prayers, his way lighted by a taper. A man was spotted sleeping like a drunkard in the corner of the oratory and wearing a sword, his spear leaning against the wall. At the sight the king shouted out that it was not natural for a person to be sleeping in the dark of night in such a place. The man was overwhelmed, bound with cords, and asked the meaning of his actions. There was no delay in subjecting him to torture, and he said that he had been sent by the envoys who had just been there and that he was supposed to kill the king.

The envoys were seized but would admit to none of the matters about which they were asked.

"We were sent for no other reason than to deliver the message we presented," they said.

While the man was subjected to various punishments and imprisoned, the envoys were condemned by the king's orders to exile in various places.

And so it was quite obvious that envoys were sent by Fredegund as a subterfuge so they could kill the king, but the mercy of God would not allow it. Among them, Baddo was considered the leader.

The End of Desiderius (VIII 45)

On Desiderius, see V 13, 39; VI 12, 31; VII 10, 27, 34, 43; VIII 27.

Envoys were repeatedly coming from Spain to King Guntram, but they could not get him to grant peace. Hostility actually got worse. Meanwhile, King Guntram restored the city of Albi to his nephew Childebert.

Seeing the situation, Desiderius, who had especially stored his more valuable possessions in the territory of this town, became afraid that vengeance would be sought because of an ancient quarrel stemming from his mauling an army of King Sigibert, of glorious memory, in that same city. He moved into the territory of Toulouse along with his wife, Tetradia, whom he took from Eulalius, now count of Clermont [see VIII 27], and all his property. Mustering an army, he made preparations to go against the Goths. First, they say, he divided his property with his sons and wife. He took with him Count Austrovald and marched on Carcasonne.

The citizens of Carcasonne learned of the attack. They had prepared themselves as if they were going to stand and fight, having heard about these fellows beforehand. Then the fight began. The Goths began to flee and Desiderius and Austovald cut the enemy down from behind. As the Goths fled, Desiderius and a few of his men reached the city, for the horses of his companions were exhausted. Then, as he reached the gate, he was cut off by citizens from within the walls and killed along with all the men who had followed him. A small number somehow got away to report what happened.

When Austrovald learned of Desiderius's death, he turned back on the road, and went to the king. He was soon appointed duke in Desiderius's place.

Death of Leovigild and Succession of Reccared (VIII 46)

After this Leovigild, king of the Spaniards, began to grow ill, but, as some maintain, he did penance for his heretical error: objecting to anyone being found party to this heresy, he went over to the Catholic faith. For the course of seven days he wept for the wicked things he had tried to do against God and then breathed his last [recte a. 586].

And Reccared his son reigned in his place.

End of Book VIII.

CHAPTER EIGHT

REVOLT IN AUSTRASIA AND THE FALL OF

EGIDIUS

AUGUST 587–591 (BOOKS IX–X)

Treason doth never prosper; what's the reason?
For if it prosper, none dare call it treason.

Sir John Harington, *Epigrams*

Year XII of Childebert II, a. 587 (continued)

Reccared and Goisuinth. More Peace Overtures (IX 1)

After the death of Leovigild, king of the Spaniards, Reccared his son made an
alliance with Goisuinth, widow of his father, and accepted her as his mother.
She was the mother of Queen Brunhild, mother of the younger Childebert.
Reccared was the son of Leovigild by another wife.

Then Reccared took counsel with his stepmother and sent envoys to King
Guntram and Childebert to say, "Make peace with us and let us enter into an
alliance so that having received your assistance, I shall in the same way out of
friendship provide you with protection when the need arises."

The envoys who were sent to King Guntram were ordered to remain at
the town of Mâcon. There the king sent his people to learn of the mission but
would not receive the envoys' presentation. For this reason such great hostility later sprang up between the kings that they would allow no one from
Guntram's kingdom to travel to the cities of Septimania.

The envoys who came to Childebert, however, received a friendly reception.
They presented gifts, attained a peace agreement, and went back home bearing
gifts.

Death of Radegund (IX 2)

In this year the most blessed Radegund passed away from this world. In the
monastery that she had founded she left behind great grief. I myself was present at her burial. She died on the thirteenth day of the sixth month [August],
and was buried three days later. In my book of wonders I have endeavored
to write more fully about the miracles that happened on that day and of the
circumstances of her funeral [GC 104].

21. Radegund and Agnes entertain Venantius Fortunatus at the monastery of the Holy Cross in Poitiers.

Assassination Attempt on King Guntram (IX 3)

Meanwhile, time came for the festival of Saint Marcellus, which is celebrated in the seventh month [September 4] in the city of Chalon. King Guntram was present. When the solemnities were over and he was attending the holy altar to take communion, a certain man came up as if to make some kind of request. As he was rapidly approaching the king a weapon slipped from his hand. He was quickly seized and they found another naked blade in his hand. He was led from the holy basilica without delay, bound, and tortured. He confessed he was sent to kill the king.

"This was the thinking of the person who sent me," he said. "The king knows that the hatred of many has built up against him, and fearing he might be struck down, he has had himself completely surrounded with his own men. There is no way we can get at him with swords, unless he is stabbed in church where he is thought to be safe and fears nothing."

Those to whom he was referring were arrested. Many were killed but the assassin, though beaten, was left alive, since the king thought it impious to execute someone who had been taken from the church.

Birth of Theuderic II (IX 4)

In this year another son was born to King Childebert. Veranus, bishop of Cavaillon, received him from the baptismal font and gave him the name Theuderic. At the time Veranus was a bishop endowed with great power of miracle, so that when he made the sign of the cross over the sick they were often immediately restored to health by God's grace.

Death of Guntram Boso and the Revolt of Rauching, Ursio, and Berthefred against Childebert (IX 8–12)

Rauching was Childebert's duke, likely for the Soissons region, which had been taken from the kingdom of Chilperic's son Chlothar (see V 3; VIII 26, 29; and IX 36). On Ursio and Berthefred, see VI 4.

Since the queen hated Guntram Boso, he began to canvass the bishops and leading men, begging rather late in the day for the pardon that to this point he had scorned to ask. During the minority of King Childebert, he had often provoked Queen Brunhild with reproaches and taunts; he had also been in favor of the injustices that her enemies had inflicted on her. To revenge the wrong done to his mother, King Childebert ordered him to be hunted down and killed.

When Guntram Boso saw that the critical point was upon him, he made for the cathedral church of Verdun, believing he could obtain a pardon through the mediation of Bishop Ageric, the king's godfather. The bishop now hurried to the king to intercede for him. The king was unable to refuse the petition.

"Let him come before us," said the king, "and then, when he's given sureties, let him go before my uncle; we'll follow whatever judgment our uncle makes."

Guntram Boso was then conducted to the place where the king was staying. Stripped of his arms and manacled, he was presented to the king by Bishop Ageric.

"I have done you and your mother wrong by not obeying your commands and by acting contrary to your will and to the public good," he said falling at the king's feet. "Now I ask you to forgive the evil that I have committed against you."

The king told him to rise from the ground and put him into the hands of the bishop.

"Let him remain in your charge, holy bishop," said the king, "until he appears before King Guntram." He then told him to withdraw.

After these events, Rauching allied himself with the leading officials in the kingdom of Chlothar, son of Chilperic. He pretended that he was carrying on discussions with them about maintaining the peace and preventing attacks and raids being carried out between the territories of the two kingdoms. They planned in fact to kill Childebert; Rauching would then control a kingdom of Champagne with Theudebert, the king's elder son; Ursio and Berthefred were to take charge of Theuderic, the younger son recently born, and control the rest of the kingdom, shutting out King Guntram. They also muttered many times that they would humiliate Queen Brunhild, as they had earlier done during her widowhood. Rauching, carried away by his great power and, as I would say, vaunting the glory of the regal scepter itself, made preparations to travel to King Childebert to carry out the plot he had entered into.

But the goodness of God brought word of these plans beforehand to the ears of King Guntram, who sent messengers in secret to King Childebert, bringing the entire affair to his attention, and saying, "Quickly, let us have a meeting, for there are issues to be discussed."

Childebert carefully investigated what had been told to him and, finding it to be true, sent for Rauching. As soon as Rauching arrived, but before the king had him admitted to his presence, the king issued letters and dispatched his servants with a warrant for use of the public post to take possession of Rauching's property in its various locations; then he ordered the duke to be admitted to his chamber. He talked with him about one thing or another and dismissed him. As he was coming out, two doorkeepers grabbed him by the legs, and he fell on the steps of the entranceway, one part of his body lying inside it, the other outside. Those who had been ordered to finish the job fell upon him with swords and beat his head into so many bits that it looked entirely like brain. He died immediately. The body was stripped, flung from a window, and committed to the grave.

Rauching lacked character and, greedy beyond human measure, was envious of the property of others. He was arrogant in the extreme because of his wealth, so much so that at the time of his death he was claiming to be the son of King Chlothar. Much gold was found on him.

As soon as he was killed, one of his servants dashed away at full speed and told his wife what had happened. She was on a street in Soissons at the time, on horseback, decked out with large pieces of jewelry and precious stones and covered with flashing gold, with an escort of servants before and behind; she was riding to the basilica of Saints Crispin and Crispinian to hear Mass, for it was the day of the passion of these blessed martyrs [October 25]. After meeting with the messenger, she turned back by another street, threw her jewels to the ground, and took refuge in the basilica of the holy Bishop Medard, thinking to find safety there under the protection of that blessed confessor. The servants sent by the king to claim the property of Rauching discovered more among his treasures than they could find even in the coffers of the public treasury; all of it was brought before the king for him to look at.

On the day of Rauching's death there were many citizens of Tours and Poitiers with the king. The plan was that, should the plotters have been able to carry out their crime, they would have subjected these people to torture, saying, "It was one of you who caused the death of our king." Then having put them to death with various punishments, the plotters would have boasted of being the avengers of the king's murder. But Almighty God confounded their plans, for these were wicked, and fulfilled that which is written: "The pit which you prepare for your brother, into it you yourself will fall [cf. Prov. 26:27]."

Magnovald was sent as duke in place of Rauching.

Ursio and Berthefred, sure that Rauching would be able to carry out what they had discussed, had collected an army and were already coming. Hearing how he had died, they reinforced the host of followers that was still with them and, with guilty consciences, fortified themselves with all their property in a fortress on the Woëvre near the villa of Ursio. If King Childebert tried to take measures against them, they intended to defend themselves against his forces from a position of strength. Ursio was their chief and the cause of the evil.

Queen Brunhild sent a message to Berthefred.

"Separate yourself from my enemy," she said, "and you'll have your life; otherwise you'll die with him." For the queen had received Berthefred's daughter from the baptismal font and for this reason wanted to have mercy on him.

"I'll never abandon him," said Berthefred, "unless death tears me away."

While these events were taking place, King Guntram again sent a message to his nephew Childebert, saying, "Enough delay, come so I may see you. There is a reason for us to see one another; it concerns both your own life as well as the public welfare."

When Childebert heard, he took his mother, sister, and wife and hurried to meet his uncle.

Bishop Magneric of the city of Trier was also present at the meeting, and Guntram Boso, whom Bishop Ageric of Verdun had taken into his charge, came as well. But the bishop, who had promised to stand surety for him, was not present, for there had been an agreement that Guntram Boso should appear before the king without an advocate. The point of the agreement was that, if the king decided that he must die, he would not be pardoned due to the bishop's intervention; and if the king granted him life, he would go free.

The kings met and Guntram Boso was judged guilty on various grounds. The order was given for him to be killed. He found out and rushed to Magneric's lodging, closing the doors and shutting out the clerics and servants.

"Most blessed bishop," he said, "I know that the kings have great respect for you. And now I take refuge with you to escape death. Look, the executioners are at the door. Clearly understand from this that, if you don't rescue me, I'll kill you and then go outside to meet my own death. Know plainly that either we both live or we die as one. Holy bishop, I know that you share with the king the place of father to his son [see VIII 37]. Since you get whatever you ask of him, I know he'll not be able to deny at all whatever your holiness requests. Therefore obtain a pardon or we shall die together." He said this with his sword unsheathed.

Alarmed at what he heard, the bishop said, "What can I do if I am kept here by you? Let me go beg the king's mercy, and perhaps he will take pity on you."

"Forget that," Guntram Boso replied. "Send abbots and men you trust to report what I am saying."

The king was not told, however, how matters really stood. The messengers said that Guntram Boso was being protected by the bishop. This made the king angry.

"If the bishop will not come out," he said, "let him be destroyed along with that traitor."

When the bishop heard of his reply, he sent messengers to the king. Although they recounted what was happening, King Guntram said, "Set fire to the building, and if the bishop cannot come out, they can both be burned together."

Hearing this, the clergy forced open the door and dragged the bishop outside.

The wretched Guntram Boso then saw that he was hemmed in by raging flames on every side and went to the door armed with his sword. As soon as he crossed the threshold of the house and stepped outside, a soldier threw a spear and struck him in the forehead. He was thrown into confusion by the blow and, as if out of his mind, tried to thrust with his sword. Those standing around wounded him with so many spears that the heads sticking in his body and the shafts supporting him prevented him from falling to the ground. The few who were with him were also killed and exposed on the field at the same time. Permission to bury them was obtained from the princes only with difficulty.

Guntram Boso acted without consideration and was avaricious, desiring other men's property beyond measure. He swore oaths to all and kept his promises to none. His wife and children were sent into exile and his property confiscated by the fisc. A great quantity of gold, silver, and valuable items of various kinds was found in his coffers. Also what he had concealed underground out of consciousness of his wrongdoing did not remain hidden. He often made use of soothsayers and lots and, in his desire to learn the future, was always deceived by them.

King Guntram concluded peace with his nephew and the queens [Treaty of Andelot, 28 November 587; see IX 20]. Having exchanged gifts and set the affairs of state on a firm footing, they sat down together at a banquet. King Guntram began to praise the Lord.

"I give you most hearty thanks, Almighty God," he said. "You have allowed me to see the sons of my son Childebert. For this reason I don't think I have been completely forsaken by your majesty, for you have allowed me to see the sons of my son."

Then Childebert received Dynamius [see VI 7, 11] and Duke Lupus [see VI 4], who had been handed over to him, and gave back Cahors to Queen Brunhild. And so, having signed the agreements, the kings gave each other presents, exchanged kisses, and went off each to his own city in peace and rejoicing, rendering thanks again and again to God.

King Childebert mustered an army and ordered it to march to the place where Ursio and Berthefred were waiting behind fortifications. In the district of the Woëvre there was a villa commanded by a steep hill. On the summit, a basilica had been built in honor of the holy and blessed Martin. They say that in antiquity there was a fortress there, but these days it had been fortified, not by art, but by nature. The two men had shut themselves up in this basilica, with their property, wives, and servants. The army having been assembled, as we said, Childebert ordered it to proceed there. Even before the force that had been mustered reached Ursio and Berthefred, it burned and looted everything wherever it could find their villas and property. Reaching the spot, the troops climbed the hill and surrounded the basilica with armed men. The commander of the force was Godegisel, son-in-law of Duke Lupus.

When the troops were unable to get the besieged out of the basilica, they tried setting the building on fire. Seeing what they were doing, Ursio came out armed with a sword and created such havoc among the besiegers that no one he caught sight of could get away alive. Trudulf, count of the royal palace, fell there and many soldiers were laid out. But when Ursio was seen to be out of breath from the slaughter, someone wounded him in the thigh, and he fell crippled to the ground; others rushed on him, and he was killed.

Godegisel saw this and began to shout out, "Let there be peace now. Look, the chief enemy of our lords has fallen. Let Berthefred have his life."

At these words, and since all the troops were longing to plunder the property amassed in the basilica, Berthefred mounted his horse and rode to Verdun. He thought he would be protected in the oratory located in the church manse, especially as Bishop Ageric was living in the manse.

When King Childebert was told that Berthefred had escaped, he was heartsick.

"If he gets away alive," said the king, "Godegisel shall not escape my grasp."

But the king did not know that Berthefred had entered the church manse, thinking instead that he had fled to some other region.

Godegisel was now afraid. Once more mustering his force, he surrounded the church manse with armed men. Since the bishop could not surrender Berthefred, and even tried to protect him, the attackers climbed the roof and killed him by hitting him with the tiles and materials covering the oratory; he died with three of his servants. The bishop was greatly pained by this, not only because he could not give him protection, but also because he had seen the place where he was accustomed to pray, and where relics of the saints were gathered together, polluted with human blood. King Childebert sent him gifts to cheer him up, but he would not be comforted.

In these days many withdrew to other regions out of fear of the king. Not a few were deprived of the dignity of the ducal office, and others were promoted in their place.

Release of Baddo (IX 13)

Guntram ordered Baddo into his presence and then sent him on to Paris. As I said above [VIII 44], Baddo had been detained for high treason.

"If Fredegund along with appropriate co-swearers clears him of the charge made against him, he may depart a free man and go where he wants," said the king.

Baddo arrived in Paris, but no one who could demonstrate his innocence from Fredegund's side put in an appearance. He was then held, loaded with chains, and taken back to Chalon under strict custody.

But after messengers went back and forth, in particular Bishop Leudovald of Bayeux [see VIII 31], Baddo was released and returned home.

Gregory mentions his journey via Rheims to Metz to see the king. See further IX 20.

Reconciliation between Bishop Egidius and Duke Lupus (IX 14)

Egidius, bishop of Rheims, was considered a suspect in the crime of high treason for which the above-mentioned men [Rauching, Ursio, and Berthefred] had lost their lives. He came to Childebert with rich gifts to plead for mercy, having first received assurances on oath in the basilica of the holy Remigius that he would suffer no harm on the way. He was received by the king and departed in peace.

He also obtained peace with Duke Lupus, who, as I recorded above [VI 4], had been driven from the ducal office of Champagne at his instigation. As a result King Guntram became very bitter; Lupus had promised him never to make peace with Egidius, a known enemy of the king.

Conversion of Reccared. A Spanish Embassy to Burgundy and Austrasia (IX 15, 16)

Reccared, King of Spain, summoned a council of Arian and Catholic bishops [January/February 587] and converted to Catholicism (IX 15)

After [the conversion], Reccared sent an embassy to Guntram and King Childebert for the sake of peace: just as they were one in faith, he said, so he would show that he was also united in friendship with them.

But the envoys were rebuffed by Guntram who said, "What kind of good faith can they promise me? Why should I believe people who have delivered my niece up as a prisoner and whose machinations brought about her husband's killing and her own death abroad? I will therefore not receive Reccared's embassy until, at God's command, I have vengeance on these enemies."

On hearing this response, the envoys proceeded to Childebert who welcomed them.

"Our lord, your brother Reccared, wishes to clear himself of the crime imputed to him of being privy to the death of your sister," they said. "He can establish his innocence should you want oaths or some other demonstration. Then, having given to your grace 10,000 solidi, he desires to have your friendship so he may have recourse to your assistance and you may gain his good offices, should the need arise."

When they said this, King Childebert and his mother promised to preserve fully peace and friendship with him.

Having received and given gifts, the envoys added, "Our lord commands that we raise with you the subject of giving your daughter and sister Chlodosind in marriage to him so that the peace promised between us can be more readily confirmed."

Childebert and Brunhild said, "Our promise will come readily on this matter, but we dare not give it without the advice of our uncle, King Guntram. We have promised to do nothing on major questions without his advice."

With this answer, the envoys went home.

Attacks by the Bretons (IX 18)

The Bretons raided the territory of Nantes, driving off animals, overwhelming villas, and taking away captives.

When this was told to King Guntram, he ordered an army mobilized, and sent a message to the Bretons that if they did not fully compensate for their bad behavior, they would be put to the sword by his forces. Frightened, they promised they would make amends for all the bad they had done.

When Guntram heard, he sent to them an embassy composed of Namatius [bishop] of Orleans and Bertram, bishop of Le Mans, as well as counts and other important officials; also in attendance were important officials from the kingdom of Chilperic's son, Chlothar [II]. They arrived in the territory of Nantes and communicated to Waroc and Vidimaclis everything the king had instructed.

"We know," they responded, "that those cities belong to the sons of Chlothar [I] and we should be their subjects; we won't delay compensating for all the unreasonable things we have done."

Giving sureties and signing promises, they undertook each to pay a thousand solidi in compensation to King Guntram and Chlothar [II], pledging never again to attack the territories of those cities....

But Waroc forgot about his oath and pledge, set aside everything he had promised, and took the vineyards away from the inhabitants of Nantes, gathering the grape harvest and taking the wine to Vannes.

This caused King Guntram to get quite furious again and muster a force, but he calmed down.

Year XIII of Childebert II, a. 588

Gregory as an Envoy to Guntram. The Goodness of Guntram (IX 20–21)

Although Guntram and Childebert were supposed to be reconciled and Guntram had adopted his nephew, relations between the two remained tense. Among the issues dividing the kings was the old problem of relations with the Visigothic monarchy of Spain, whose new Catholic king Reccared now sought marriage with Childebert's sister Chlodosind; Guntram remained hostile to the Visigoths, ostensibly over Septimania and the treatment of Ingund. The question of the control of cities was not satisfactorily settled either, despite a treaty. Joint assemblies of the bishops of the two kingdoms, which Guntram dearly wanted, were resisted by Childebert. And last but not least, the status of Chlothar II, Fredegund's son, remained a trouble spot. Would Guntram recognize him and make him an heir?

These problems came up in the following conversation between the envoys of Childebert—namely Gregory himself and an unknown bishop Felix (likely of Châlons-sur-Marne)—and King Guntram. Although the Treaty of Andelot was signed in November 587, Gregory refrained from giving the text until his account of the following interview with Guntram. Immediately afterwards (IX 21) is a description of what Gregory calls Guntram's goodness.

In that year, the thirteenth of King Childebert, when I had gone to meet the king in the city of Metz [see IX 13], I was ordered to go on an embassy to King Guntram.

I found him at Chalon.

"Famous king," I said, "your glorious nephew Childebert sends you bountiful greetings and renders thanks beyond measure for your dutiful goodness. You remind him continually to do what is pleasing to God, acceptable to you, and beneficial to the interests of the people. With respect to the matters you discussed together, he promises to fulfill everything and pledges to break no item of the agreements drawn up between you [cf. IX 11]."

To this the king replied, "I don't offer him the same thanks, because he has broken the promises that were made to me. My part of the city of Senlis has not been relinquished; they have not discharged the people whom in my interests I wanted moved, since they are my enemies. How can you say that my dearest nephew does not wish to break any of his written agreements?"

"He wishes to do nothing contrary to those agreements," I replied, "but promises to fulfill all of them. So if you wish to send representatives to divide Senlis, do not delay for a moment; you shall immediately receive what's yours. And as to the people you mention, give me a list of their names and all that is promised shall be fulfilled."

When we had discussed these matters, the king ordered the agreement itself to be read over again before those who were present.

COPY OF THE AGREEMENT

In the name of Christ, the most excellent lords Kings Guntram and Childebert and the most glorious lady Queen Brunhild met out of regard for each other at Andelot to settle in a broader forum all matters that might in any way cause quarrels between them. With the mediation of bishops and leading officials and the help of God, it was settled, resolved, and agreed between them, out of regard for each other, that they would be loyal to each other and maintain a mutual affection pure and sincere as long as almighty God preserved their lives in the present world.

§ Likewise, since Lord Guntram claimed, in accordance with the agreement he had made with Lord Sigibert of good memory, that the entire share that Sigibert had acquired from Charibert's kingdom belonged completely to him, and since Lord Childebert wanted to recover everything his father had possessed, they have, after deliberation, agreed to the following: that the third portion of the city of Paris, with its territory and people, that had come to Lord Sigibert from Charibert's kingdom by written agreement, with the fortresses of Châteaudun and Vendôme, and whatever the said king received of the districts of Étampes and Chartres for right of passage, with their lands and people, were to remain perpetually under the jurisdiction of Lord Guntram, along with whatever Guntram previously held from Charibert's kingdom during Lord Sigibert's lifetime.

Equally, however, King Childebert from this day forward has the right to Meaux, two-thirds of Senlis, Tours, Poitiers, Avranches, Aire, Saint Lizier, Bayonne, and Albi, with their territories.

The above terms are conditional on the following: whichever of these kings the Lord should allow to survive, the other shall vindicate fully and forever the kingdom of the one that passes on from the light of the present world without children and, with God's help, leave it to his successors.

§ The following special agreement is to be faithfully observed in all its details. Whatever the lord king Guntram has bestowed, or yet by God's favor shall bestow, upon his daughter Chlothild in all kinds of property and persons, in cities, lands, and revenues, shall remain under her ownership and control. And if she wishes of her own free will to dispose of properties of the fisc, valuable articles or movables, or to bestow them on any one, let that gift, with God's help, be protected forever and not be taken by anyone at any time. Let her possess with full honor and respect under the defense and protection of Lord Childebert everything of which he finds her in possession at her father's death.

Equally, the lord king Guntram promises that, if during his lifetime, owing to the uncertainty of human life, Lord Childebert should happen to pass from the light—may the divine goodness not allow such a thing and Guntram has no desire to see it—Guntram will receive under his care and protection, like a good father, Childebert's sons Theudebert and Theuderic and any others that God wishes to give him, so that they shall possess their father's kingdom in its entirety. And he will receive under his care and protection with a spiritual love Lord Childebert's mother, Queen Brunhild, and her daughter Chlodosind, sister of King Childebert, as long as she might be in the country of the Franks, and his queen Faileuba, like a good sister and daughters, and they shall possess with full honor and respect, secure and without disturbance, all their property, namely, cities, properties, revenues, and all rights and powers of that property, both what they possess at the present time and what they may justly add in the future by Christ's aid. If they wish to dispose of any of the fiscal properties or precious articles or movables of their own free will or to bestow them on anyone, let the gift be permanent and perpetual, and let their will in this respect not be upset by anyone at any time.

As to the cities, namely, Bordeaux, Limoges, Cahors, Béarn, and Cieutat, which Galswinth, Lady Brunhild's sister, acquired as a marriage portion and as *morganegyba*, that is, as morning gift, when she came to Francia, and which Lady Brunhild acquired by the judgment of the most glorious lord King Guntram and of the Franks in the lifetime of Chilperic and King Sigibert, it is agreed that from this day forward Lady Brunhild shall take possession of the city of Cahors with its lands and all its people. As for the other cities named above, Lord Guntram shall possess these as long as he lives, on condition that, after his death, they shall by God's grace be restored in their entirety to the control of Lady Brunhild and her heirs. During Lord Guntram's lifetime, however, they shall not at any time, or under any pretext, be claimed by Lady Brunhild or her son King Childebert or his children.

§ Likewise, it is agreed that Lord Childebert shall hold Senlis in its entirety; and as far as the one-third share due from there to Lord Guntram is concerned, the latter shall be compensated by the third share belonging to Lord Childebert in Ressons.

§ Likewise, in accordance with the agreements made between Lord Guntram and Lord Sigibert of blessed memory, with respect to the *leudes* who originally took oaths to Lord Guntram after the death of Lord Chlothar, if they are proven to have afterwards gone over to Sigibert, it is agreed that they shall be removed from the places where they live. Likewise, those who are proven to have first sworn allegiance to Lord Sigibert after the death of King Chlothar, and then to have passed over to Guntram, shall also be removed.

§ Likewise, whatever the aforesaid kings have bestowed on churches, or on their followers, or, in the future, shall bestow by God's grace in accordance with the law, shall be held permanently.

As regards whatever is owed justly and according to law to any of their followers in either kingdom, let the matter not be treated prejudicially, but let their followers be permitted to possess and to obtain the property that is their due; and if anything is taken from anyone who is without fault on account of divisions of the kingdom, a hearing shall be held and the property shall be restored.

As regards what each follower possessed through the generosity of previous kings down to the death of the lord king Chlothar of glorious memory [a. 561], let each have secure possession. And as regards whatever has been taken from followers since then, let each immediately get it back.

§ And since the friendship binding the aforementioned kings together is pure and honest, it is agreed that neither kingdom will deny passage to the followers of the other king who wish to travel on public or private business.

§ It is likewise agreed that neither king shall entice away the other's *leudes* or receive them when they come. And if it happens because of some transgression that a follower thinks he has to flee to the other kingdom, let him be absolved according to the nature of the offense and sent back.

§ It has been decided also to add this to the agreement. If either party shall at any time violate the present provisions on some artful pretext, he shall lose all the benefits conferred, both prospective and present, and let the advantage be his who faithfully maintains all the terms written above, and let him be absolved in all matters from the obligations of his oath.

All these matters having been decided, the parties swear by the name of almighty God, the inseparable Trinity, all that is divine, and the fearful day of judgment, that they will faithfully observe all that is written above without any fraud or deceit.

This treaty was made four days before the Kalends of December [November 28] in the twenty-sixth year of the reign of Lord King Guntram and in the twelfth year of Lord Childebert [a. 587].

When the agreements were read over the king said, "May I be struck by God's judgment if I violate any one of the terms contained here."

And he turned to Felix, who had come with me as an envoy.

"Tell me, Felix," he said, "have you finished creating ties of friendship yet between my sister Brunhild and that enemy of God and man, Fredegund?"

When he denied this, I said, "Let the king have no doubt that the friendship that was made many years ago is being kept up between them. Surely you know that the hatred once established between them still grows; it is not withering. Most glorious king, would that you yourself had less friendly dealings with Fredegund. For, as we have learned repeatedly, you give her embassies greater consideration than ours."

"You should know, bishop of God," he said, "that I receive her embassies in such a way as not to neglect the affection I have for my nephew King Childebert. For I cannot have friendly ties with someone from whom regularly come assassins looking to take my life."

When he had said this, Felix said, "I believe the news has reached you, glorious king, that Reccared has sent an embassy to your nephew to ask for your niece Chlodosind, your brother's daughter, in marriage. But your nephew would not promise anything without your advice."

The king said, "It's hardly the best idea for my niece to go to the same place where her sister was killed [see VIII 28]. It seems inconceivable to me that the death of my niece Ingund is not avenged."

"They want very much to clear themselves of her death either by oath or by any other means you demand," answered Felix. "Only give your consent for Chlodosind to be betrothed to him as he asks."

"If my nephew fulfills the terms that he wished inserted in the agreements," said the king, "then I will do what he wants in this matter."

We promised that he would fulfill everything, and then Felix added, "He begs your goodness to help him against the Lombards. If they can be driven from Italy, the part which his father claimed possession of during his lifetime can be restored to him, and the other part can be returned by your help and his to the dominion of the emperor."

"I can't send my forces to Italy. That would be consigning them to death. A devastating plague is now wasting the country."

I said, "You have indicated to your nephew that all the bishops of his kingdom should meet together, since many matters need investigation. However, your glorious nephew thinks in accordance with the canons that each metropolitan should meet with the bishops of his province, and whatever wrongs were being done in each district could then be set right by the authority of the bishops. What is the reason for so great a number assembling together? The faith of the church is not rocked by any danger; no new heresy is arising. Why is there need for so many bishops meeting together?"

"Many wrongs have been done that should be investigated, both incestuous relations as well as matters in dispute between us," answered the king. "In particular, there is an issue greater than all others, that of God. You must investigate why Bishop Praetextatus was put to the sword in his church. Also there should be an investigation of those who are accused of licentiousness, so that, if they are found guilty, they can be corrected by the sentence of the bishops, and if they are found to be innocent, the false charge can be publicly removed."

He gave orders at that time for the synod to be delayed until the Kalends of the fourth month [June 1].

After this conversation we went to church; it was the day celebrating the Lord's resurrection [Sunday]. After mass he invited us to a dinner that was no less laden with food than it was rich in cheer. For the king talked constantly of God, of building churches, and of protection for the poor. Now and then he would laugh and make a pious joke, even throwing in a suitable quip so we might enjoy some of the merriment.

And he said this: "If only my nephew will keep his promises! Everything I have is his. Still, if it disturbs him that I receive my nephew Chlothar's envoys, am I so far gone that I am unable to mediate between them and stop the quarreling going further? I know it's better to cut strife short than to have it spread. If I acknowledge that Chlothar is my nephew, I will give him two or three cities somewhere so that he shall not seem to be disinherited. Leaving him this will not disturb Childebert."

He said this, and other things, and, treating us warmly and loading us with gifts, told us to depart, charging us always to give King Childebert advice that would benefit him.

King Guntram, as we have frequently said, was generous in almsgiving and disposed to vigils and fasting. At the time, there were reports that Marseilles was suffering greatly from a plague affecting the groin and that the disease had spread swiftly as far as the village of Saint-Symphorien d'Ozon in the Lyons district. The king, like a good bishop providing remedies that cure the wounds of a sinful people, commanded all to assemble in the cathedral and celebrate rogations with the utmost piety. He ordered that no food should be eaten but barley bread and clean water, and that all should continually attend vigils. And all was done as he said. For three days he gave alms with more than his usual generosity, and he showed such concern on behalf of all the people that he was at this time already regarded as not only a king but also as a bishop of God. Placing all his hope in the mercy of God, he directed the thoughts that came to him towards God from whom he believed with perfect faith they could be given effect. A common story was told at the time among the faithful about a woman whose son was suffering from a four-day fever and was lying sick in bed. Slipping behind the king in a throng of people, she secretly tore off a fringe from the king's garments, put it in water, and gave it to her son to drink. Immediately the fever died down, and he was cured. I do not doubt this story, since I myself have heard the demons of those possessed being compelled by the wonderful power of this man to call out his name and confess their own crimes.

Bishop Ageric and Guntram Boso's Children (IX 23)

Ageric, bishop of Verdun, grew seriously ill because of the lasting depression he felt at the death of Guntram Boso for whom he had stood as surety [see IX 8, 10]. An added cause of sorrow was the killing of Berthefred in the oratory of the church manse [see IX 12]. But worst of all was the fact that he kept with him the sons of Guntram Boso.

"You have been left as orphans because of animosity toward me," he would say, daily lamenting.

Disturbed for these reasons, as I said, and weighed down by depression and wasted by fasting, he died and was laid in the grave....

Austrasian Defeat in Italy (IX 25)

Although King Childebert had promised his sister [Chlodosind] to the Lombards, who were asking that she marry their king, and took gifts from them, he promised her again when envoys of the Goths arrived, on the basis of his recognizing that they had converted to the Catholic faith; and he sent an embassy to the emperor [see X 2] saying that he would wage war on the Lombards and with his guidance remove them from the peninsula, which he had not earlier done [see VIII 18]. He nonetheless also sent his army to take the region.

The generals were roused and went off to Italy with their forces, and all engaged the enemy. But our forces were battered, many were laid low, a good number taken captive, and a greater number fled, only returning home with difficulty. So great was the slaughter of the Frankish forces that its like could not be recalled.

Year XIV of Childebert II, a. 589

Guntram's Suspicions of Brunhild, Dubious Peace with the Lombards, and Another
Failed Campaign in Septimania (IX 28, 29, 31, 32)

Queen Brunhild ordered a shield of wondrous size to be made with gold and gems. She had it sent to the king in Spain along with two wooden bowls, commonly called 'basins', which were likewise made with gems and gold. The delivery was entrusted to Ebregisil who had often visited this region on embassies.

Guntram found out about his journey when someone told the king that Queen Brunhild was sending gifts to the sons of Gundovald. On hearing this, he ordered strict watches to be set up on the roads of his kingdom so that no one could get by without being interrogated. They examined people's clothing, shoes, and other goods to see if they were carrying secret letters.

On reaching Paris with the treasures, Ebregisil was arrested by Duke Ebrachar and taken to Guntram.

The king said to him, "Isn't it enough, you miserable wretch, to shamelessly counsel sending an offer of marriage to that Ballomer [see VII 33, 34] whom you call Gundovald and whom I subdued when he tried to take control of my kingdom. Now you send gifts to his sons to invite them to commit murder in Gaul once again. You are not going where you think you are but are to be put to death, because your embassy is a danger to our lineage."

Ebergisil rejected the charge, saying it had nothing to do with him and that these gifts were being sent to Reccared who was to be married to Chlodosind, the sister of King Childebert.

Believing him, the king let him go, and Ebergisil resumed his journey taking the gifts with him.

Then King Childebert at the invitation of Sigimund, bishop of Mainz, decided to celebrate Easter [April 10] at the aforementioned city. At the time his eldest son Theudebert was gravely ill with a tumor of the throat, but he got better.

Meanwhile King Childebert mobilized an army and prepared to accompany it to Italy to fight the Lombards. But the Lombards heard about it and sent envoys with gifts to say, "Let there be friendship between us and may we not suffer destruction. We shall render a fixed tribute to your authority, and it shall be no trouble for us to provide you with assistance against your enemies if it is needed."

When Childebert heard this, he sent an envoy to King Guntram to report their offer directly to him. Guntram was not averse to this agreement and gave advice to establish peace.

Childebert for his part ordered the army to remain in place and sent envoys to the Lombards to say that if they would confirm the promises the army would go back home. But nothing came of this....

As for Guntram, he sent a force against Septimania. Duke Austrovald had earlier gone to Carcasonne and, taking oaths from the population, had subjected them to royal control. Now the king sent Boso [see VII 38] and Antestius [see VIII 27, 43] to take the other cities.

Boso approached, leading there the forces of Saintes, Périgueux, Bordeaux, Agen, and even Toulouse, and arrogantly disparaged Duke Austrovald, denouncing him for daring to enter Carcasonne without him. While his overweening behaviour in this matter carried him along, the Goths heard about these events and prepared an ambush. Boso pitched his camp by a small river not far from the city, sat down to dinner, fell to drinking, and heaped abuse and curses upon the Goths. The Goths attacked, finding Boso's forces eating and ill prepared. At that point they rose up with a shout against the Goths, who fought back only a little and pretended to flee. The Goths who were ready in ambush fell upon the pursuers, and catching them between two forces, slaughtered them. Those who got away fled with difficulty on horseback and left all their gear lying on the ground, taking away nothing of their own and thinking themselves lucky just to be alive. The pursuing Goths found and seized all their property and led away all the troops on foot as captives. About five thousand men fell there and more than two thousand prisoners were taken. Many of the prisoners, however, were released and returned home.

King Guntram was stirred to order the roads in his kingdom closed to prevent passage through his territory of anyone from Childebert's kingdom.

"Because of his wickedness in concluding a treaty with the king of Spain, my army was brought to ruin," he said. "His interference caused those cities to reject subjecting themselves to my authority."

To this reason, he added another cause of his bitterness—that King Childebert was thinking about sending his eldest son Theudebert to Soissons, a course of action that made King Guntram suspicious.

"My nephew is sending his son to Soissons for the purpose of entering Paris and trying to take my kingdom away," he declared.

If it is permissible to say so, this is an action that Childebert could never even have conceived of.

He hurled a lot of abuse at Queen Brunhild, saying it was by her advice that this was done, and adding also that she wanted to call in the son of the late Gundovald and marry him.

On this matter, he ordered a synod of bishops to meet on the Kalends of November. Many bishops hurrying from the furthest parts of Gaul to this assembly turned back on the road when Brunhild cleared herself of this crime by oath. And so the roads were reopened and passage given to those who wished to go to King Childebert.

Quarrels between Fredegund and Her Daughter (IX 34)

Rigunth, Chilperic's daughter, kept insulting her mother, saying that she herself was the mistress and would return her mother to servitude, and repeatedly provoking her with heaps of abuse. Sometimes they punched and hit each other.

"Why do you annoy me so, daughter?" said her mother. "Here, take the things of your father that I have in my possession and do with them as you please."

She went into the storeroom and opened a chest full of necklaces and costly jewelry.

When for some time she had taken various items from the chest and handed them to her daughter, who was standing by, she said, "I am tired now. You put in your hand and take out what you find."

As Rigunth thrust her arm in and was taking things from the chest, her mother seized hold of the lid and slammed it down on her daughter's neck. She forced it down and the chest's lower edge pressed against Rigunth's throat so that even her eyes were ready to burst.

One of the female servants who was in the storeroom shouted out, "Please come quickly, come quickly. My mistress is being throttled to death by her mother."

Those waiting for them to come out burst into the room, rescued the girl from imminent death, and took her outside.

After this affair the hostility between mother and daughter increased in intensity. There were continual quarrels, and blows were exchanged between them. The main reason for the trouble was Rigunth's fondness for adulterous relationships.

The End of Waddo (IX 35)

Beretrudis has the same name as the wife of a certain Duke Launebodis mentioned by Venantius Fortunatus. For Waddo, see VI 45; VII 27, 34–38, 39, 43.

Beretrudis died and appointed her daughter as heir, leaving some property to the monasteries of girls she had founded, as well as to churches and basilicas of the holy confessors.

But Waddo, whom I have mentioned in an earlier book, claimed that his horses were stolen by Beretrudis's son-in-law. He thought he would go to one of the villas she had left to her daughter located in the territory of Poitiers.

"This fellow came from the territory of another king and seized my horses," he said. "I shall take his villa away from him."

Meanwhile he sent orders to the administrator of the villa, saying he was coming and to get ready everything necessary for his stay. When the administrator heard the news, he joined up with some people from the household and got ready to fight.

"Waddo will not enter the house of my lord," he said, "except over my dead body."

Waddo's wife learned of the warm welcome they had prepared for her husband.

"Don't go there, dear husband," she said. "You shall die if you go and I and the children shall be miserable." She tried to hold him back.

Then a son added, "If you go, we too shall die and you shall leave my mother a widow and my brothers orphans."

These words had no effect on him. Roused to a fury against his son, he called him a craven weakling and threw his ax at him almost caving in his head. But the boy was knocked to one side and escaped the blow.

Waddo's party mounted their horses and left; again he issued orders to the administrator to sweep the house and to put coverings over the bare planks. But the administrator had little regard for his orders, and stood at his lord's door with a crowd—as I said—of men and women, awaiting Waddo's arrival.

Waddo came and immediately entered the house.

"Why are the boards not covered and the place not swept?" he said. Raising his arm he cleaved the man's head in two with his sword. The fellow fell down dead.

The dead man's son saw what happened and brought his lance to bear on Waddo from the front. It hit him right in middle of the gut and came out the back. Waddo fell to the ground and the crowd that had gathered came up and started to stone him. Some of those who had accompanied Waddo approached under the hail of stones and covered him with a cloak. When the crowd settled down, his son, loudly wailing, raised Waddo on to his horse and brought him home still alive.

But thereupon he breathed his last amid the tears of his wife and sons. And so ended a most futile life. His son went to the king and obtained his father's property.

Childebert Sends his Son Theudebert to Soissons (IX 36)

In the same year, Childebert was staying with his wife and his mother in the territory of the town called Strasbourg. At this time some of the better fighting men who lived in Soissons and Meaux came to him.

"Give us one of your sons," they said, "so that we may serve him. That way if we have among us one of the offspring of your line, we shall the better resist the enemy and diligently defend the territory of your city."

The king was pleased with the request and decided to send them his elder son Theudebert, to whom he assigned counts, *domestici*, mayors, governors, and all the persons required for serving a king. In the sixth month [August] of this year, he dispatched Theudebert in accordance with the wishes of those who had asked the king to send a son. The people received Theudebert with joy and with prayers that the divine goodness might grant him and his father a long life.

A Plot against Faileuba, Brunhild, and Childebert (IX 38)

While Faileuba, King Childebert's queen, was weak from giving birth to a child that soon died, she got word that certain people were plotting against herself and Queen Brunhild. As soon as she had regained her strength, she went before the king and revealed to him and to his mother all that she had heard.

This is roughly what she had been told. Septimina, her children's nurse, would advise the king to drive out his mother, leave his wife, and take another spouse; the conspirators would then do with him as they liked or obtain from him whatever they wanted. If the king would not agree to what she suggested, they would kill him by witchcraft, raise his sons to the throne, and rule the kingdom themselves, while the children's mother and grandmother would be driven out just the same. Associates in this plot, declared Faileuba, were Sunnegisil, count of the stables, Gallomagnus the referendary, and Droctulf, who had been appointed to aid Septimina in raising the king's children.

Next, these two, Septimina and Droctulf, were seized. Without delay they were spread between posts and beaten severely. Septimina confessed that she had killed her husband Jovius by witchcraft out of love for Droctulf, with whom she played the whore. They both confessed to all the matters which I have related above and denounced the people I have mentioned as involved in the plot.

A search was made at once for them also, but guilty consciences caused them to seek refuge in the enclosures of the churches. The king himself went to them.

"Come out," he said, "and stand before a tribunal so we may examine whether the charges brought against you are true or false. I am of the belief that you never would have fled to this church, if a bad conscience had not terrified you. Nevertheless, you may have a promise that your lives shall be spared, even if you are found guilty. For we are Christians, and it is wrong even for criminals to be punished [with death] if they have been taken out of a church."

They were then led outside and came with the king before the court. When they were examined, they protested innocence.

"Septimina and Droctulf revealed this plot to us," they said. "But we, cursing and shunning it, would never consent to this crime."

"If you hadn't just winked at this," said the king, "surely you would have brought the matter to our attention. Is it not so, therefore, that you gave consent in this matter, when you decided to conceal this from my knowledge?"

Immediately they were driven outside and once more they made for the church.

Septimina was severely flogged, together with Droctulf, and her face was branded with hot irons. Everything she had was taken from her. She was led away to the villa of Marlenheim to turn the mill and to prepare each day flour for the food of the women in the gynaeceum. Droctulf's hair and ears were cut off, and he was assigned to work in the vineyards; but after a few days he slipped off and fled. Search was made by the steward, and he was again brought before the king. He was severely beaten and sent back to the vineyard that he had left.

Sunnegisil and Gallomagnus were stripped of all the property they had received from the fisc and were sent into exile. But envoys, among whom were bishops, came from King Guntram to intercede for them, and they were recalled from exile, though they were left nothing but their private property.

Year XV of Childebert II, a. 590

Gripo's Embassy to Maurice and War against the Lombards (X 2, 3, 4)

Gripo returned from the Emperor Maurice [see IX 25] and related the following.

In the previous year he had boarded ship and, along with his colleagues, had sailed to the port of Africa and entered the city of Carthage. While they were staying there, awaiting the order of the resident [praetorian] prefect for them to go on to the imperial court, one of the retainers, specifically a servant of Evantius who was accompanying Gripo, grabbed a costly object from the hands of a certain merchant and brought it to their lodgings. The owner followed him, demanding he return his property. But the retainer contradicted him and day after day the dispute grew more serious until one day the merchant came across the retainer on the street, grabbed him by his clothing, and tried to hold him.

"I won't let you go," he said, "until you restore the property you took from me by force."

Trying to shake off the merchant's grip, the retainer had no hesitation in drawing his sword and cutting the man down. He immediately went back to

the lodgings but did not reveal to his fellows what he had done. In the delegation there was, as I said, the envoy Bodygisil the son of Mummolin of Soissons,
Evantius the son of Dynamius of Arles, and Gripo himself, who was a Frank by
birth. They had just gotten up from the table and were having a nap.

When the deed of the retainer was told to the leading official of the town,
he gathered soldiers and proceeded to the lodgings surrounded by a whole
crowd of townsmen under arms. Unexpectedly woken up, the delegation was
confused as to what was going on.

"Put down your weapons," shouted the commander, "and come out so we
can learn without recourse to violence how this killing took place."

When they heard this, the delegation, stricken with fear and still not knowing what had gone on, asked for assurance that they would be safe if they came
out unarmed. The Carthaginians took an oath, but impulsiveness prevented
them keeping it. Soon Bodygisil came out and was struck by a sword blow, and
the same thing happened to Evantius. When they were laid low at the entrance
to the lodging, Gripo seized his weapons and came forth with the retainers
who accompanied him.

"We have no knowledge of what was done," he said. "Look, my traveling
companions who were sent to the emperor, have been struck down by the
sword. God shall judge the outrage done to us and the death of those men at
your hands, for you have cut us down though we are innocent and come in
peace, with the consequence that no longer shall there be peace between our
kings and your emperor. We have come on a mission of peace and to bestow
assistance on the empire. Today I call on God as a witness that your crime will
cause the promised peace between the princes to fail."

When Gripo said this and words of that sort and the hostility of the Carthaginians dissipated, everyone returned home.

The prefect came to Gripo, trying to soothe his feelings over what had
happened, and arranging for him to proceed to an audience with the emperor.
When he arrived, Gripo delivered the message as he had been instructed and
reported the fate of his colleagues. The emperor got quite angry over the matter and promised to avenge their deaths according to a judgment delivered by
King Childebert. Then rewarded by the emperor, Gripo peacefully returned
home.

Gripo reported these events to King Childebert and immediately the king
ordered an army to go to Italy, sending twenty dukes to fight the Lombards. I
have not thought it necessary to list all their names in my account.

Duke Audovald along with Wintrio assembled the forces of Champagne.
When he came to Metz, which was on his march, he perpetrated so much
pillaging, killing, and slaughter that one would think he was leading an enemy
force through his own country. And the other dukes did the same with their

forces, afflicting their own region and its inhabitants even before gaining any kind of victory against an enemy people.

Reaching the Italian frontier, Audovald with six dukes turned right, advanced on Milan, and camped there some distance away in open country. Duke Olo ineptly approached Bellinzona, a fortress of that city located in the fields of Canini; he was struck by a javelin below the breast and fell down dead. When the forces went forth to pillage for food, they were attacked by the Lombards and cut down wherever they went. There was a body of water in the territory of Milan that is called Ceresium [Lake Lugano], from which a small but deep river emerges. They heard that on the banks of the lake the Lombards had dared take up a position. When the Franks approached it, and before crossing the river I mentioned, there was one of the Lombards standing on the bank, wearing body armor and a helmet and brandishing a spear.

"Today," he said, addressing the Frankish forces, "it will be apparent to whom God grants victory." It was understood from this that the Lombards had arranged this encounter as a sign.

Then a few Franks crossed the river, contended with the Lombard and cut him down. And look!—the entire army of the Lombards turned in flight and got away. Those who crossed the river could find no one but detected only the campground where the Lombards had their hearths and had pitched their tents.

Since the Franks could not catch anyone they returned to their own camp where envoys of the emperor had come to meet them and to report that an [imperial] army was present to assist them.

"We will come with it in three days," they said, "and this shall be your signal. When you see the houses of this villa on the hill set on fire, and the smoke of the fire rises to the sky, you will know that we are at hand with the army we have promised."

But waiting on the agreed spot for six days, they saw not one of them come.

Chedinos with thirteen dukes entered Italy on the left, and took five fortresses from which they also exacted oaths. Dysentery also seriously afflicted the army because the air was ill-suited and strange to the men, a good number of whom died as a result. The wind rose and the rain came down and when the air began to cool a little, sickness gave way to good health.

What more is there to say? They wandered about Italy for almost three months, accomplishing nothing. They could not take vengeance on their enemies (they were holed up in quite defensible locations) or capture the king on whom vengeance might be wreaked (he was safe within the walls of Pavia), and the army became ill, worn down by the extreme climate, as I said, and hunger. As a consequence, they decided to return home, subjecting to royal authority the area that Childebert's father [Sigibert] had once possessed, from which area they led away captives and other spoils. And so traveling home, they were so worn down by hunger that they were ridding themselves of their weapons and clothing to buy food before they reached their native land.

Aptachar [Authari], king of the Lombards, sent an embassy to King Guntram with a message of this sort: "Most pious king, we wish to be loyal subjects to you and your dynasty, as we were to your fathers. And we do not abandon the oath that our forerunners swore to your predecessors. But stop afflicting us and let there be peace and harmony with us so we can provide you with assistance against your enemies, should the need arise, and so once your people and ours are safe and sound and we recognize peacemakers, the enemies who circle howling will have more reason to be terrified than to rejoice in our discord."

King Guntram received these words graciously and sent the envoys to his nephew King Childebert. When they had delivered their message and were still in attendence, others arrived with news of Aptachar's death [5 September 590] and his replacement by Paul, and bearing a message similar to the one I mentioned above. King Childebert set a meeting date with the envoys so the king could later specify what would satisfy him and ordered the envoys to depart.

Now Maurice sent before King Childebert the Carthaginians who killed the king's envoys the year before. There were twelve of them, loaded with chains and with their hands tied. The stipulation was that the king had the right to kill them if he wished, but if he set them free in return for compensation, three hundred solidi would be received for each and the matter would rest. And so the choice was his of what would best lay the quarrel to rest and provide no opportunity for hostilities arising between them.

But King Childebert was averse to accepting the bound men.

"It is regarded as uncertain by us whether those you have brought are the homicides or other people," he said. "Perhaps they are someone's slaves, although our people who were killed by you were well-born freemen."

Chief among those present was Gripo who at the time had been sent as an envoy with the men who had been killed.

He said, "The prefect of the city with a band of two or three thousand men attacked us and killed my colleagues. I myself would have died in this slaughter if I had been unable to defend myself like a man. If I went there I could recognize the men. If your emperor wants to preserve peace with our king, as you say, he should take vengeance on them."

And so the king ordered the envoys to depart, deciding to send a message to the emperor in their wake.

Campaign against the Bretons. Fredegund, Waroc, and the Saxons. The End of Beppolen (X 9)

While these events were transpiring and the Bretons were on the rampage around the cities of Nantes and Rennes, Guntram ordered an army to march against them. To lead it, he chose Dukes Beppolen [see VIII 42] and Ebrachar [see IX 28].

Ebrachar, suspecting that if Beppolen was victorious, the latter would obtain the command he himself administered as duke, quarreled with him, and so throughout the march the two attacked one another with oaths, insults, and curses. Truth be told, the army burned, slew, and plundered along the path it traveled, committing many crimes. Meanwhile, they arrived at the river Vilaine, crossed it, and came to the river Oust, where they demolished the dwellings in the neighborhood and built a bridge by which the whole army could cross over.

At that time a certain priest joined Beppolen and said to him, "If you follow me, I will take you to Waroc [see V 16, 26] and show you all the Bretons gathered together in one place."

Since Fredegund's hatred for Beppolen was already longstanding, when she heard he would be on this campaign, she ordered the Saxons of Bayeux [see V 26] to come to Waroc's assistance, with their hair cut in Breton fashion and wearing Breton clothing.

Beppolen arrived, leading the troops that chose to follow him, and engaged; for two days he killed large numbers of the above-mentioned Bretons and Saxons. Ebrachar had withdrawn with the greater part of the force without the slightest intention of coming up until he heard of Beppolen's death. By the third day, when those that accompanied Beppolen had been killed and he himself, though wounded by a lance, continued to defend himself, Waroc and his forces overwhelmed him and killed him. He had forced them onto narrow paths among the marshes so that more drowned in the mire than were put to the sword.

Ebrachar for his part reached Vannes. There Bishop Regalis had sent clerics holding crucifixes and singing psalms to meet him and led his forces to the city. It was said at the time that Waroc tried to take refuge on the islands in ships laden with gold and silver and other property; when they reached the high seas, a storm arose sinking the ships, and they lost all the goods stowed aboard them. Waroc came to Ebrachar seeking peace and handed over hostages and many gifts, promising that he would never act against the interests of King Guntram.

When he departed, Bishop Regalis, along with the clergy and laity of his city, gave a similar oath, "We are guiltless with respect to our lord kings, and we have never been so proud as to do anything against their interests, but finding ourselves captives of the Bretons, we were subject to a heavy yoke."

Then peace was concluded between Waroc and Ebrachar.

"Go now," said Waroc, "and announce that I shall willingly endeavor to fulfill everything the king has ordered. And so you may better believe me, I hand over my nephew as a hostage."

And so he did and the war came to an end. But a huge number of the royal and Breton armies had been killed.

The army left Brittany and the hardier troops crossed the river, but both the lesser ones and the poor, who were with them, could not get over and were left on the bank of the river Vilaine. Waroc, forgetting about the oath and the hostages he gave, sent his son Canao with a force to seize those left on the bank of the river. They were bound and those who resisted were killed, while a few who tried to swim their horses across the rushing waters, were swept away by the current into the sea. Many were later released as freemen by Waroc's wife in the rite of taper and tablet [a procedure of Roman law for the manumission of slaves] and returned home.

The army of Ebrachar that had earlier crossed the river, fearing to return by the road they had come in case they suffered for the evils they had inflicted, proceeded to Angers and tried to cross the bridge over the river Mayenne. The small band that first crossed was despoiled, beaten, and reduced to a completely disgraceful condition at the bridge I just mentioned. Those going through Tours committed robberies, despoiling many people; they took the locals by surprise.

Still, many from this army reached King Guntram, declaring that Ebrachar and count Willachar [see VII 13] had taken money from Waroc and caused the destruction of the army. For this reason, when presented before the king, Ebrachar was subjected to heaps of abuse by the king and ordered out of the king's sight. Count Willachar fled and went into hiding.

Judicial Duel in the Vosges (X 10)

In the fifteenth year of King Childebert, which is the twenty-eighth of Guntram, as King Guntram was hunting in the Vosges forest, he came on the traces of a wild ox that had been killed. When the king compelled the forester to reveal who dared do this in the royal forest, he revealed that it was Chundo, the chamberlain of the king. On this accusation, the king ordered Chundo seized and led to Chalon tightly bound. As both the forester and Chundo disputed in the presence of the king and Chundo said that the accusations laid against him were groundless, the king adjudged proof by battle.

The chamberlain presented his nephew to fight on his behalf and then both combatants stood upon the field. The young man threw his lance and pierced the foot of the forester, who soon fell on his back. The youth drew the blade that hung at his belt, and as he tried to cut through the neck of the fallen man, he was stabbed in the belly with a sword and transfixed. Both fell down dead.

Seeing this Chundo tried to flee to the basilica of Saint Marcellus. But the king shouted for him to be seized, and he was caught before he reached the holy threshold. He was bound to a post and stoned.

Later the king's action caused him to repent deeply that anger had made him so hasty as to rashly kill a loyal and trusted servant for a minor offense.

Explaining Chlothar's Recovery. Fredegund and Waroc (X 11)

Chlothar, the son of the late King Chilperic, grew severely ill and was thought to be in such a desperate condition that his death was announced to King Guntram. For that reason Guntram left Chalon and came to the Sens region, intending to go to Paris. But when he heard that the boy had recovered, he returned to Chalon.

When Chlothar's mother Fredegund saw that her son looked beyond hope, she pledged a great deal of money to the basilica of Saint Martin [in Tours], and so the boy improved. She also sent a message to Waroc to release for the sake of her son those still held captive from the army of King Guntram [see X 9]. Waroc did so. This shows clearly that both Beppolen was killed and the army battered to pieces by the collusion of this woman.

Attempt to Assassinate Childebert (X 18)

As the king entered the oratory of his house at Marlenheim, his servants saw a man unknown to them standing at a distance.

They said to him, "Who are you and where do you come from? What's your business? We don't know you."

"I am one of you," he answered.

He had no sooner said this than he was thrown out of the oratory and interrogated. It was not long before he confessed, saying that he had been sent by Fredegund to kill the king.

"Twelve of us have been sent here by her," he said. "Six have arrived, while the other six have stayed behind at Soissons to snare the king's son. As for me, while I was waiting my chance to strike down King Childebert in the oratory, fear came over me, and I decided not to carry out my purpose."

When he said this, he was immediately subjected to savage tortures and named his accomplices. Search was made for them in various quarters. Some were consigned to prison, some were left with their hands cut off; some were released, shorn of their ears and noses, to be laughed at. Many of those who were confined, fearing various kinds of torture, stabbed themselves with their own weapons. Not a few also succumbed under torture so that the king could get vengeance.

Removal of Egidius, Bishop of Rheims (X 19)

Sunnegisil's confession regarding Chilperic's death sometimes occasions surprise (and emendation). While in the context we might expect a reference to a plot against Childebert, the text as it stands is unobjectionable. Ennodius, the prosecutor in Egidius's trial, was a former duke of Tours and Poiters removed at the request of the counts of these towns in 587.

Sunnegisil [see IX 38] was once more subjected to torture and was flogged daily with rods and whips. His wounds festered, but, as soon as the pus cleared up and the wounds began to close, he was tortured again. Under these torments he confessed not only to the assassination of Chilperic but also of having committed various crimes. In these confessions he also added that Egidius, bishop of Rheims, had been an accomplice in the plot of Rauching, Ursio, and Berthefred to kill King Childebert.

The bishop was instantly arrested and taken to Metz, though he was at the time quite worn out by a prolonged illness. There he was kept in custody while the king ordered the bishops to be summoned to examine him; they were to meet at Verdun at the beginning of October. The king was blamed at the time by the other bishops for having ordered this man to be carried off from his city and kept in custody without a hearing. For this reason he allowed Egidius to return to his city, but issued letters, as I have said, to all the bishops of his kingdom, requiring them to be present in the aforesaid city in the middle of November to investigate the matter. There were heavy rains and immeasurable torrents, the cold was unbearable, the roads were awash in muck, and the rivers overflowed their banks; but the bishops could not disobey the king's command. Finally, they met and were obliged to continue to Metz, where the aforesaid Egidius also appeared.

The king at that time declared him his enemy and a traitor to the country. He directed Ennodius, the former duke, to conduct the prosecution.

Ennodius's first question was this: "Tell me, bishop, why was it that you did forsake the king in whose city you enjoyed the episcopal dignity to place yourself among the friends of King Chilperic, who has always proven himself to be the enemy of our lord king, who killed our lord king's father, sentenced his mother to exile, and overran his kingdom? And in these cities which, as we have said, he subjected to his authority by unjust invasion, why was it that you received from him farms from the property of the fisc?"

To these points Egidius responded: "That I was the friend of King Chilperic,

I cannot deny, but this friendship never grew to prejudice the interests of King Childebert. The villas that you mention I received through written authorizations of King Childebert."

At this he produced them before the court, but the king denied having granted them. Otto was summoned. He had been the referendary at the time and a likeness of his signature was on the documents. He appeared and denied that it was his signature. For his hand had been forged in the writing of this document. On this charge the bishop was for the first time found guilty of deception.

After this were produced letters of his to Chilperic that contained many criticisms of Queen Brunhild; likewise letters of Chilperic sent to the bishop, in which, among other things, was this passage: "If the root of anything is not cut, the stalk that grows from the earth will not wither." Here it was quite clear that this was written with the meaning that, when Brunhild was overthrown, her son could be destroyed.

The bishop denied sending these letters in his own name or receiving them as an answer from Chilperic. But a confidential servant of the bishop was present with shorthand copies for the records of correspondence. There remained no doubt to those sitting there that they were sent by the accused.

Next, agreements were produced in the names of Kings Childebert and Chilperic containing a clause that the two kings, after expelling King Guntram, would divide his kingdom and his cities between themselves [see VI 3, 31; VII 6]. The king denied that he had been a party to this.

"You set my uncles against each other, stirring up civil war," he said. "As a result an army was mustered that devastated and laid waste the city of Bourges, the district of Étampes, and the town of Châteaumeillant. In this war many were killed. God's judgment, I believe, shall hold you responsible for their deaths."

This charge the bishop could not deny. For these documents were found together in one of the letter-cases in the vault of King Chilperic and had passed into King Childebert's possession at the time he took delivery of the treasure removed from Chelles, the royal villa in the territory of Paris, following Chilperic's death [see VII 4].

The discussion of matters of this kind dragged on for some time when Epiphanius, the abbot of the basilica of the holy Remigius, appeared and said that Egidius had received two thousand pieces of gold and many valuable items to preserve his friendship with King Chilperic. Envoys who had accompanied the bishop to the aforesaid King Chilperic also testified.

"He left us and conferred for a long time alone with the king," they said. "We knew nothing of what they said, until later we learned that the above-mentioned devastation had been carried out."

The bishop denied these charges, but the abbot, who had always been a party to his secret plans, named the place where the gold pieces were delivered and the person who brought them. He recounted how it happened, step by step, that an agreement was reached to devastate the region and kill King Guntram.

Convicted, Egidius now confessed to the charges.

On hearing this and seeing that a priest of the Lord had been an abettor of such great evil, the bishops who had been summoned sighed deeply and begged a space of three days to consider what they had heard, thinking that Egidius might recover himself and find some means of clearing himself of the charges brought against him. At dawn on the third day, they gathered in the church and asked the bishop, if he had any excuse, to declare it.

"Do not delay passing sentence on a guilty man," he said, confounded. "For I know that I deserve death on the charge of high treason. I have always opposed the interests of the king and his mother, and on my advice many campaigns were conducted in which not a few parts of Gaul were devastated."

When the bishops heard this and mourned the disgrace of a brother, they obtained his life, but removed him from the priesthood after reading the sanctions prescribed by the canons. He was immediately taken to Argentoratum, now called Strasbourg, and placed in exile. Romulf, son of Duke Lupus, already in priest's orders, succeeded to his position as bishop. Epiphanius, who presided over the basilica of the holy Remigius, was removed from his post as abbot. Many pounds of gold and silver were found in the vault of Egidius. The proceeds from his actions in the service of evil were handed over to the royal treasury. The proceeds from taxes or other business of the church were left there.

Waddo's Sons and Gundovald's Treasure (X 21)

The sons of Waddo [cf. IX 35] were wandering about the Poitiers region, committing crimes, homicides, and a number of thefts. Earlier they had fallen on merchants in the dark of night, put them to the sword, and taken their property. They even laid a trap for a man of tribune rank, killing him and taking his property.

When Count Macco [of Poitiers] tried to check them they went to the king. Just as the count was in the regular process of delivering the renders due the fisc, they too were before the king, presenting a great baldric decorated with gold and precious stones and a marvelous sword, the hilt of which was decorated with Spanish jewels. When the king learned that the crimes he was told about were committed by Waddo's sons openly, he had them clamped in irons and tortured.

In the course of the examination, they began to reveal the hidden treasure which their father had taken from the property of Gundovald, whom we have mentioned before. Without delay, men were sent to investigate and found a countless hoard of gold, silver, and precious objects decorated with gold and jewels, which they delivered to the royal treasury.

Afterward, the eldest son was executed, and the younger one exiled.

Year XVI of Childebert, a. 591

Fredegund Buries the Hatchet (X 27)

A not insignificant dispute arose among the Franks of Tournai because the son of one of them kept angrily criticizing the son of another, who had married his sister, for leaving his wife and going to a whore. When accusations failed to mend the behavior, the anger of the boy reached the point that he and his men rushed upon his brother-in-law and killed him. The boy himself was struck down by his brother-in-law's followers and there was only one man left from both parties without an adversary to do him in.

Relatives on both sides were in fury at each other as a result, but Fredegund kept telling them to give up their enmity and make peace because persistence in the quarrel would only lead to a greater public disgrace. But when she was unable to pacify these people with soft words she suppressed both sides with the ax.

She invited many guests to a feast and had three of these people sit on the same bench. When the dinner had gone on beyond nightfall, the table was taken away, as is the custom of the Franks, and the guests remained sitting on the benches in the places they had been assigned. A lot of wine had been consumed, and they were so far gone that their retainers were drunkenly sleeping wherever they had fallen down in the corners of the room. At that point, as the woman had arranged, three of her men with axes stepped up behind the three occupying the same bench. They were talking together as the hands of the queen's retainers swung their axes, in one movement, as I would say, striking the three men down and ending the banquet. The names of the dead were Charivald, Leodovald, and Valeden.

When this was told to their relatives, they began to watch Fredegund closely and sent messengers to King Childebert asking him to arrest her and put her to death. The forces of Champagne were mustered over this matter, but time was wasted, and Fredegund, saved by the help of her men, went somewhere else.

The Baptism of Chlothar (X 28)

After this Fredegund sent envoys to King Guntram with a message saying, "Let my lord king come to Paris. Summon my son, his nephew, and have the boy consecrated with the grace of baptism. Let him take the child from the sacred font and be so kind as to treat him as his own foster son."

When he heard this the king gathered bishops, namely, Aetherius of Lyons, Syagrius of Autun, Flavius of Chalon, and others he wanted, and told them to go to Paris, saying that he would follow later on. Also present at this assembly were many officials from his kingdom, *domestici* as well as counts, involved in making the necessary preparations for the king's expenses. Though the decision to go to the assembly had already been made, the king was held up by a foot ailment. Upon his recovery, he came to Paris and from there quickly went off to the villa of Rueil in the territory of that city; summoning the boy, he ordered a place of baptism made ready in the village of Nanterre.

While this was going on, envoys came to see him from King Childebert.

"Your recent promise to your nephew Childebert hardly included establishing ties of friendship with his enemies," they said. "As far as we can tell, you are keeping no part of your word. Rather, ignoring your promise, you are making this boy king with his throne in the city of Paris. God shall judge you for not recalling what you promised of your own accord."

"I don't disregard the promise that I made to my nephew Childebert," replied the king. "There is no need for him to take offense if I receive his cousin, my own brother's son, from the sacred font; no Christian should refuse the request to do so. And God knows very well that I undertake the duty without ulterior motives and in the simplicity of a pure heart, for I fear angering God. Our line suffers no disparagement if I accept this child. For if masters take up their servants at the sacred font, why can't I receive a near relation and make him a son by the spiritual grace of baptism? Be off and tell your lord that I am anxious to preserve intact the agreement I made with him, and if your side does it no harm, it shall certainly not be set aside by me."

After these words, the envoys withdrew, and the king approached the sacred font, presenting the boy for baptism. On receiving him from the font, he said he wanted him to be called Chlothar.

"Let the boy grow and fulfill the meaning of this name," he said. "And may he enjoy such power as the former Chlothar whose name he has received."

At the end of the ceremony he invited the boy to his table and honored him with many gifts. When in turn, he had been invited by his nephew and loaded with numerous presents, he departed, deciding to return to Chalon.

The above chapter is the last political event of Gregory's narrative. King Guntram died in March 592. Gregory mentions the king's death in his VM 37, but does not record it in his Histories.

EPILOGUE AND POSTSCRIPTS

Gregory's account of political events ended in 591 with the baptism of Chilperic's son Chlothar II, Guntram's sponsorship—finally—of his nephew, and the older king's wishes that his nephew's success rival that of his namesake Chlothar I (IX 28). Neither Gregory nor Guntram could have known how prophetic those words (however they were meant) would turn out to be. In 613, Chlothar II reconstituted a unified kingdom of the Franks for the first time since the last years of his grandfather Chlothar I († 561), laying the groundwork for what is usually regarded as the apogee of Merovingian power under his son Dagobert I (629–39). The line of Chilperic and Fredegund, not of Sigibert and Brunhild, produced the Merovingian kings of the seventh and eighth centuries.

When Gregory died in 594, such an outcome hardly seemed to be in the stars. Guntram had predeceased him by two years and Childebert II, now twenty-four and with two sons, had succeeded to the Burgundian kingdom as his uncle had promised. Chlothar II was ten years old and, with his mother Fredegund and his Neustrian supporters, was holding on to a small kingdom based on Rouen that might have looked not long for this world. Soissons, the seat of his father's and grandfather's kingdom, had been taken by Childebert, who like Guntram also continued to operate in the regions adjacent to the Breton march. To judge from the second-to-last event given by Gregory (IX 27), Chlothar's and Fredegund's hold on Tournai may have looked shaky. Following Guntram's death, Wintrio, duke of Champagne, launched an unsuccessful attack on Chlothar's kingdom.

For the narrative of events after 591 we depend on a compendium of historical materials made around 660 by an anonymous author, conventionally known as Fredegar. He included in his work a chronicle of his own that began with the last years of Guntram and broke off abruptly in 642, likely because the author died before bringing it up to the present. The events dealing with the fall of the house of Sigibert are relatively full and must have been based on a source (or sources) no longer extant. This account, and a version of Jonas's *Life of Columbanus* which Fredegar integrated into his narrative, are hostile to Brunhild; Fredegar retains Jonas's reference to her as a second Jezebel.

Briefly, this is what Fredegar's chronicle tells us about the principal players in Frankish affairs after Gregory's death:

Childebert died in 596. His eldest son Theudebert, aged eleven, received Austrasia and his younger son Theuderic, aged nine, got Burgundy. Immediately Chlothar and Fredegund took Paris and won a victory at Laffaux against Austrasian and Burgundian forces. Fredegund died the next year in 597.

As for her rival Brunhild, on the division of Childebert's kingdom, she stayed initially in the court of her grandson Theudebert but was eventually expelled and joined her other grandson Theuderic in Burgundy. Fredegar portrays her influence thereafter as pernicious. Beginning in 602, she plotted repeatedly to have her enemies eliminated (including Saint Desiderius of Vienne, who was exiled in 603 and finally stoned to death in 607) and had her favorite Protadius appointed patrician for the Transjuran region in 604 and then mayor of the palace in 605, receiving in return his sexual favors. By 605 she was urging war against Theudebert, despite considerable resistance on the part of the Burgundian forces to comply, and poisoning the mind of Theuderic by casting doubt on the paternity of his brother Theudebert, who she claimed was the son of a gardener. In 607 she caused Theuderic to reject a royal Visigothic bride in favor of his concubines, raising the ire of the Spanish king Wetteric. The excerpt from Jonas represents her in her dealings with Saint Columbanus as vindictive and controlling. It is worth noting that Fredegar's serializing of Brunhild's bad behavior has her influence beginning when Theuderic reached the age of majority and her expulsion from the court of Theudebert occurring around the time he reached his majority. Fredegar implies that Theudebert was simple-minded.

Despite the hostility that developed between Theudebert and Theuderic, the two courts at first worked together successfully. After the setback of Laffaux, they ganged up on Chlothar in 600 at the battle of Dormelles, retaking for Theuderic the region from the Seine to the Loire up to the Breton march and acquiring for Theudebert the northern duchy of Dentelin around Tournai. Chlothar was forced back into an even smaller kingdom around Rouen. Two years later the two brothers had some success in the south against the Gascons. A counterattack by Chlothar in 604 against Theuderic failed at the battle of the river Louet, and the Burgundian king entered Paris. Theudebert made a separate peace with Chlothar. Thereafter relations between Austrasia and Burgundy deteriorated, especially after Theuderic was forced to give up Alsace to Theudebert in 610. In 612 Theuderic, now in his mid 20s, attacked his older brother Theudebert, keeping Chlothar neutral with a promise of a return of the duchy of Dentelin. Theudebert was captured (he was dead the next year, but the circumstances of his demise are not told) and the brains of his young son Merovech smashed out against a rock. Theuderic then moved against Chlothar but died before forces could engage.

Now the denouement. In Austrasia and Burgundy Brunhild tried to establish Theuderic's young son Sigibert (her great grandson) as king of both kingdoms, but her support among the aristocracy collapsed. Important Austrasian magnates led by Bishop Arnulf of Metz and Pippin of Landen (the ancestors of the Carolingians, as it turned out) invited Chlothar to enter Austrasia. Before

Chlothar's army and Brunhild's Austrasian and Burgundian forces could engage, her side abandoned the field, leaving Chlothar victorious.

Chlothar had two of Theuderic's sons killed— Sigibert and Corvus. A third, Merovech, was spared because Chlothar, who had stood sponsor at his baptism, was his godfather. A fourth, Childebert, escaped by flight. Brunhild was brought into Chlothar's presence. According to Fredegar, Chlothar harbored the deepest hatred toward her and accused her of the death of ten kings of the Franks, including Sigibert I, Chilperic's son Merovech, and Chilperic himself. The list by any count is too long and the charge exaggerated, since it included the young princes whom Chlothar himself had just eliminated. The meaning of the slightly puzzling accusation may be to show that Chlothar regarded the internal troubles plaguing the Merovingian house since the 560s as being somehow all Brunhild's fault.

Chlothar had Brunhild tortured for three days and then paraded on a camel before the army. She was then tied by her hair and one foot and hand to the tail of a vicious horse, which was then loosed, and she was "torn to pieces by the hooves and the pace of the galloping horse."

★ ★ ★

Gregory's history became the foundation of Frankish history. Fredegar and the anonymous *History of the Franks* (*Liber historiae Francorum*) of ca 727 used a six-book version of the *Histories* as the basis for their history of Frankish affairs. In so doing they not only continued from where Gregory left off (or where they thought he left off) but supplemented his narrative.

In Fredegar's case, he included the *Histories* in his compendium as a separate item, which he identified and abbreviated. Most of his stories of early Frankish history are added to this abbreviated version as if they were originally part of Gregory's history.

Among his notable additions on early Frankish history are the following:

1. A tale deriving the Franks from the Trojans, dispersed following the fall of Troy. This addition radically clarifies the hesitant search for early Frankish kings in the *Histories*. It is also the earliest reference to a motif that became a standard feature of Frankish/French history down to the sixteenth century.

2. A brief anecdote (ultimately derived from a false etymology of Merovech's name) casting the founder of the Merovingian dynasty as the offspring of Chlodio's wife and a sea beast.

3. A more elaborate version of the story of Childeric and the broken token, identifying Childeric's friend as Wiomad, and taking Childeric to Constantinople.

4. A well-developed tale added to Gregory's brief story of Childeric and Basina. On Basina's advice the couple refrained from intercourse the first night of their union. Childeric saw apparitions of animals whose significance was interpreted by Basina: Clovis, their son to be, is a lion, and subsequent generations of the Merovingians are successively leopards and unicorns, wolves and bears, and as the kingdom collapses, dogs and lesser beasts.

5. An elaborate tale about Clovis contacting Chlothild and forcing her uncle Gundobad to allow him to marry her.

6. A statement by Clovis uttered at his baptism, that if he and his Franks had been at the crucifixion, they would have avenged Christ.

7. A tale of the dealings of Paternus, Clovis's envoy, with Alaric, king of the Visigoths, and Theoderic the Great (this is added not to the *Histories* but Hydatius's *Chronicle*, which is also included in Fredegar's compendium.)

For events contemporary with Gregory's lifetime, Fredegar's details tend to be slightly less colorful. His abbreviated version of the *Histories* provides:

1. Reasons for Guntram's dismissal of Marcatrude. She was too fat, but the excuse used to dismiss her was her mother's misbehavior as a slut and concocter of potions.

2. The identity of the emissary who brought Brunhild from Spain as Gogo. Fredegar has him killed by Sigibert at the instigation of Brunhild (Gogo, as Gregory tells us, died in 581[VI 1], after Sigibert) and also portrays a certain Chrodin as Sigibert's mayor of the palace in the mode of a seventh-century mayor. Chrodin, who died in 582 at the age of seventy, must have been an important figure; Gregory gives a brief obituary (not translated in these selections).

3. The circumstances leading to Sigibert's attack on Chilperic in 575. A truce was signed between Sigibert and Guntram to halt the conflict, but Sigibert's troops wanted to attack somebody.

4. A distinct version of Childebert's rescue following Sigibert's assassination. Fredegar prefers Gundovald putting the child in a sack and passing him out through a window to a retainer, who shows the boy in Metz.

5. The identification of Chilperic's assassin as Falco, an agent of Brunhild.

The *Liber historiae Francorum* integrates the *Histories* into its account without identifying it. Here are a few instances of how it supplements its main source.

1. Another version of the Trojan origin of the Franks, independent of that in Fredegar.

2. Another version of Clovis's wooing of Chlothild, independent of that in Fredegar.

3. Comical anecdote of Saint Martin's hard bargaining with Clovis over the gift of a horse.

4. Humorous tale of how Fredegund displaced Audovera in the affections of Chilperic by tricking Audovera into being the godmother of her own child (and thereby being ineligible by church law from sleeping with Chilperic, with whom she was now spiritually related).

5. Humorous tale of Fredegund's adultery with the mayor of the palace Landeric, leading to Chilperic's murder. On returning unexpectedly from the stables, Chilperic approached Fredegund from behind as she was bent over washing her hair and slapped her affectionately across the buttocks with his riding crop. Fredegund's response, "What are you doing Landeric?" sealed the king's fate, for Fredegund realized the secret was out and had assassins do in the king.

6. A tale of Fredegund victoriously leading the Neustrians in battle against the Austrasians, cradling a young Chlothar in her arms. The story contains an early version of the Birnam Wood motif in Shakespeare's *Macbeth*.

7. An account of the fall of the house of Sigibert, featuring Brunhild's wickedness. Following Theudebert's death at the hands of Theuderic's men, Theuderic's lustful eye fell on Theudebert's daughter. When Brunhild blurted out in disgust, "How can you take the daughter of your brother?", Theuderic now realized he had indeed killed his own brother, deceived by his grandmother's lie about Theudebert's spurious paternity.

As delightful as most of these stories from Fredegar and the *Liber historiae Francorum* are, it would be hard to underestimate their historicity. These tales tell us about the elaboration of an image of the early Merovingians that has considerable interest for our understanding of the age that cultivated them and which still lived under Merovingian kings, but they are not repositories of additional information that can be used to flesh out the narrative of the bishop of Tours.

The imaginative representation of the Merovingians has been and, of course, remains ongoing. Distant (as opposed to contemporary) history is not a subject that past ages—ancient, medieval, or modern—have handled at all well. Present-day scholarship self-consciously struggles with the problem. Though it is true, as Horace said long ago, "scholars dispute and still judgment is pending," at least the discourse occurs within a critical process. Modern media, film, pseudo-history, and novels continue to handle the past with a heedless, fanciful abandon not dissimilar to the approach of Gregory of Tours's continuators, though alas, usually without the humor or dramatic sense of the scene.

APPENDIX

THE MEROVINGIAN BISHOP

All have not the gift of martyrdom.

John Dryden, *The Hind and the Panther*

The Histories *constitute a remarkably detailed source for the sixth-century episcopate, richer by far than for the secular offices of the Merovingian state. Gregory's interests and vocation are only part of the reason for the bias. For historical reasons the bishop as leader of the* civitas *was a central figure in what might be called the Merovingian system. When bishops emerged as leaders of local Christian communities in the early church, the episcopal office became a flash point of contention among competing interests, a feature of the office that only increased, and was consequently regulated, as the power of the position grew. The importance of the office from a very early date transcended its spiritual significance. By the late empire it became, in effect, an organ of local government as secular communities were forced to yield power to appointees of the central authority and the growing influence of the Christian church and its clergy. By the Merovingian period, it is not inconceivable that the church, presided over by its bishops, controlled resources comparable in importance to those of municipal government in its heyday.*

The following selections merely supplement and contextualize a little more fully the role of episcopacy in the life of the sixth-century civitas.

Episcopal Appointments

Canon law provided for the participation of various sectors of the community in the selection of the bishop, but its norms, which had developed in political circumstances increasingly distant from those of Gallic communities and kingdoms, were imprecise or variously interpreted. Divergent and genuine interests intersected, not always harmoniously, when a new bishop needed to be appointed. Such circumstances, combined with many of the less wholesome characteristics of human society, made the process of episcopal appointment a disruptive feature of political life in the Gallic cities. Yet for all the discord, episcopal appointment in the sixth century was still a process marked with very distinct institutional continuities with the preceding century—and the impending seventh, just on the horizon at the time of Gregory's death.

The following selections cover about twenty years, from 551 to about 571, and concern Clermont, Tours, and Saintes. As usual, Gregory's own perspective is as germane to the subject as the events he recounts.

The Rivalry of Cato and Cautinus in Clermont (IV 5–7)

When Saint Gallus [bishop of Clermont] had passed from this life [a. 551], and his body had been washed and taken into the church, the priest Cato immediately gained the nomination of the clergy for the post of bishop. He took control of all church property as if he were already bishop, dismissing its superintendents and discharging its officials, arranging everything on his own.

The bishops who came to Saint Gallus's funeral said to the priest Cato after the interment, "We see that you are by far the most popular choice for bishop; come then, agree with us, and we will bless and consecrate you as bishop. As for the king, he is still a boy, and, if any blame falls on you, we will take you under our protection, deal with the leaders and chief officials of Theudebald's kingdom, and see to it that no wrong is done to you. You can put your confidence in us because we promise that, should you suffer loss, we will make it all up to you from our own resources."

Cato, fiercely proud, replied, "You know from what people say that from the very beginning I have always lived a religious life. I have fasted, I have been happy to give alms, I have often kept long vigils. I have even stayed at my post continually singing psalms all night. My Lord God, to whom I have given such service, will not allow me to be deprived of this office. Also I have always attained the various grades of the clergy according to the rules of the canons. I was reader for ten years. I tended to the duties of the subdiaconate for five years. For fifteen years I was assigned to the diaconate. I have held the dignity of the priesthood now for twenty years. What else is there for me but to attain the office of bishop, which my faithful service deserves? You should return to your cities and do whatever is in your interest. As for me, I intend to get this office in the manner prescribed by the canons."

Hearing this, the bishops left, cursing his pointless vanity.

When the clergy had agreed to elect Cato as bishop and he had taken charge of everything, though he was not yet ordained, he then began to make threats against the archdeacon Cautinus.

"I will discharge you," he said, "I will humble you, I will have death prepared for you in many ways."

"I desire your favor, pious lord," replied Cautinus. "If I am worthy of that, there is one kindness I can do for you. Without your troubling yourself, and without deception, I will go to the king and get the office of bishop for you. I ask nothing for myself but to earn your favor."

Cato suspected Cautinus was trying to trick him and quite scornfully rejected the offer.

When Cautinus saw that he was being humiliated and subjected to false charges, he pretended to be sick and, leaving the city in the middle of the night, went to King Theudebald and reported the death of Saint Gallus. When the king and his court heard this, they assembled bishops at the city of Metz, and Cautinus the archdeacon was ordained bishop. By the time the messengers of the priest Cato arrived, Cautinus was already bishop. Then, by command of the king, these clerics and everything they brought with them from church property were handed over to Cautinus, and bishops and chamberlains were appointed to accompany him on his journey back to Clermont. Cautinus was readily accepted by the citizens and clergy and Clermont was provided with a bishop.

Later intense hostility arose between Cautinus and the priest Cato because no one could ever persuade Cato that he was subject to his bishop. A split among the clergy developed, some following Bishop Cautinus and some the priest Cato, a situation that was completely disastrous for Cato's party. Cautinus saw that there was no way to make Cato obey him, and so he took away all church property from Cato and his friends, or whoever agreed with him, leaving them penniless and destitute. However, any of them who came over to his side received back what he had lost.

Cato and Tours (IV 11, 15)

Cato got a second chance at an episcopal appointment after the death of Theudebald in 555, when Chlothar I assumed the kingdom. The following events took place around the time Chramn was misbehaving in Clermont.

Bishop Gunthar died at Tours, and the priest Cato was asked to assume direction of the church of Tours, at the suggestion, it is said, of Bishop Cautinus. And so it happened that the clergy assembled and, accompanied by Leubastes, *martyrarius* and abbot, made a great show of going to Clermont. When they had made known the king's will to Cato, he kept them hanging around for a few days waiting for an answer.

Anxious to go home, they said, "Tell us your decision so we know what we're doing; otherwise we're going back home. It wasn't our idea to approach you; the king commanded it."

Cato, in his pointless desire for glory, got together a crowd of poor folk and had them cry out, "Good father, why do you abandon us, your children, whom you have raised up to now? Who will give us food and drink if you go away? We, whom you are accustomed to nourish, ask you not to leave us."

At that point, turning to the clergy of Tours, he said, "Now you see, dear brothers, how this multitude of poor people loves me. I can't leave them and go with you."

With this answer, they returned to Tours.

Now Cato had made friends with Chramn and got a promise from him that the moment King Chlothar died Cautinus would be tossed out of the bishop's office and Cato given control of the church. But he who scorned the throne of the blessed Martin did not get what he wanted, and in this was fulfilled the song of David, "He refused the blessing and it shall be taken far from him [cf. Ps. 109:17]."

Cato struck vain poses, thinking that no one was his superior in holiness. For example, he once hired a woman to cry out in church as if possessed and say that he was a great holy man, beloved of God, and that Bishop Cautinus was guilty of every sort of crime and unworthy of attaining episcopal rank.

Gregory recounts the excesses of Bishop Cautinus (IV 12), before returning to the story of Cato.

The family of Eufronius, mentioned below, was also that of Gregory of Tours. The consensus drawn up on Eufronius's behalf was a form of petition; a model of such a document is preserved in the formulary of Marculf, dating from the following century.

The people of Tours on hearing that King Chlothar had returned from slaughtering Saxons [a. 555] drew up a consensus nominating Eufronius and went to the king.

When they delivered their request, the king answered, "I have given instructions for the priest Cato to be ordained at Tours. Why has my order been rejected?"

"We asked him," they replied, "but he wouldn't come."

As they were saying this, the priest Cato suddenly turned up asking the king to have Cautinus expelled from Clermont and him appointed instead. The king laughed at that suggestion, and Cato made a second request, that he be ordained to the bishopric of Tours, which he had earlier scorned.

"My first instructions were for them to consecrate you bishop of Tours, but, from what I hear, you disdained that church. So you shall be kept well away from control of it."

And so Cato went off confounded.

When the king asked about the holy Eufronius, they told him that he was a grandson of the blessed Gregory [bishop of Langres], whom I have mentioned before [III 15].

"This is a great and prominent family," said the king. "May the will of God and the blessed Martin be done; let the selection process be brought to an end."

He issued a directive and the holy Eufronius was ordained bishop, the eighteenth after the blessed Martin.

Doing it the Wrong Way: A Bishop for Saintes (IV 26)

In the times of King Charibert [a. 561–67], Leontius [metropolitan bishop of Bordeaux] gathered the bishops of his province at the city of Saintes and deposed Emerius from the bishopric, claiming that Emerius had not been appointed to this position in accordance with the canons. Emerius had received a directive issued by King Chlothar allowing him to be consecrated without the consent of the metropolitan, since the metropolitan was not present. They expelled Emerius from office and drew up a consensus in favor of Heraclius, then a priest of the church of Bordeaux, signed it with their own hands, and sent Heraclius with the document to King Charibert. Heraclius came to Tours and informed the blessed Eufronius what had been done, requesting him to sign the document. The man of God flatly refused to do so.

After the priest Heraclius entered the gates of the city of Paris and came before the court, this is how he addressed the king, "Greetings, glorious king. An apostolic see sends your eminence best wishes."

"Have you been to Rome, then, that you bring us greetings from its pope?" asked the king.

"It is your father Leontius who, together with the bishops of his province, sends you greetings," said Heraclius. "He is announcing that Cymulus"—this was what Emerius used to be called as a child—"has been expelled from office because he attained the episcopacy of the city of Saintes by ignoring the stipulations of the canons. And so they have sent you a consensus nominating another in his place. Thereby violators of the canons may be censured according to its rules and the power of your reign may be known in ages to come."

When Heraclius said this, the king in a rage ordered him dragged from his sight, placed in a wagon full of thorns, and taken off into exile.

"What do you think—" asked Charibert, "no son of King Chlothar is around to uphold the actions of his father just because these people have, without my consent, cast out a bishop whom my father chose?"

Immediately he sent men of religion to restore Bishop Emerius to his post and also dispatched some of his chamberlains to exact a thousand gold pieces from Bishop Leontius and to fine the other bishops as much as was feasible. And so the insult to the prince was avenged.

Doing it the Right Way: Avitus, Bishop of Clermont (IV 35)

These events took place after both Cautinus and Cato died in the plague (see IV 31). The king in question was Sigibert. Gregory had been a pupil of Avitus in Clermont. Avitus held the bishopric from 571 to some time after 592.

When, as I have said, Bishop Cautinus had died at Clermont, many candidates contended for the bishopric, offering much and promising more. The priest Eufrasius, son of the late senator Euvodius, for instance, acquired from the Jews many a costly item, which he sent to the king by means of his kinsman Beregisil, with the hope of obtaining by bribery what he could not get by merit. His manners were agreeable but his actions were indecent, and while he would often make barbarians drunk, he seldom refreshed the poor. I think the stumbling block in the way of his success was that he tried to attain this dignity not through God but through men. But what the Lord said through the mouth of holy Quintianus cannot be changed, "The line of Hortensius will never produce anyone to govern the church of God."

When the clergy assembled in the church of Clermont, the archdeacon Avitus made no promises to them, but he still received the nomination and went off to see the king. Firminus, who had received the office of count of Clermont, then tried to block Avitus's appointment. But he did not go in person to the king; instead, friends of his whom he had sent on this mission asked the king to postpone Avitus's consecration for at least one Lord's Day; if this delay were announced, they would give the king a thousand pieces of gold. But the king would not listen to them.

So it happened that the citizens of Clermont assembled together and the blessed Avitus, at the time, as I said, archdeacon, was elected by the clergy and people and received the episcopal throne. The king held him in such high esteem that he bypassed for a moment the strictness of the canons, and ordered Avitus's consecration to take place in his own presence.

"May I deserve to receive the blessed bread from his hands," said the king.

Avitus was consecrated at Metz by royal favor.

When Avitus had received the bishopric, he showed himself a great man in every respect, providing people with justice, the poor with support, the widow with assistance, and the orphan with all the help he could give.

A Bad Bishop and a Worse Wife (VI 9, VIII 39)

A revealing sketch of episcopal appointments in Le Mans. Baudegisel (see also VII 15) is the first official we know of to bear the title mayor of the palace. Gregory as metropolitan bishop almost certainly ordained him. Bishops gave up relations with their wives on ordination. Red-hot plates (laminae) were Roman instruments for the torture of slaves. The first part of the selection is from 581, the second from 586.

Domnolus, bishop of Le Mans, began to grow ill. In the time of King Chlothar I [†561] he was the head of a monastic community at the basilica of Saint Laurence in Paris. The elder Childebert I [† 558] was still alive, but Domnolus always remained loyal to King Chlothar and repeatedly hid the agents that Chlothar sent as spies. For this reason the king was waiting for a vacancy in a bishopric that Domnolus could fill.

The bishop of the city of Avignon died and Chlothar decided to give the position to Domnolus. But when Domnolus heard the news, he went to the basilica of the holy priest Martin, where Chlothar had come at the time to pray, and spent the whole night in vigils. Through the leading men who were in attendance, he conveyed a request to the king that he not banish him like a captive from his sight or allow his simple nature to be worn down among sophistic senators and philosophizing judges, claiming that the post would be more of a humiliation to him than an honor. The king agreed and, on the death of Innocentius of Le Mans, appointed Domnulus bishop of that church.

Once he had taken up the episcopacy, he proved to be someone so remarkable that he was carried to the very height of sanctity, restoring the use of his limbs to a lame man and sight to a blind one.

After twenty-two years in office [a. 581], he recognized that he was being seriously debilitated by jaundice and the stone and chose Abbot Theodulf to succeed. The king [Chilperic] gave his consent, but not long after, changed his mind and the choice passed to Baudegisel, mayor of the royal palace. Baudegisel was tonsured and, rising through the clerical grades, succeeded on the bishop's death after a period of forty days....

In this year [586] many bishops died. Baudegisel, bishop of Le Mans [was one], a man exceptionally savage to the citizenry, unjustly seizing and taking away the property of various people. His wife, even more savage, had attended to his bitter and harsh spirit with advice inciting him to commit the most vile crimes. He missed neither a day nor even a moment in which he failed to go about despoiling his citizens or engaging in various disputes. Day in day out he never ceased from investigating matters with the judges and engaging in secular administration, raging at some people, having others beaten, even striking them with his own hands, riding rough-shod over many.

"Shall I not avenge wrongs done to me just because I have been made a cleric?" he would ask.

But why speak of strangers when he would not even spare his brothers and plundered them even worse? They were never able to get justice from him regarding their paternal and maternal inheritance.

When he had finished the fifth year of his episcopacy and was beginning the sixth, he was preparing a banquet for the citizens with a great deal of merriment when he was seized by a fever. Sudden death cut short the new year for him just as it began.

Bertramn, an archdeacon from Paris, was appointed in his place. He ended up involved in many disputes with Baudegisel's widow because she retained as personal property assets that had been given to the church in the time of her husband's episcopacy.

"This office," she said, "was my husband's."

She restored all of it, however, although unwillingly.

Her wickedness was unspeakable. With men [slaves], she frequently cut off their genitals completely along with the skin of their bellies, and with females, she burned their private parts with red hot metal plates. And she did many other wicked things that I have thought it better to be silent about.

The widow's name was Magnatrude, and in 590 she foiled the attempt of Chuppa, former master of the stables, to abduct her daughter, driving him and his men off with the help of her household servants (X 5).

A Successful Outsider, a. 591 (X 26)

The episcopacy tended to be the preserve of the local and especially the Gallic aristocracy but not a monopoly. Occasionally others made it through the selection process. Faremod appears in Parisian episcopal lists as Eusebius's successor.

Ragnemod, bishop of the city of Paris, died. When his brother, the priest Faremod, ran for the episcopal post, a certain merchant called Eusebius, a Syrian by birth, gave many gifts and was appointed in Ragnemod's place. Once he got the episcopacy, Eusebius dismissed the entire body of his predecessor's followers and appointed Syrians of the same origin as himself as the servants of the cathedral household.

The Competition

The Other Pretenders: False Prophets and a False Christ (IX 6, X 25)

In 580, the time of the second story, Gregory was under threat of a treason charge before Chilperic.

In this year [587] there was in Tours a certain Desiderius, who said he was some kind of great man, claiming he could perform many wonders: he boasted there were intermediaries scurrying back and forth between himself and the apostles Peter and Paul. As I was not around, a great horde of peasants flocked to him, bringing with them the blind and disabled, whom he sought not to cure by holiness but to delude by the error of clever necromancy. For he would order those who were paralysed or crippled with another affliction forcibly stretched out so that he could pretend to restore by effort those whom he could not straighten by the gift of divine power. His servants would seize the hands of a man while others grabbed his feet, pulling him in different directions so that the sinews looked as if they were broken. When the fellow was not cured, he was left for dead. And so it happened that many a person breathed their last in the midst of this punishment.

The wretched man was so puffed up that he said that the blessed Martin was his inferior and, in fact, that he himself was equal to the apostles. No wonder he would say he was like the apostles since the very author of wickedness from whom such deeds proceed shall proclaim he is Christ at the end of the world [2 Thess. 2.4].

It was noticed that he was steeped in the art of necromancy, as I said above, since, as those who saw him assert, when anyone would say something bad about him from afar and in secret, he would stand before the people and reproach him.

"You have said such and such a thing about me which is insulting to my sanctity," he would say.

How else did he know this but through the agency of demons?

He wore a hood and tunic made of goat hair and abstained from food and drink when in view, but in secret when he came to his lodgings he so stuffed his mouth that a servant could not keep up with his grasping requests for more.

Still, his deceit was uncovered, and I had him arrested and expelled from the city territory. I do not know where he went, but he said he was a citizen of Bordeaux.

Seven years earlier [a. 580] there was another charlatan who deceived a great many with his tricks. He wore a short-sleeved tunic, with a mantle of fine cloth on top, and carried a cross from which hung ampullas that he said contained holy oil. He said he came from Spain and was bringing relics of the blessed martyrs Vincent the Levite and Felix the Martyr.

When he reached the basilica of Saint Martin it was evening and we were sitting at dinner. He sent a message to say, "Let them come to greet the holy relics."

I replied to him, since it was late, "Place the blessed relics on the altar until we can come to see them in the morning."

But he arose right at dawn and, without waiting for us, he came in with his cross and appeared in my cell. I was amazed and, wondering at his effrontery, asked him what was the point of his behavior. His response was that of a proud man.

"You should give us a better welcome," he said in a pompous voice. "I shall bring this personally to the attention of King Chilperic. He shall avenge this contemptuous treatment of me."

He went into the oratory, quite ignoring me. He spoke one, then a second and a third verse of a psalm, offered a prayer, and then finishing, raised his cross once again and left.

He spoke like a peasant and his expression was base and obscene; not a reasonable word came out of his mouth.

He went to Paris. Public Rogations were being celebrated at the time [May 27–29] which customarily take place before the holy day of the Lord's ascension [May 30]. It happened that Bishop Ragnemod was leading a procession of his people and going about the holy sites. He arrived, showing off his strange outfit to people, joined by women from the country and those of dubious reputation. He drew up his chorus and attempted to visit the holy places with his own host. The bishop saw this and sent his archdeacon.

"If you bring relics of the saints," the archdeacon said, "place them for a while in the basilica and celebrate the holy days with us; when the ceremonies are over, be on your way."

Barely considering the archdeacon's words, he proceeded to abuse and curse the bishop.

The bishop understood he was a deceiver, and ordered him shut up in a cell. All his possessions were searched, and it was discovered that he had a large sack full of the roots of various plants; as well, there were mole teeth, mouse bones, and bear claws and fat. Seeing this to be witchcraft, the bishop ordered it all thrown in the river, had his cross taken away, and ordered him expelled from the territory of Paris.

But this fellow began to do what he had done before and made another cross. He was seized by the archdeacon, bound in chains, and ordered to be kept in confinement.

I had come to Paris during this period and had my lodging in the basilica of the blessed Julian the Martyr. The following night the wretched fellow broke out of his prison and headed for the aforesaid basilica of Saint Julian, still in the chains with which he had been bound. He fell down on the pavement in the spot where I was accustomed to stand, and overcome by drowsiness and wine, fell asleep. Unaware of this we arose in the middle of the night to render thanks to the Lord and found him sleeping. Such a stink arose from him as might conquer that of every sewer and privy. We could not get into the basilica for the smell. One of the clerics, nevertheless, approached, holding his nose, and in vain tried to rouse him; the wretch was sodden with wine. Then four clerics approached, lifted him up, and tossed him in a corner of the basilica. They brought water and washed the pavement and sprinkled sweet-smelling herbs, and so we entered to pray. Nor could he be roused by our singing, until daylight and the sun rose into the heavens. Thereafter I handed him over to the bishop once he had been pardoned.

Bishops gathered in Paris, and since I recounted these events at table, we ordered him to appear so he could be corrected. As he was standing there, Aemilius, bishop of Cieutat, raised his eyes and recognized him as a servant who had run away; and so he pardoned the fellow, took him back, and returned home.

Many there are who carry out these deceptions and continually bring the country people into error. I believe the Lord means them when he says in the Gospel that false christs and false prophets will rise up in the last days, who providing signs and prodigies, may lead even the elect into error [cf. Matt. 24:24]. But enough of such things; let me get back to my subject.

...[a. 591] In Gaul, in the province of Marseilles, the disease I have often mentioned, took hold. Severe famine overwhelmed Angers, Nantes, and Le Mans. These are the beginnings of the sufferings the Lord spoke of in the Gospel—there shall be pestilences and famine and earthquakes in places; and false christs and false prophets shall arise and provide signs and prodigies in the heavens, leading the elect into error [cf. Matt. 24:7–8, Mk. 13:22]—just as happened in the present day.

A certain man from Bourges, as he himself later declared, entered a forest to cut wood needed to finish some job he was doing, and a cloud of flies engulfed him; as a result he was out of his mind for two years. From this one can tell that this evil was sent by the devil. Afterwards, traveling through the neighboring cities, he came to the province of Arles, and there he dressed in hides and prayed like a holy man. To delude him, the enemy provided him with the power of divination.

Then removed from there so that he could advance to a greater crime, the man left the aforesaid province and entered the territory of Javols, making out that he was a great man and unafraid of declaring himself to be Christ; he had a certain woman with him as a sister and had her called Mary. A host of people flocked to him bringing the sick, whom he touched and restored to health. Those who came to him gave him gold and silver and clothing. To deceive them more readily, he distributed this wealth to the poor, prostrating himself on the ground, pouring forth prayers with the aforesaid woman; rising he ordered those standing about him to worship him. He predicted the future and announced that death would come to some, injury to others, and to a few future health. He did all this by means of diabolical arts and what tricks I know not. A huge host of people was fooled by him, and not only the more countrified, but even priests of the church. More than three thousand people followed him.

Meanwhile, he began to despoil and rob certain people he encountered on the road; the loot he gave to those who had nothing. He threatened bishops and citizens with death because they disdained worshipping him. He entered the territory of the city of Le Velay and reached the place called Anicium [Puy-en-Velay], halting at the neighboring basilicas with his entire force, which he drew up for battle against Aurilius, who was bishop at the time. He sent messengers ahead, naked men dancing and frolicking, to announce his arrival.

The bishop was amazed and sent vigorous men to him asking what he thought he was doing. The leader of the group, as he knelt to kiss his knees and impede his passage, gave an order for him to be seized and despoiled. Then without delay, drawing his sword, he cut him to pieces, and that christ, who might better be called anti-christ, fell to the ground dead. All who were with him were scattered. The Mary in question was subjected to torture and revealed all his apparitions and deceptions.

Now all those people whom he had confounded into believing in him by means of a diabolical trick never fully recovered their senses, but always professed him to be Christ and Mary to have a share in his divinity. And throughout all Gaul many came forth who likewise deceived certain females into joining them and into deliriously proclaiming them holy men and who put themselves forward among the populace as great men. I have seen many of them with whom I have disputed and tried to recall from their error.

A Prosperous Seeress, s.a. 585 (VII 44)

Cf. the seeress in V 14, s.a. 577. On Ageric: IX 8, 12, 23.

At that time there was a woman who possessed the spirit of Pytho and profited her masters a great deal by divining [cf. Acts 16:16]; gaining their appreciation for that, she was set free by them and released to her own devices. If anyone was a victim of theft or something untoward, she revealed immediately the thief's location, the receiver of the goods, or what he had done with the stolen property. She daily accumulated gold and silver and traveled about in jewels so people might suppose there was something divine about her.

But when this situation was reported to Ageric, bishop of Verdun, he issued orders to arrest her. When she was arrested and brought before him, he recognized, in accordance with what we read in Acts, that the unclean spirit of Pytho was in her. Then as he said an exorcism over her and anointed her forehead with holy oil, the demon spoke out and revealed what he was. But since he could not drive the demon out of the girl, she was allowed to go. The girl, however, saw she could not live in Verdun and went off to Queen Fredegund and hid out there.

Disputes

Bishops and dispute settlement is a virtually inexhaustible topic and is illustrated many times in the main text of the present selections. The following tend to concern examples of disputes that modern literature calls feuds. Feud should be understood, not as a synonym for vengeance, but as a state of hostility existing between two parties as the result of a legal wrong deemed to have been inflicted by one upon the other. It certainly could lead to vengeance and bloodshed, as these excerpts show, but in social and institutional conditions like those of Frankish Gaul it was regularly resolved by settlement. Nor was it at all exempt from coercive jurisdiction, if one could be brought to bear on it. Feud is not an adjunct of lawlessness but a recurrent feature of compensation-based legal systems, such as that which operated among the elites, both Roman and Frankish, of the Merovingian kingdom. For Gregory's account of a feud among Gallic Jews, see VI 17. It is worth noting that the principal participants in the hostilities described by Gregory were all important people. Many features of feud as found in Gregory's pages show correspondences not only with Frankish law, but also with the norms of Roman and canon law and the ancient legal practices of Roman provincials. Gregory does not use the Germanic term 'feud' (which did have Latinized analogues in the period), but a series of conventional Latin terms for 'dispute', 'quarrel', and 'conflict'.

The final selection on the dispute between the estranged couple Tetradia and Eulalius deals with a matter of family law that would become standard fare for ecclesiastical courts.

A Feud in the Family:
Silvester's Son and Gregory's Brother Peter, a. 576 (V 5)

Gregory places this account ostensibly under the year 576, when he got Felix's letter, but the narrative recounts events of the previous number of years and is written from a perspective of at least the middle part of the 580s. Peter was Gregory's elder brother.

At this time [a. 576] Felix, bishop of Nantes [a. 549–82], wrote me a letter full of insults, even saying that my brother [Peter, deacon in Langres] had been killed because he had killed his bishop out of a greedy desire for the bishopric. The reason Felix would write such a thing is that he coveted a villa belonging to the church; when I refused to give it up, full of anger, he vomited up a thousand insults against me, as I said.

I finally replied to him, "Remember the saying of the prophet: 'Woe unto those who join house to house and unite field to field! Are they alone going to inhabit the earth? [cf. Isaiah 5:8].' If only you were bishop of Marseilles! Ships would never bring oil or other goods there, only papyrus, so you could have all the more opportunity of writing disgraceful accusations against honest men. Only a lack of papyrus puts an end to your wordiness."

He was a man of incredible greed and boastfulness.

I shall put aside these matters, however, not to appear like him, and just relate my brother's passing from this world and the swift vengeance the Lord took upon his killer.

At a time when the blessed Tetricus [†ca 572], bishop of the church of Langres, was getting on in years, he dismissed the deacon Lampadius, whom he had employed in a position of trust. My brother, wanting to aid the poor whom Lampadius had wickedly despoiled, agreed with the humbling of Lampadius and for this reason incurred his hatred. Meanwhile the blessed Tetricus had a stroke. Nothing the doctors could give him did any good. The clergy were alarmed, and, since they were deprived of a pastor, they asked for Munderic. The king granted their request and Munderic was tonsured and ordained bishop [ca 568], with the stipulation that as long as blessed Tetricus survived, Munderic would govern the stronghold of Tonnerre as archpriest and have his residence there; when his predecessor died, however, then he would succeed him.

While Munderic was living in Tonnerre, he incurred the king's anger. He was charged with furnishing King Sigibert with supplies and assistance when the king was marching against his brother Guntram [see IV 47]. Munderic was dragged from the stronghold and exiled to a cramped roofless tower on the bank of the Rhône. Here he lived for nearly two years in considerable hardship; then through the intercession of the blessed bishop Nicetius, he returned to

Lyons and lived with the bishop for two months. But since he could not persuade the king to restore him to the position from which he had been expelled, he fled in the night and went over to Sigibert's realm. He was made bishop of the town of Alais with fifteen parishes more or less under him. The parishes were once held by the Goths but were now being administered by Dalmatius, bishop of Rodez.

Now that Munderic was gone, the people of Langres again asked for a bishop in the person of Silvester, a kinsman of mine and of the blessed Tetricus. Their asking for Silvester was the doing of my brother. Meanwhile the blessed Tetricus passed away and Silvester was tonsured, ordained a priest, and given control of the property of the church. He made preparations to go and receive episcopal consecration at Lyons. In the midst of the preparations, he was seized by an attack of epilepsy, a disease he had long been susceptible to, and, quite bereft of his senses and bellowing constantly for two days, died finally on the third day.

After these events, Lampadius, who, as I said above, had been deprived of his post and his means, joined with Silvester's son in hatred of Peter the deacon, contriving an allegation that Peter had killed Silvester by witchcraft. Silvester's son, who was young and not too bright, was incited into accusing Peter in public of parricide. When Peter heard the charges, a date was set for a hearing before Saint Nicetius, bishop [of Lyons], my mother's uncle; Peter made his way to Lyons. There in the presence of Bishop Siagrius [of Autun] and many other bishops and leaders of the laity he cleared himself by oath of ever having been involved in Silvester's death.

Two years later [a. 574], again goaded by Lampadius, Silvester's son pursued the deacon Peter along the road and stabbed him with a spear, killing him. Peter's body was then carried from there and taken to the town of Dijon and buried beside Saint Gregory, our great-grandfather. As for Silvester's son, he fled and went over to King Chilperic, leaving his property to the treasury of King Guntram.

Silvester's son traveled through a number of districts, but on account of the crime he had committed there was no safe place for him to settle down. At last, as I believe, innocent blood cried out to the divine power against him [cf. Gen. 4:10], and, as Silvester's son was traveling somewhere, he drew his sword and killed a man who had done nothing to him. The man's relatives, in a terrible state at the death of their kinsman, raised a commotion, and, drawing their swords, cut Silvester's son to pieces, scattering bits of his body around. This is the kind of end this wretched man met by the just judgment of God, so that he who slew an innocent kinsman, such a criminal did not himself survive for long, for this happened to Silvester's son in the third year [after the killing of Peter].

Langres finally got a bishop, by the name of Pappolus (ca 572–ca 580). Gregory passes over his misdeeds, which he has heard by report, "in case I appear to be a disparager of my fellow bishops," though he does linger on the details of Pappolus's death.

Following Pappolus, the abbot Mummolus, surnamed the Good, was made bishop [ca 580–post 585]. Many praise him highly, saying that he is chaste, abstemious, and temperate, always ready to do a good deed, a friend of justice, and lover of charity with all his heart.

When he took the bishopric, he was aware that Lampadius had taken a lot of church property by fraud, and had piled up fields, vineyards, and slaves from the spoil of the poor. He ordered him stripped of everything and driven from his presence. Lampadius now lives in the worst poverty and makes his living by manual labor.

I have said enough on these matters.

Sacrilege in the Church of Saint Denis (V 32)

The process leading to the initial appearance of the disputants in Saint Denis was probably not as casual as might appear from Gregory's account. The effects of episcopal excommunication gained much from being accompanied by royal disapproval.

In Paris a certain matron fell into criminal behavior, many claiming that she had left her husband and was having intercourse with another man. Then her husband's kinsmen approached her father.

"Demonstrate your daughter's innocence," they said, "or let her die before her criminal behavior causes disgrace to our family."

"I know my daughter is quite innocent," said her father. "This is a false rumor spread by malicious people. To stop this slander going any further, I will prove her innocence with an oath."

"If she is blameless, support your oath by swearing at the burial place of the blessed Dionysius [Saint Denis]," they replied.

"I will do that," said the father.

They reached an agreement and then gathered at the basilica of the holy martyr. The father lifted his hands over the altar and swore that his daughter was without fault. But others from the husband's side declared on the contrary that he had sworn falsely. As they quarreled, swords were drawn and the parties assaulted one another, cutting each other down before the very altar. They were well born and very close to King Chilperic. Many were lacerated by swords and the holy basilica was stained with human gore; the entrances were pierced by javelins and swords; and weapons were wielded with wicked fury right up to the tomb itself. The situation could scarcely be alleviated, and the liturgy in the church was suspended, until the whole matter was brought to the attention of the king.

The parties hurried off to see the king but were not warmly received, being sent back to the bishop of Paris. The decision was that if they were not found responsible for their outrageous action, they might be admitted to communion. They paid compensation for their bad behavior to Bishop Ragnemod, who presided over the church of Paris, and were readmitted to the communion of the church.

As for the matron, not many days after she was summoned to a hearing, she hanged herself.

The Feuds of Sichar, a. 585 and 588 (VII 47, IX 19)

With the exception of the account of Clovis, the feud between Sichar and Chramnesind is probably the most famous passage in the Histories *and has often been taken as an exemplar of both Gregory's primitive prose style and the crude legal institutions of his day. A different reading of Gregory's prose and the events he narrates is possible.*

The iudex, or judge, acting in concert with Gregory, was the count. The 'judges' determining the sums owed by Chramnesind and Sichar were assessors and citizen-members of the court, often called 'rachineburgs' or 'good men', who advised tribunals on the law and assisted in its administration.

At this point a serious internal conflict arose among the citizens of Tours.

While Sichar, son of the late John, was holding Christmas celebrations in the village of Manthelan [near Tours], with Austrighysel and other people of the district, the local priest sent round a servant to invite some people to have a drink at his place. So the servant arrived and one of the men he was inviting thought nothing of drawing a sword and striking him with it. The servant fell down dead on the spot. Sichar was connected to the priest by friendship, and as soon as he heard that the servant had been killed, he grabbed his weapons and went to the church to wait for Austrighysel. When Austrighysel heard about this, he grabbed his arms and went after Sichar. In the general commotion of the fighting that ensued when the two sides came together, Sichar was saved by some clerics and escaped to his villa, leaving behind in the priest's house money, garments, and four wounded servants. After Sichar had fled, Austrighysel attacked again, killing the servants and carrying off the gold and silver and other property.

After this the parties appeared before a tribunal of citizens. It found that Austrighysel was subject to legal penalty because he had committed homicide, killed servants, and seized property without obtaining judgment. An agreement was reached [for Austrighysel to pay compensation], and a few days later Sichar heard that the stolen property was being held by Auno, his son, and his brother Eberulf. Setting the agreement aside, Sichar, accompanied by Audinus, created a public disturbance by attacking them at night with an armed force. Sichar broke apart the quarters where they were sleeping, did in the father, brother, and son, killed slaves, and took off with property and cattle.

I was very upset when I heard news of the attack and, acting in conjunction with the count (*iudex*), sent a delegation with a message for the parties to come before us so that a reasonable settlement could be made and they could depart in peace without the dispute going any further.

When they arrived, and the citizens had assembled, I said, "Men, stop this criminal behavior and prevent the evil spreading further. We have already lost sons of the church; now I fear we shall be deprived of even more of them by this quarrel. Be peacemakers, I beg of you; let whoever did wrong pay compensation out of brotherly love, so that you may be peaceable children and worthy, by God's gift, to occupy His kingdom. For He Himself said, 'Blessed are the peacemakers, for they shall be called the children of God [Matt. 5:9].' Listen carefully! If anyone who is liable to a penalty has insufficient resources, church money will be paid out on his behalf. In the meantime, let no man's soul perish."

In saying this, I offered money of the church, but the party of Chramnesind, who had a claim for the death of his father [Auno], his brother, and his uncle, refused to accept it.

When they went away, Sichar made preparations for a journey to visit the king; with this in mind he first went to see his wife in Poitiers. While admonishing a slave at his labors, Sichar beat him with a rod. The fellow drew a sword from his baldric and without hesitation wounded his master with it. Sichar fell to the ground, but his friends ran up and caught the slave. They beat him viciously, cut off his hands and feet, and hung him up on a gibbet.

Meanwhile rumor reached Tours that Sichar was dead. When Chramnesind heard, he mustered his kinsmen and friends, and rushed to Sichar's home. He plundered it, killing some slaves and burning down all the buildings, not only Sichar's, but those of other landlords in the villa, and took off with the herds and anything he could move.

At this point the parties were brought into the city by the count and pleaded their own causes. The judges found that the side that had earlier refused compensation and then put houses to the torch should forfeit half the sum formerly awarded to it—this was done contrary to law only to ensure that they would be peaceable; as for the other side, Sichar was to pay the other half of the compensation. He paid it, the church providing the sum that the judges had determined, and he received a notice [from Chramnesind] discharging him from future claims. Both sides took oaths to each other that neither would ever so much as mutter a word against the other.

And so the dispute came to an end.

The conclusion of the story comes three years later, under the year 588.

The conflict among the citizens of Tours that I said above had ended arose again with renewed madness.

Sichar had struck up a great friendship with Chramnesind after having killed his relatives. They had such affection for each other that they often ate together and slept together in the same bed. One day Chramnesind had an evening dinner prepared and invited Sichar to the feast. He came and they sat down at the meal together.

Sichar got stinking drunk on wine and bragged a lot at Chramnesind's expense, until at last, so we are told, he said, "Dear brother, you owe me a great debt of gratitude for doing in your kinsmen. There's certainly no lack of gold and silver around here since you got compensation for them. If this business hadn't given you a bit of a boost, you'd now be naked and poor."

Chramnesind took Sichar's words badly and said to himself, "If I don't avenge my kinsmen's death, I should lose the name man and be called a weak woman."

He immediately extinguished the lights and split open Sichar's head with his sword (*sica*). Emitting a little cry at the end of his life, Sichar fell down dead. The servants who had come with him scattered. Chramnesind stripped the lifeless body of its clothes, hung it on a fence post and, mounting his horse, rode off to see the king [Childebert].

He entered the church and threw himself at the king's feet.

"Glorious king," said Chramnesind, "I ask for my life because I have killed men who slew my kinsmen in secret and stole their property."

When the details of the matter were brought to light, Brunhild took it badly that Sichar, who was under her protection, had been killed in this way, and the queen became angry at Chramnesind. When he saw that she was against him, he went to the Vosagus district in the territory of Bourges where his kinfolk lived, because it was considered part of Guntram's kingdom.

Sichar's wife Tranquilla left her sons and her husband's property in Tours and Poitiers and went to her family in the village of Mauriopes, and there she got married again.

Sichar was about twenty years old when he died. In his life he was a foolish, drunken killer, who inflicted harm on not a few people when he was drunk.

As for Chramnesind, he came back to the king, and the judgment he received was that he prove his killing of Sichar was unavoidable. This he did. But since Queen Brunhild had placed Sichar under her protection, as I have said, she ordered Chramnesind's property confiscated, but it was later restored by the *domesticus* Flavian. Chramnesind also went quickly to [Duke] Agynus and got a document from him guaranteeing no one would interfere with him, since Chramnesind had been granted his property by the queen.

Eulalius and Tetradia the Widow of Desiderius (X 8)

Despite the opening sentence, the tribunal later appears to be mixed. For Eulalius's earlier venture on this matter at the court of Guntram, see VIII 26. Eulalius was count of Clermont. On Desiderius, see VIII 45.

A synod of bishops was held on the border between Clermont, Javols, and Rodez to deal with Tetradia, the widow of the late Desiderius. It assembled as a result of Eulalius suing her for the property she had taken with her when she fled from him [see VII 27, 45]. I think the matter needs to be recounted from an earlier point, tracing how she left Eulalius and how she took refuge with Desiderius.

Eulalius as a youth acted, typically enough, somewhat unreasonably. His mother often chided him and as a result he hated her whom he should have loved. She used to prostrate herself in supplication in the oratory of their house and, as the servants slept, repeatedly keep nightly vigils of tearful prayers. In the end she was found there strangled, wearing the hair shirt in which she prayed. No one knew who did it, but the crime of parricide was laid at the doorstep of the son. When the bishop of Clermont, Cautinus [† 571], learned of the event, he excommunicated Eulalius.

Then the citizens and the bishop gathered at the feast of the blessed martyr Julian [August 28], and Eulalius prostrated himself at the feet of the bishop complaining he had been excommunicated without being heard. At that point the bishop allowed him to watch the ceremony of the mass along with everyone else. When the time came to take communion, Eulalius approached the altar.

"Public opinion proclaims you a parricide," said the bishop. "For my part, I don't know if you committed the crime or not. I declare the judgment of God and Saint Julian in this matter. If, as you say, you are innocent, come near and take part of the eucharist and put it in your mouth. God shall be the examiner of your conscience."

Eulalius took the eucharist, communicated, and went away.

He married Tetradia, who was noble on her mother's side and of lesser rank on her father's. But, since he would lie with the servant girls in his own house, he began to neglect his wife, and when he would return from his debauch, he often severely beat her. He even incurred a number of debts on account of his crimes and to pay them off repeatedly squandered his wife's jewels and gold. Finally put in the awkward position of having lost every honor due her in the house of her husband and of her husband having gone to see the king, Tetradia excited the desire of Virus—that really was his name—the nephew of her husband; since he had lost his wife, he wanted to marry Tetradia.

Virus however feared the hostility of his uncle and sent the woman to Duke Desiderius, thinking he would marry her later. She took all her huband's property, in gold, silver, and clothing, and anything that could be moved, as well as her eldest son. She left a younger one in the house. Eulalius came back from his journey and found out what had happened. When his distress subsided and he had settled down a little, he attacked and killed his nephew Virus among the narrow passages in the valleys of the Auvergne. Desiderius had recently lost his wife too, and when he heard that Virus was killed, he married Tetradia himself.

As for Eulalius, he got a wife by seizing a girl from a nunnery in Lyons. But his concubines, out of jealousy it is said, confused his senses with witchcraft. After a good period of time, Eulalius secretly attacked and killed Emerius, the girl's cousin. Likewise he killed Socratius, his mother-in-law's brother; their father had him by a concubine. He did many other wicked things which would take too long to describe.

Eulalius's son John, who had gone off with his mother, slipped away from Desiderius's house and came to Clermont. It so happened that at the time Innocentius had managed to get a hold of the episcopacy of Rodez [see VI 37, 38, s.a. 584]; Eulalius sent him a power of attorney, hoping the bishop would help him recover property owed to him in the city's territory.

But the bishop replied, "If I receive one of your sons, whom I can make a cleric and keep in my entourage, I shall do what you ask."

Eulalius sent him his son John and got his property.

Innocentius received the boy, clipped the hair of his head, and assigned him to the archdeacon of his church. John was so given to abstinence that he ate barley instead of wheat, drank water instead of wine, rode an ass instead of a horse, and wore the most menial clothing.

And so, as I said, bishops and important laymen assembled on the border of the above-mentioned cities. Tetradia was represented by Agynus and Eulalius appeared as the complainant. When he sought the property that Tetradia took from his house when she went to Desiderius, the judgment given Tetradia was that she restore what was taken away by a four-fold amount and the children she had by Desiderius were to be considered illegitimate. It was also stipulated that if she paid the amount to Eulalius ordered by the court, she would have permission to go to Clermont and there enjoy the property she had inherited through her father, exempt from litigation.

And this was what was done.

Bishop as Intercessor

The role of bishops as intercessors on behalf of the imperiled or the condemned is illustrated many times in the main text of the selections in the context of treason cases. The freeing of common criminals and the rejection of afflictive penalties were motifs of hagiography, and could also be models for episcopal action.

Lucky Thieves before Chilperic, a. 581 (VI 10)

In these days the basilica of Saint Martin was broken into by thieves. They placed at the window of the choir a railing from someone's grave, and mounting it, broke the glass and got in. They removed a great deal of silver and gold and silk robes and took off, without fear of stepping on the holy tomb where we scarcely dare place our lips.

But the power of the saint wanted to reveal this rashness with a dreadful judgment. Those who had committed the crime went to the city of Bordeaux where a quarrel arose and one of them killed another. And so the deed was revealed and the theft was discovered, and their silver, which had been broken up, and the robes were taken from their lodging.

The affair was reported to Chilperic who ordered them bound in fetters and delivered to his presence. Then fearing that the men would die on account of him who while alive prayed for the lives of the condemned, I sent a letter of entreaty to the king, saying I to whom prosecution of the suit belonged was not laying charges and asking for them not to be killed. The king generously received it and granted their lives. As for the precious material which had been dispersed, he carefully gathered it together and had it returned to the holy place.

GENEALOGIES

Note

Not all offspring, wives, or consorts are included in the following genealogies.

The abbreviation m. stands for a recognized sexual union between a king and his consort, whether or not it entailed marriage in a formal sense or the queenship. Descent lines are connected where possible to m. or the appropriate consort, but in many cases such precision is beyond our knowledge.

The names of Frankish kings are capitalized in genealogies 1–4, but only those who ruled in their own right. King's sons entitled to bear the royal title are in lower case.

Sequences of siblings, from left to right, do not necessarily correspond to the birth order, which is not always known; the sequence has sometimes been determined by graphical requirements.

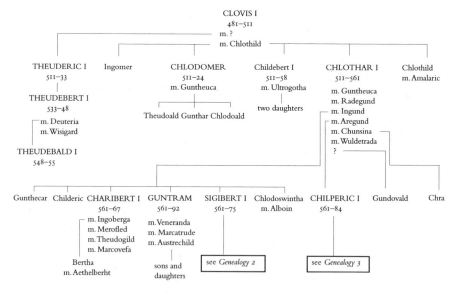

Genealogy 1. *The Early Merovingians: Clovis, his Sons, and Grandsons*

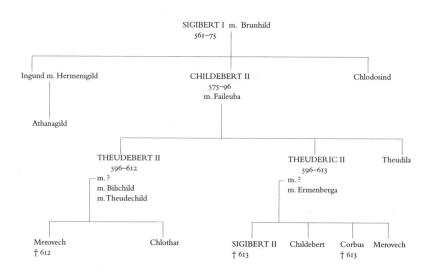

Genealogy 2. *The Early Merovingians: Sigibert I, Brunhild, and their Descendants*

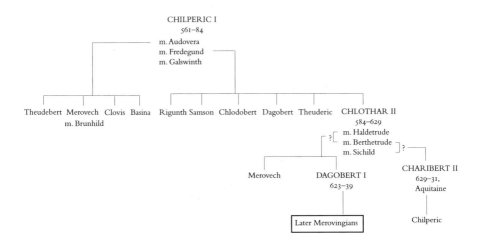

Genealogy 3. The Early Merovingians: Chilperic I, Fredegund, and their Descendants

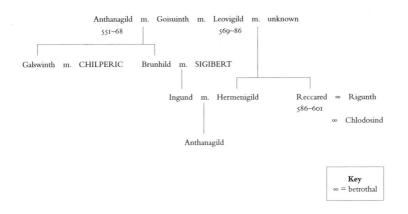

Genealogy 4. The House of Chlothar I and the Visigothic Monarchy

MAPS

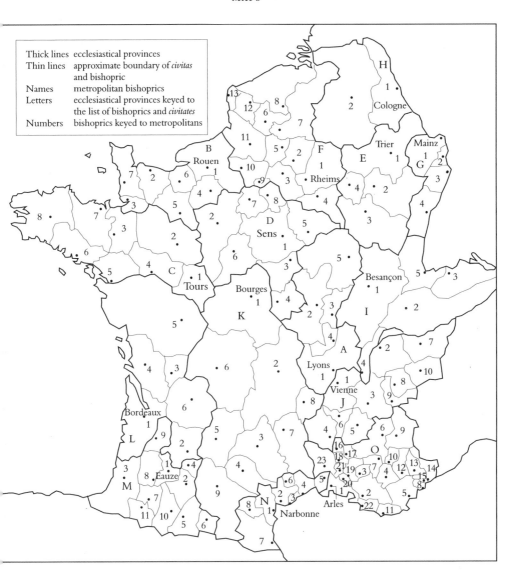

Map 1. Bishoprics of Gaul

Bishoprics and Civitates *of Gaul in the Merovingian Period*

The Roman-period *civitates* were in large measure the basis for the secular and ecclesiastical divisions of the Merovingian kingdom. As a result, the Merovingian ecclesiastical province and its bishoprics reflected the provincial groupings of the late Empire. The seats of most, but not all, Merovingian bishoprics were located in the old *civitas* capitals; the seats of most metropolitans were located in old provincial capitals.

The following list of Merovingian-period bishoprics (column 1) has been keyed to the *Notitia Galliarum*, a fifth-century list of Gallic cities grouped by provinces and (secular) dioceses (column 2). Note that while the the the list of ecclesiastical metropolitans and suffragans of the Merovingian period follows in its main outlines the *Notitia*, some reorganization has had to be made to the *Notitia* to bring it into line with the episcopal list. The map and the list that accompanies it are also essentially composite, representing information from the Merovingian period as a whole, not just the age of Gregory of Tours.

In the list each bishopric has been given its modern name (column 1), followed by the name of the *civitas* according to the *Notitia* (column 2). The see of the metropolitan in column 1 has been placed in capital letters as has the name of the Roman province and diocese, which has also been put in boldface, in column 2. The few Roman period *civitates* unattested as bishoprics have been left out. Bishoprics whose towns are not mentioned in the *Notitia* as *civitates* or *castra* have been placed in italics. Some of these were added in the course of the seventh century. Brackets in column 2 identify the original placement of a *civitas* in the *Notitia*, if that differs from the order of metropolitan and suffragan bishops in column 1. Parentheses in column 1 mark alternate, or fuller, forms of a name, and occasionally the name of the region; in column 2 they mark alternate, and later, names added to the *Notitia Galliarum*. A slash separating names in column 1 indicates the movement of a bishop's seat from one town to another.

In the *Notitia* the term *civitas* (meaning not just 'city', as an urban area, but also the dependent countryside) is usually followed by the name of the people in the genitive plural. Thus the *civitas Parisiorum*, is the 'city of the Parisii'. The term for a Roman provincial capital was *metropolis civitas*.

THE GALLIC PROVINCES

A. LUGDUNENSIS PRIMA

1. LYONS	Metropolis civitas Lugdunensium
2. Autun	Civitas Aeduorum or Augustodunum
3. Chalon(-sur-Sâone)	Castrum Cabillonense
4. Mâcon	Castrum Matisconense
5. Langres	Civitas Lingonum

B. LUGDUNENSIS SECUNDA

1. ROUEN	Metropolis civitas Rotomagensium
2. Bayeux	Civitas Baiocassium

3. Avranches	Civitas Abrincatum
4. Evreux	Civitas Ebroicorum
5. Sées	Civitas Saiorum
6. Lisieux	Civitas Lexoviorum
7. Coutances	Civitas Constantia

C. LUGDUNENSIS TERTIA

1. TOURS	Metropolis Turonorum
2. Le Mans	Civitas Cenomannorum
3. Rennes	Civitas Redonum
4. Angers	Civitas Andecavorum
5. Nantes	Civitas Namnetum
6. Vannes	Civitas Venetum
7. Corseul	Civitas Coriosolitum
8. Osismes (Carhaix)	Civitas Ossismorum

D. LUGDUNENSIS SENONIA

1. SENS	Metropolis civitas Senonum
2. Chartres	Civitas Carnotum
3. Auxerre	Civitas Autisioderum
4. *Nevers*	*Civitas Nivernensium*
5. Troyes	Civitas Tricassium
6. Orleans	Civitas Aurelianorum
7. Paris	Civitas Parisiorum
8. Meaux	Civitas Melduorum

E. BELGICA PRIMA

1. TRIER	Metropolis civitas Treverorum
2. Metz	Civitas Mediomatricum (Mettis)
3. Toul	Civitas Leucorum (Tullo)
4. Verdun	Civitas Verodunensium

F. BELGICA SECUNDA

1. RHEIMS	Metropolis civitas Remorum
2. *Laon*	*Civitas Lugduni Clavati*
3. Soissons	Civitas Suessionum
4. Châlons(-sur-Marne)	Civitas Catalaunorum
5. Vermand/Noyon	Civitas Veromandorum
6. Arras	Civitas Atrabatum
7. Cambrai	Civitas Camaracensium
8. Tournai	Civitas Turnacensium

9. Senlis	Civitas Silvanectum
10. Beauvais	Civitas Bellovacorum
11. Amiens	Civitas Ambianensium
12. Thérouanne	Civitas Morinum
13. Boulogne	Civitas Bononiensium

G. GERMANIA PRIMA

1. MAINZ	Metropolis civitas Magontiacensium
2. Worms	Civitas Vangionum (Vuarmacia)
3. Speyer	Civitas Nemetum (Spira)
4. Strasbourg	Civitas Argentoratensium (Stratoburgum)

H. GERMANIA SECUNDA

| 1. COLOGNE | Metropolis civitas Agrippinensium (Colonia) |
| 2. Tongres/Maastricht | Civitas Tungrorum |

I. MAXIMA SEQUANORUM

1. BESANÇON	Metropolis civitas Vesontiensium
2. Avenches	Civitas (H)Elvitiorum, Aventicus
3. Windisch/Constance	Castrum Vindonissense
4. Belley	Civitas Belisensium
5. Basel	Civitas Basiliensium

THE SEVEN PROVINCES

J. VIENNENSIS

1. VIENNE	Metropolis civitas Viennensium
2. Geneva	Civitas Genavensium
3. Grenoble	Civitas Gratianopolitana
4. Alba/Viviers (Vivarium)	Civitas Albensium
5. Die	Civitas Deensium
6. Valence	Civitas Valentinorum
7. Martigny (Valais) /Sion	Civitas Valensium, Octodurum [Alpes Graiae et Poenninae]
8. Tarentaise	Metropolis civitas Centronium, Darentasia [Alpes Graiae et Poenninae]
9. *Maurienne*	*Civitas Mauriennensis*
10. *Aosta*	*Civitas Augusta*

K. AQUITANICA PRIMA

1. BOURGES	Metropolis civitas Biturgium
2. Clermont(-Ferrand)	Civitas Arvernorum
3. Rodez	Civitas Rutenorum
4. Albi	Civitas Albigensium
5. Cahors	Civitas Cadurcorum
6. Limoges	Civitas Lemovicum
7. Javols	Civitas Gabalum
8. Velay	Civitas Vellavorum
9. Toulouse	Civitas Tolosatium [Narbonensis prima]

L. AQUITANICA SECUNDA

1. BORDEAUX	Metropolis civitas Burdigalensium
2. Agen	Civitas Agennensium
3. Angoulême	Civitas Ecolisnensium
4. Saintes	Civitas Santonum
5. Poitiers	Civitas Pictavorum
6. Périgueux	Civitas Petrocoriorum

M. NOVEMPOPULANA

1. EAUZE	Civitas Elusatium
2. Auch	Metropolis Civitas Ausciorum
3. Dax	Civitas Aquenesium
4. Lectoure	Civitas Lactoratium
5. St-Bertrand-de-Comminges	Civitas Convenarum
6. Couserans (St-Lizier)	Civitas Consorannorum
7. Lescar	Civitas Bernarnensium
8. Aire	Civitas Aturensium
9. Bazas	Civitas Vasatica
10. Cieutat	Civitas Turba ubi castrum Bigorra
11. Oloron	Civitas Illoronensium

N. NARBONENSIS PRIMA

1. NARBONNE	Metropolis civitas Narbonensium
2. Béziers	Civitas Beterrensium
3. *Agde*	*Civitas Agatensium*
4. *Maguelonne*	*Civitas Magalonensium*
5. Nîmes	Civitas Nemausensium
6. Lodève	Civitas Lutevensium
7. Elne	Civitas Elnensium
8. Carcassonne	Civitas Carcassonensium

O. NARBONENSIS SECUNDA, ALPES
MARITIMARUM, PARTS OF VIENNENSIS

1. ARLES	Civitas Arelatensium [Viennensis]
2. Aix-en-Provence	Civitas Aquensium
3. Apt	Civitas Aptensium
4. Riez	Civitas Reiensium
5. Fréjus	Civitas Foroiuliensis
6. Gap	Civitas Vappencensium
7. Sisteron	Civitas Segestericorum
8. Antibes	Civitas Antipolitana
9. Embrun	Metropolis Civitas Ebrodunensium
10. Digne	Civitas Diniensium
11. *Toulon*	*Civitas Telonensium*
12. Senez	Civitas Sanisiensium
13. Glandève	Civitas Glannatena
14. Cimiez/Nice	Civitas Cemelensium
15. Vence	Civitas Vintiensium
16. St-Paul-Trois-Châteaux	Civitas Tricastinorum [Viennensis]
17. Vaison	Civitas Vasiensium [Viennensis]
18. Orange	Civitas Arausicorum [Viennensis]
19. Carpentras	Civitas Carpentoratensium [Viennensis]
20. Cavaillon	Civitas Cabellicorum [Viennensis]
21. Avignon	Civitas Avennicorum [Viennensis]
22. Marseilles	Civitas Massiliensium [Viennensis]
23. Uzès	Castrum Uceciense (Civitas Ucetecensium, Eucetica) [Narbonensis prima]

Map 2. Gaul in the Sixth Century

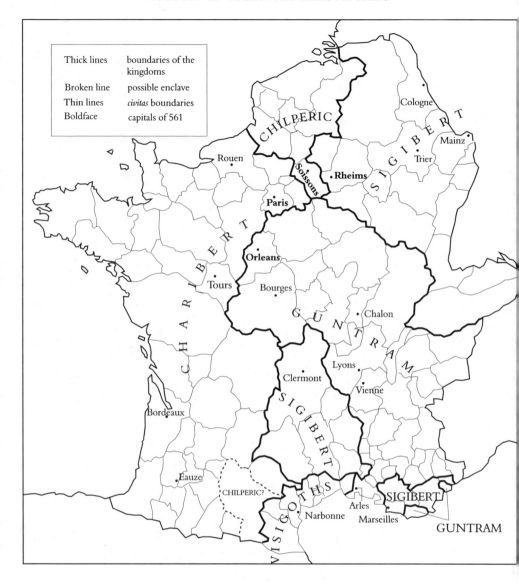

Map 3. The Division of 561 (cf. Gregory, *Hist.* IV 22)

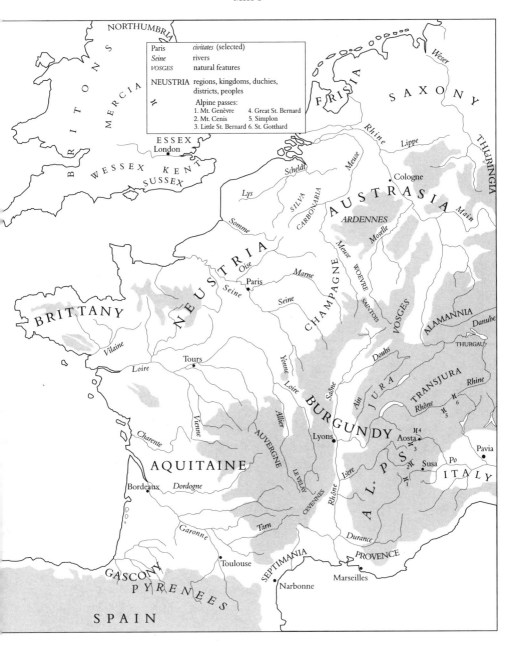

Map 4. Regions of Gaul and its Neighbors in the Merovingian Period

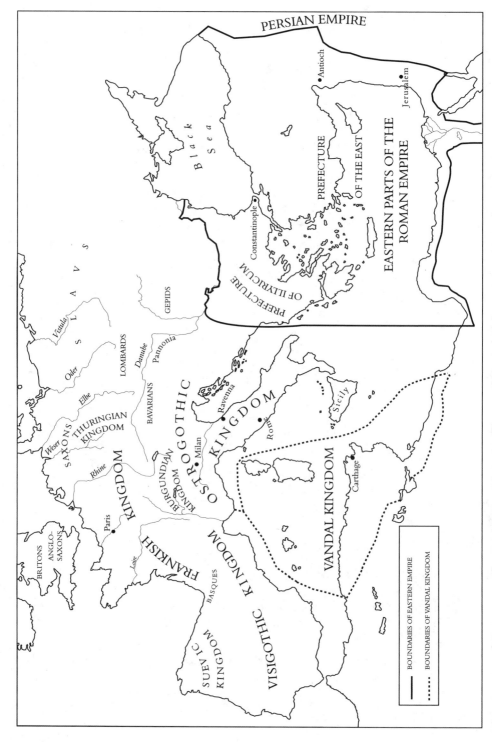

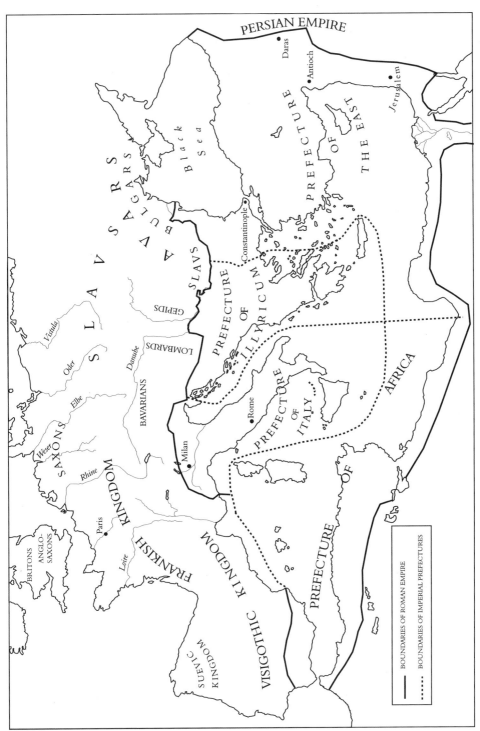

Map 6. West and East around the Deaths of Chlothar I (a. 561) and Justinian (a. 565)

INDEX OF PERSONS

This is essentially an index of the *dramatis personae* of the *Histories*, with the addition of the historians whom I have mentioned in passing. References are to page numbers. They refer first to the body of the political narrative (chapters 1-8), then to the Appendix (App.), then to the Epilogue and Postscripts (Ep.), and finally to the Introduction (Intro.).

BOOKS CURRENTLY AVAILABLE IN THE READINGS IN MEDIEVAL CIVILIZATIONS AND CULTURES SERIES